Postm

£4.49

Post-Contemporary

Interventions

Series Editors: Stanley Fish and

Fredric Jameson

POSTMODERNITY IN LATIN AMERICA

The

Argentine

Paradigm

Santiago

Colás

Duke University Press

Durham and London

1994

For Emily

© 1994 Duke University Press

All rights reserved

Printed in the United States of America on acid-free paper ∞

Designed by Cherie Holma Westmoreland

Typeset in Plantin and Gill Sans by Keystone Typesetting, Inc.

Library of Congress Cataloging-in-Publication Data appear on the last

printed page of this book.

It is safest to grasp the concept of the postmodern as an attempt to think the present historically in an age that has forgotten how to think historically in the first place.

¿Como podríamos soportar el presente, el horror del presente, me dijo la última noche el Profesor, si no supiéramos que se trata de un presente histórico. Quiero decir, me dijo esa noche, porque vemos cómo va a ser y en qué se va a convertir podemos soportar el presente.

Contents

Preface and Acknowledgments

Tired of postmodernism already? The term seems to have lost whatever meaning it once had when MTV launched—already several years ago—its special program, "Postmodern MTV." Consider the introduction, in the pages of *Vogue* (in early 1988), of the "postmodern ski jacket": What was the "modern ski jacket"? Was there a "realist ski jacket"? Surely *this* dissolved the critical significance of the term for observers of contemporary culture. Why, then, would I write another book about postmodernism? And if we think *we* are tired of postmodernism, why then, especially, would I write a book that dumps the concept—like so much First-World toxic waste—onto Latin America?

Probably the criteria most often agreed upon for distinguishing between the modern and postmodern cultural sensibilities is their respective attitudes toward mass culture. Modernism defined itself in opposition to mass culture. Postmodernism embraces its forms and contents, incorporating them within new artifacts that blur the distinction between high and low culture. If so, then only as modernists would we discard the term *postmodernism* solely on account of its migration into seemingly banal mass cultural arenas. By contrast, this very migration is sufficient cause for postmodernists to continue critical discussion of the term. Many postmodernists no longer believe in a pure modernist or avant-garde locus of consciousness outside the range of mass culture. Yet such a space was a precondition for the modernist rejection of mass culture. Therefore, postmodernists conclude that although critical analysis of mass culture is still possible, provided one attends to one's own enmeshment in the phenomena, rejection from without is certainly not. We may attempt to forget or ignore mass culture, but it will neither forget nor ignore us.

Of course we feel tempted to walk away from a term that has lent itself so easily to commercial and imperialist abuse. But perhaps *because* the term has come to occupy a central position—however nebulous or vague—in our social and cultural vocabulary (unlike, by the way, so many of the more specialized terms of our profession), we should invest more energy in shaping its meaning and function. This seems not only useful but also a matter of strategic necessity, especially if the debate over postmodernity in culture and politics is really about "new ways of thinking or imagining democracy."[1] If so, and if " 'liberal democracy' is being touted as the *ne plus ultra* of social systems for countries that are emerging from Soviet-style state socialism, Latin American military dictatorship, and Southern African regimes of racial domination,"[2] then we find ample justification for continuing to talk about postmodernity and for talking about its relationship to Latin American culture.

As always, there is also a personal story behind this project. Initially, I felt both attracted to and concerned by theoretical writings on postmodernism. Postmodernism's dissolution of the boundaries between high and mass culture seemed to me to echo, if not historically explain, the work of one of my favorite Latin American authors, the late Manuel Puig. Puig, in novels from *La traición de Rita Hayworth* (1967) to *Cae la noche tropical* (1990), directly incorporated the language, themes, and fragmentary forms of radio, B movies, soap operas, and popular music. And he did this for the most part as his contemporaries of the boom generation were spinning their massive modernist epics of the region. In turn, my attraction to both postmodernism theory and Puig seem partly explained by the circumstances of my own upbringing. I was the youngest, and only U.S.-born, son of well-educated Spanish immigrants in a politically progressive midwestern university town. I grew up (and remain) caught between an instilled appreciation for the loftier forms of an "Old-World" high culture and a somewhat embarrassed enjoyment of U.S. mass culture, even in its most maligned forms. I was raised on Watergate, disco, MTV, yuppies, CNN, and the Reagan-Bush era, but also on chess, *Don Quixote* and Unamuno, St. Teresa of Avila, NPR, and classical music on every radio in the house at what seemed to me like every waking hour.

This appreciation for high culture, along with a romantic notion of literature as the expression of human intellectual vitality, led me to experience a shock upon entering graduate school in the late 1980s. There, debates in contemporary theory intimidated me and struck me as abstract, esoteric, and distracting from the proper appreciation of literature. This initial impression changed as, impelled by the requirements of the program, I deepened my study of theory. But I never completely shed a skepticism for theory's excesses, particularly with regard to the literary products of other parts of the world. This tension between theory and Latin American fiction became the fundamental impulse behind this work. For, as I further investigated the concept of postmodernism, I felt frustrated by what seemed to be unnecessarily abstract and reductive, universalizing readings of some of my cherished Latin American texts. At the same time, I suspected the outright rejection of all postmodernism theory as a foreign, imperialist imposition, perhaps because of my own peculiar non-nativist initiation into Latin American literature via the mass cultural novels of Puig. If Latin American culture didn't quite fit the categories of postmodernism theory, neither did these seem to be quite alien to it. Perhaps the proper approach lay somewhere in between.

In fact, I came to realize, the proper approach lay not in between, but altogether elsewhere: in a different view of the relationship of theory to reality, in this case cultural reality. I discovered, in the writings of the late Caribbean writer and political activist C. L. R. James, a formal, but engagingly colloquial, expression of my concerns about this relationship. James wrote novels, plays, literary and cultural criticism, and histories, as well as pointed articles, essays, and books on urgently important political matters. But I found my methodological guideposts in his philosophical reflections on Hegel and Marxism. "Thought is not an instrument you apply to a content," James warned in 1948. "The content moves, develops, changes and creates new categories of thought, and gives them direction. . . . Now one of the chief errors of thought is to continue to think in one set of forms, categories, ideas, etc., when the object, the content, has moved on, has created or laid the premises for an extension, a development of thought."[3] James tells us that our thinking about reality—or theory— works through frozen categories, whereas reality continues to flow and thus escapes our attempts to represent it in theory. He was talking about the movement of reality over time. Yet his passionate interest in decolonization lend his words a spatial dimension. In that case, he might have been warning us against the instrumental application of theory to the raw materials of culture and, more specifically today, to the application of site-specific theories of postmodernism to international culture without regard for the locally determined specifics of that culture.

Many theorists of literary postmodernism and of social and cultural postmodernity inadequately interpret Latin American literature and culture in the process of substantiating their theoretical models. They do so by excluding the specific social and political conditions out of which that culture has emerged.[4] Where they do include social and political considerations, they oversimplify and reduce these to fit the requirements of an explanation of the political situations in Europe and the United States in the post–World War II era. These inadequate interpretations result in theories incapable of accounting for real and concrete, historical developments in regions such as Latin America, as well as in partial misunderstandings concerning the causes and characteristics of recent Latin American culture. Both postmodernism theory and Latin American culture are impoverished. Furthermore, such *ex*propriations might be seen as the latest in a long line—stretching back five hundred years—of European (and North American) self-fashioning at the expense of Latin America. This book, concerned with these problems, will therefore perform double duty. It will, on the one hand, criticize the limitations of postmodernism theory, and, on the other, suggest an alternative account of recent Latin American culture. This account does not reject the contributions of postmodernism theory, but does adjust them. In what follows, in other words, I have tried to heed James's caution and sensibly mediate the confrontation between the suggestive contributions of a variety of theoretical interventions and the exigencies of concrete historical developments in the economy, politics, and culture of Latin America.

This mediation involves two steps. In the first step, in chapter 1, I clear some ground for a different engagement of postmodernism theory and Latin American culture. This takes the form of a critique, from the point of view of Latin American culture, of existing theories of postmodernism. I will review the theories of Linda Hutcheon and Fredric Jameson—two of the most influential theorists of the postmodern. I ground my modifications of certain aspects of their contributions in recent developments in Latin American society and culture, including critical theory. At the same time, I will establish some points toward a new theory of postmodernism and Latin America. With this revised theoretical framework established, the challenge lies in properly grasping recent Latin American culture and its relationship to postmodernity. I address this in a second step of cultural analysis comprising the next six chapters of the book. I center a history of three moments of Latin American, especially Argentine, society and culture since 1960 on readings of four novels. Julio Cortázar's *Rayuela* (1963) will serve as the centerpiece for discussing Latin American modernity (chapters 2 and 3), Manuel Puig's *El beso de la mujer araña* (1976) as the focal point for examining a second, transitional, moment between Latin American modernity and Argentine postmodernity (chapters 4 and 5), and finally, Ricardo Piglia's *Respiración artificial* (1980) exemplifies the social and cultural coordinates of postmodernity as found in Argentina (chapter 6). Tomás Eloy Martínez's *La Novela de Perón* (1985) provides an occasion to recapitulate the nature of Argentine postmodernity (chapter 7), inflecting its rewriting of history in the particular direction of that crucial Argentine historical figure, Juan Perón. In chapter 8, I articulate the specific features of Argentine narrative and political postmodernity with certain features it shares with Central American testimonial narrative and politics and with women's writing and politics in Argentina during the same period. Ultimately, I hope to provoke first, a revised understanding of the multiple meanings of postmodernity when viewed globally, and second, a reconsideration of recent Argentine social and cultural history that is informed by this revised understanding of postmodernity. Such an understanding will include recognition of the relevance of all this to the emergence of new and more just democratic institutions not only in Argentina but also throughout Latin America.

I have many people to thank for their contributions to this book. I thank first my parents for encouraging and facilitating my interest in reading, writing, and thinking about culture in general. This book was originally a dissertation completed under the direction of Professors Fredric Jameson and Ariel Dorfman of the Graduate Program in Literature at Duke University. They combined their respective expertise with intellectual dexterity and generosity, and with a genuine concern for my own development. Their influence on my thinking will be evident throughout the book, but I am especially grateful that they encouraged me to disagree with them and develop my own positions on some of these issues. Stephanie Sieburth also read many versions of this book when it was still in the process of becoming a dissertation. Her attention to the details of textual meaning was a most helpful corrective to my tendency to paint with an excessively broad brush. Frank Lentricchia and Michael Moses, of Duke's English Department, also read an earlier version and offered useful suggestions for understanding these Latin American texts in a broader context. I also thank Professor Sylvia Molloy, of New York University, who very generously agreed to read the dissertation version of this manuscript. Of the many brilliant students with whom I shared classes and less-formal discussions at Duke, I wish to single out Michael Speaks for his particularly insightful and challenging comments on my ideas. Initial work on this book also could not have been completed without the various forms of support offered by the staff of the Graduate Program in Literature, in particular Sandy Mills.

I would like to thank graduate students from the Departments of Comparative Literature, Spanish and Portuguese, History, and Architecture and Urban Planning at UCLA and to students from Comparative Literature, Spanish, American Culture, and Sociology at the University of Michigan, all of whom contributed to the reformulation of some of the theoretical points of the book through their participation in my seminars at these institutions. Also at UCLA, a grant from the faculty senate provided the funding for the able research assistance of Jennifer Loeb. To George Yúdice, whose name appears throughout the notes, I owe gratitude not only for introducing me to the debates over postmodernity within Latin America but also for warm friendship and encouraging discussions. Doris Sommer, John Beverley, Neil Larsen, Alberto Moreiras, and Julio Ramos also read substantial sections of the book manuscript and helped me with specific suggestions and criticisms at various points, as did Ricardo Piglia, Mempo Giardinelli and the staff at Facultad latinoamericana de ciencias sociales in Buenos Aires. Reynolds Smith, of Duke University Press, provided the warmest and most able editorial stewardship that a novice author could have hoped for. I thank him as well. My babies, Eva and Adam, helped more than they know with their easy temperament and good sleeping habits.

The most difficult thanks to express are the deepest I owe. My wife Emily, to whom this book is dedicated, provided the most basic kinds of material support without which I could never have imagined, let alone completed, this book. But beyond this, I owe to her brilliant and constructive critical mind and her outsider's mistrust of academic jargon whatever clarity the reader finds in both the style and organization of this work. And finally, her support for this project (even at her own expense), her patience and her sense of humor, and her love and encouragement, I happily admit, put me where I am today: writing the acknowledgments for my first book.

I

Linda Hutcheon, over the course of several books, has established herself as a major authority on postmodernism, particularly in literature.[1] In *A Poetics of Postmodernism: History, Theory, Fiction*, first published in 1987, she added a literary historical dimension to her own previous work on parody and self-reflexivity. At the same time, she consolidated and organized the notoriously confusing and inflated body of scholarship on literary postmodernism.[2] Her book has become a virtual textbook on postmodernism. In more recent works, Hutcheon has increased the range of the model introduced in *A Poetics of Postmodernism* to include Canadian fiction and other international cultural forms, such as dance, photography, film, and performance art. Thus, by studying Hutcheon's representative and respected work, we may get an appropriate look at the first kind of misinterpretation, the one that extracts Latin American fiction from its local social and cultural context.

Hutcheon cites, at one time or another, such disparate Latin American novels as Gabriel García Márquez's *One Hundred Years of Solitude;* Manuel Puig's *Kiss of the Spider Woman;* Mario Vargas Llosa's *The War of the End of the World;* Carlos Fuentes's *The Old Gringo, Terra Nostra,* and *The Death of Artemio Cruz;* Augusto Roa Bastos's *I, the Supreme;* Alejo Carpentier's *Explosion in the Cathedral;* and Julio Cortázar's *Hopscotch* and *A Manual for Manual.* All these texts serve as examples of the primary mode of postmodern fiction, what Hutcheon terms "postmodern historiographic metafiction." Hutcheon includes within this category texts that use techniques such as the manipulation of narrative perspective, self-consciousness, and the incorporation of actual historical figures and texts to challenge the illusion of unified and coherent subjective identity and the distinction between art, specifically fiction, and life, specifically history or the past (105ff.). Hutcheon considers these two cultural institutions to be the moorings of what she calls "bourgeois liberal humanist" society (e.g., 179ff.). In that case, she argues, postmodernism, through its primary fictional mode "historiographic metafiction," targets that society from within, without pretending to escape from it or to inaugurate a new society. And postwar Latin America is one, if not the primary, source of this kind of fiction.

Hutcheon's claim that Latin American literature best embodies literary postmodernism depends upon several hidden presuppositions. First, she presupposes a definition—however implicit—of literary postmodernism. Second, she presupposes an identification of the constitutive features of the Latin American text or texts in question. Then, she must align the features defining postmodernism with the features identified in the Latin American text. She may *explicitly* do no more than substantiate her theory by referring to cultural examples such as Latin American texts. But she also *implicitly* pretends to explain the emergence and specific character of Latin American texts by reference to an international literary trend. The relationship thus works both ways.

The problem with this is not that postwar Latin America has not produced a body of fiction that concerns itself with history and that seeks to write Latin American history a different way and from a different perspective. On the contrary, one might argue that in the wake of the boom texts (written mostly during the 1960s) that Hutcheon primarily deals with, two new strains of narrative have emerged that seem to fit her stylistic description even more closely. Isabel Allende's *House of the Spirits* (1982), Antonio Skármeta's *I dreamt the Snow Was Burning* (1984) and *The Insurrection* (1982), Carlos Martínez Moreno's *Inferno* (1983), Luisa Valenzuela's *Lizard's Tail* (1983) and *Other Weapons* (1982), and Marta Traba's *Conversación al sur* (1981) and *En cualquier lugar* (1984)—along with the novels discussed in chapters 6 and 7—combine stylistic complexity with a concern for representing and intervening in recent history. During the same period, *testimonios* (testimonial narratives) have emerged from all over Latin America, such as Alicia Partnoy's *Little School* (1986); Hernan Valdés *Tejas Verdes* (1974); Rigoberta Menchú's *I, Rigoberta Menchú* (1982); Domitila Chungara's *Let me Speak* (1978); and Elena Poniatowska's *Until We Meet Again* (1969), *Massacre in Mexico* (1971), and *Nada, Nadie* (1988). These *testimonios* certainly question the processes by which historical facts are constructed, passed off as given, and pressed into the service of a particular class, race, gender, or institution. Thus, it's not that Hutcheon invents a trend in Latin American fiction nor even that she doesn't read Latin American texts carefully.

The problem is that Hutcheon doesn't complete her reading. And if the texts are only partially read to begin with, the theoretical category built of such partial readings will be of accordingly limited use. At the same time, therefore, her implicit account of the text's appearance and characteristics will be limited. In this case, Hutcheon's partial readings of these texts involves the exclusion of the social and political conditions out of which they emerged. This exclusion derives from certain limitations established by Hutcheon on her own theory. And it results in her misappropriation of Latin American fiction for her transnational canon of postmodern historiographic metafiction.

Hutcheon introduces her study as "neither a defense nor yet another denigration of the cultural enterprise [called] postmodernism. You will not find here any claims of radical revolutionary change or any apocalyptic wailing about the decline of the west under late capitalism. Rather than eulogize or ridicule, what I have tried to do is study a current cultural phenomenon" (ix). Ostensibly seeking to inject some calm reason into a discussion that has grown overly polemical, Hutcheon in fact excludes the concrete, historical, and political dimension of postmodern culture. She rhetorically equates "defenses," "denigrations," "eulogizing," and "ridiculing"—all things we wouldn't want to be doing in a scholarly discussion— with "claims of revolutionary change" or "wailing about the decline of the west under late capitalism." In so doing, Hutcheon bans any discussion of the concrete political consequences or affiliations of postmodern culture. We must not speak of revolution or capitalism because those things require a polemical rhetoric alien to the rational study to be undertaken here. By explicitly (and appealingly) sidestepping these caricatured (and unappealing) positions, Hutcheon also manages to repress that dimension—the concretely social and political—or postmodernism upon which such interpretations focus. If every interpretation rewrites its object of study in a different way, then Hutcheon is here writing a cultural postmodernism at the expense of a social, historical, and political postmodernism.

Aside from matters of personal preference, this exclusion severely limits Hutcheon's capacity to explain the emergence and specific function of the surface features she describes. Hutcheon cannot answer—or even ask, really—why postmodernism came *when* it did, nor why it took the form it did, nor even, finally, what function these various stylistic features serve. For example, Hutcheon rejects the explanation that the "postmodern 'return to history' " results from the U.S. bicentennial in 1976, rightly observing that this cannot explain a similar return in Canada, Latin America, and Europe (93). But in its place, she offers a similarly narrow explanation: "The members of the '60s generation . . . tend to think more historically than their predecessors," giving rise to a "desire" for "reading as 'an act of community' " (93). This only begs the question of causes. What gave rise to the " '60s generation" tendency to think more historically? Hutcheon's exclusion of social and historical causes and effects, such as revolution or capitalism, makes it impossible for her to ask, let alone answer, such a question.

At the same time, this example reveals a second problem with Hutcheon's model: its unconscious universalizing impulses. Hutcheon feels it is wrong to attribute an international return to history to one nation's bicentennial. But she fails to address the problems involved in assuming the existence of a uniform, international generation of the sixties and identifying it as the cause instead. She does not explain the emergence of any such "generation." But beyond this, Hutcheon also fails to ask whether, in spite of a certain admittedly internationalist impulse in various cultural movements in the sixties, this generation might not have different concerns and aims in different parts of the world. And also whether these differences were dictated by the many different institutional faces presented by Hutcheon's other homogeneous universal: "bourgeois liberal humanism." This tendency is striking partly because Hutcheon explicitly seeks to counter such "totalizing" impulses in other theories of postmodernism. But also, her very definition of postmodernism seems to preclude the kind of abstracting moves she makes: "Perhaps the most basic formulation possible of the paradox of the postmodern" is that "it is more a questioning of commonly accepted values of our [whose?] culture (closure, teleology, and subjectivity), a questioning that is *totally dependent* on that which it interrogates" (42; emphasis added). That definition should therefore be more self-consciously applied to her own work. For only by raising her theoretical gaze above the confusing crowd of local circumstances, cultural traditions, political projects, and historical tendencies can she align a whole series of varied international cultural artifacts and determine that they are the expression of a single postmodernism engaged in "using and abusing," "installing and subverting," "contesting, but not denying" bourgeois liberal humanism.[3]

Hutcheon thus excludes from her model the pressure that social and historical forces exert on culture. She also excludes the differentiating power that specific, local social and cultural elements might exert on dominant forces like "bourgeois liberal humanism." In the case of Latin American fiction, these exclusions lead Hutcheon to omit precisely those features of these texts that would make them resistant to inclusion in her canon of postmodernism, namely, the concrete ways these texts may reproduce or be resistant to the dominant economic, political, and cultural institutions in both the First World and the various regions and nations of Latin America. So, for example, no mention is made of possible relationships between boom fiction and the Cuban revolution or the ideology of modernization, both potent social forces for the Latin American " '60s generation." Nor, as I noted above, does Hutcheon seem to be aware of a series of texts (many untranslated) that emerged from revolutionary struggles in Central America, or from the experience of fearsome state terrorism under military rule in the Southern Cone. The reasons for these inadequate interpretations lay in the blind spots within Hutcheon's own theoretical model.

Fredric Jameson conceived of his model of postmodernism as "radically different" from what he called "stylistic" models—of which Hutcheon's might be considered the culmination—for which "postmodernism" was a style an artist might choose or reject.[4] Instead, Jameson attempted to produce a concept of postmodernism as a "cultural dominant": a dominating cultural medium within which all cultural production takes place and to which it must all, in one way or another, respond. Moreover, Jameson sought to explain the emergence of that cultural dominant in terms of Ernest Mandel's account—in *Late Capitalism*—of postwar mutations in the structure of capitalism. Hence the title of Jameson's landmark essay on the topic, as well as his more recently published collection of essays and new reflections: *Postmodernism, or, The Cultural Logic of Late Capitalism*. Jameson interwove his cultural analyses with political and economic accounts precisely to *historicize* the cultural phenomena of postmodernism: to address the question of why postmodernism came *when* it did, and of what it might mean given the economic and political circumstances in which it emerged.

Some have felt that Jameson overstated the link between postmodern culture and the social forms of late capitalism. But he undoubtedly succeeded in shifting the terms of the debate so that critics and theorists were forced to consider postmodernism within a broader field of forces than those usually associated with changes in literary or artistic practice. Of course, my own critique of Hutcheon, the possibility of seeing a gap in her theory, depends heavily on Jameson's rearranging of the debate. The importance of his model notwithstanding, the question for us to keep in mind is how Jameson—who presumably will attend to the social and historical dimensions of a text—constructs the specificity of Latin American culture within his broad version of postmodernism.

In fact, we come across the Third World often in Jameson's theory of postmodernism. For example, it functions centrally as the space whose disappearance manifests the emergence of late capitalism. "This purer capitalism of our time," Jameson writes of late capitalism, "thus eliminates the enclaves of precapitalist organization it had hitherto tolerated and exploited in a tributary way. One is tempted to speak in this connection of a new and historically original penetration and colonization of Nature and the Unconscious: that is the destruction of precapitalist third world agriculture by the Green Revolution, and the rise of the media and the advertising industry" (36). Compare this to an earlier formulation: "Late capitalism can therefore be described as the moment in which the last vestiges of Nature which survived on into classical capitalism are at length eliminated: namely the third world and the unconscious."[5] Elsewhere, it is "above all" a change in the status of the Third World with respect to capital that distinguishes late capitalism (ix). The latter finally saturates the previously colonized, but until now untransformed, "agricultural" or "precapitalist" spaces of the Third World, including Latin America.

It may be obvious that this seemingly final victory of capitalism over all resistant spaces is lamentable to Jameson. But consider the specifics of his lament. Jameson catalogues, among the baleful features of postmodernism, a "weakening of historicity" (6), defining historicity as "a perception of the present as history" (284). In modernism, historicity came from "some residual zones of 'nature' or 'being,' of the old, the older, the archaic" (ix). These zones "[threw] up the concept and the image of an older mode of agricultural production" (366) and permitted "the lived coexistence between several modes of production, the existential experience, within a single life and a single individual, of multiple 'alternate' historical worlds."[6] Latin Americanists might think of Alejo Carpentier's *Lost Steps,* whose protagonist in traveling from a northern metropolis to the heart of the Orinoco, passes backward—by his own accounts—in time through several historical periods. In postmodernism, late capitalism obliterates the nature of the Third World and paralyzes our sense of historicity. Since we cannot recall the past out of which our present was shaped, we lose our sense of the present as changeable. We therefore weaken our capacity to formulate projects for new futures. We are left immobile as political subjects. Jameson therefore advocates a concept of postmodernism, as well as a postmodern cultural practice of cognitive mapping, that will, in the first words of the book, "think the present historically in an age that has forgotten how to think historically in the first place" (ix). The urgency of this call is underscored when we go back to his best-known work, *The Political Unconscious.* There, we find a similar version—"Always historicize!"—characterized not only as the moral of *that* book but also as the " 'transhistorical' imperative of all dialectical thought."[7] How though, given the bleak picture of a uniformly modernized—"imploded"[8]—capitalist landscape, can we regain the leverage necessary to think historically?

Now we come across the Third World again. For the "radical difference" of the texts of the Third World have a "tendency to remind us of outmoded stages of our own first world cultural development." This reminder "challenges our imprisonment in the present of postmodernism and calls for a reinvention of the radical difference of *our own* cultural past."[9] Jameson locates these texts somehow outside the ostensibly total range of late capitalism and postmodernism, characterizing them as "forms of oppositional culture: those of marginal groups, those of radically distinct residual or emergent cultural languages . . . resistant and heterogeneous forces which [postmodernism] has a vocation to subdue and incorporate" (159). These resistant, but not postmodern, forms of culture bear a family resemblance to, but are finally contrasted with, Jameson's favored First-World cultural forms—the work of sculptor Hans Haacke, for example—which are both resistant and postmodern. The Third World returns from its annihilation, paradoxically, to serve as the cultural source for historical thinking, a source to be mined by us in the First World in order to regain our own debilitated historicizing faculties. We might reasonably ask, in light of this central and complex, but finally vexing and paradoxical role assigned the Third World, what in Jameson's theory permits such an expropriation of Third-World culture?

If Jameson makes historicity and Third-World spaces indispensable to politics, he also links them both to the concept of utopia. Indeed, the impulse to preserve at least the *concept* of utopia—along Althusserian lines[10]—forms perhaps the secret force behind Jameson's interest in historicity and the Third World. Jameson therefore writes: "One wants to insist very strongly on the necessity of the reinvention of the Utopian vision in any contemporary politics: this lesson, which Marcuse first taught us, is part of the legacy of the sixties which must never be abandoned in any reevaluation of that period and of our relationship to it" (159). Considered in light of the centrality of both "historicity" and the "emergent cultural languages," the concept of utopia now appears to take two forms for Jameson. Both of these involve paradoxes. First, an intellectual utopia is represented by the paradoxical imperative to "think the present historically in an age that has forgotten how to think historically in the first place." Second, there is the paradoxical utopian space of Third-World culture—reminiscent of a whole history of European constructions of the "New World" as utopia[11]—from which emanates "various forms of oppositional culture," despite the fact that "multinational capital ends up penetrating those very precapitalist enclaves (Nature and the Unconscious) which offered extraterritorial and Archimedean footholds for critical effectivity" (49). But these two utopias are also linked because it is precisely the loss of the Third World, as representative of our own bygone modes of production, that brings on the crisis in historicity.

This suggests one of those restrictions within Jameson's theory that determine the paradoxical character of his formulations with respect to the Third World. Jameson writes that "it is thus the limits, the systemic restrictions and repressions, or empty places, in the Utopian blueprint that are the most interesting, for these alone testify to the ways a culture or a system marks the most visionary mind and contains its movement toward transcendence" (208). Perhaps these paradoxes testify to one of the ways late capitalism marks the visionary attempt to represent it. Perhaps the paradoxical nature of Jameson's own utopian postmodern cultural politics is an "empty place in the Utopian blueprint" for *our* time. Only by insisting on doing that which contemporary culture prohibits—namely, thinking the present historically—and only by summoning the return of a seemingly eliminated space, can the *concept* of a utopian future be kept alive.

There is also something "outside" Jameson's theory that helps explain his paradoxical reliance on the Third World. I mean the dynamic of contemporary capitalism itself. Far from imploding in a landscape of pure uniformity and complete modernization, it develops strategies for generating difference from within itself. This, at least, is the image of capitalism developed in both the school of radical geography and the contributions of some Latin American scholars to the postmodernism debate.[12] This image complicates the two Marxist theories of imperialism invoked by Jameson. Jameson's argument that capitalism increasingly homogenizes the world landscape derives from the most influential classical accounts found in Marx and Lenin. In 1848, Marx wrote: "National differences and antagonisms between peoples are daily more and more vanishing, owing to the development of the bourgeoisie, to freedom of commerce, to the world market, to uniformity in the mode of production and in the conditions of life corresponding thereto."[13] Lenin extended this thesis in 1916: "The export of capital affects and greatly accelerates the development of capitalism in those countries to which it is exported."[14] For classical Marxists, capitalism was an international revolutionizing force. It would obliterate national boundaries en route to establishing an international class—the proletariat—capable of ushering in communism. But Jameson also relies on a contrary thesis, developed in the 1960s and 1970s by dependency theorists. They argued that capitalism in "metropolitan" or "core" nations "developed underdevelopment" in certain fixed "satellite" or "peripheral" regions. Samir Amin thus asserted: "During the first seventy years of the twentieth century, however, which have been marked by a speeding up of the historical process, the division of the world into 'developed' and 'underdeveloped' countries has not become less pronounced; on the contrary, the gap between them continues to grow larger."[15] In this way, Jameson's understanding of the logic of capitalist development draws from two succeeding, historically determined accounts in Marxist theory.[16]

But neither of these theories seems to account for contemporary capitalism. Consider instead geographer Neil Smith's concept of uneven development described, if rather dramatically, here: "Capital is like a plague of locusts. It settles on one place, devours it, then moves on to plague another place. Better, in the process of restoring itself after one plague the region makes itself ripe for another. . . . Differentiation as the means to a spatial fix becomes itself the problem to be fixed."[17] In this conceptualization, capitalism becomes a mobile process rather than a glacial, if methodical, leviathan. This capitalism does not lend itself to the binary conceptual structures of dependency theory either: of regions easily and permanently identified as penetrated or unpenetrated, First World or Third World, metropolis or satellite, developed or underdeveloped. As Arjun Appadurai writes, "The new global cultural economy has to be seen as a complex, overlapping, disjunctive order, which cannot any longer be understood in terms of existing center-periphery models (even those which might account for multiple centers and peripheries)."[18] Even Ernest Mandel, from whom Jameson borrows his economic model, observes that late capitalism is "an integrated unity, but . . . an integrated unity of non-homogeneous parts."[19] Finally, Norbert Lechner points out that "the development of capitalism . . . at least in the Southern Cone [of Latin America], only deepened and complicated the existing structural heterogeneity."[20]

The groundwork for this concept is already laid in Marx's *Grundrisse*. There he included the earlier image of capital as "the constant impulse to exceed its quantitative limits: an endless process," which is "destructive towards, and constantly revolutionises . . . tearing down all barriers which impede the development of the productive forces, the extension of the range of needs, the differentiation of production, and the exploitation and exchange of all natural and spiritual powers."[21] But he nuanced this with the concrete observation that "the fact that capital posits every such limit as a barrier which it has *ideally* overcome, it does not at all follow that capital has *really* overcome it; and since every such limit contradicts the determination of capital, its production is subject to contradictions which are constantly overcome *but just as constantly posited.*"[22] It is out of this line of Marx's writing that geographer David Harvey cautions that "geographic differentiations then frequently appear to be what they are not: mere historical residuals rather than *actively reconstituted features within the capitalist mode of production.*"[23] All this suggests that perhaps there is something in contemporary capitalism that produces the optical illusion to which Jameson falls prey. If he sees both a desert of complete modernization extending to the horizon and scattered, miragelike oases of Third-World resistance, perhaps it is because the saturation of the globe by capitalism, as the geographers argue, brings with it a multiplication, not an eradication or organization, of differences.[24]

The classical Marxist line that suggested an endless capitalist "explosion" leads to Baudrillard's prediction of a "fatal implosion" as well as to Jameson's vision of capital as "late capitalism" (as in nearing the end of its trajectory). The argument is that capital requires differences, an exterior, to survive. If contemporary capital has consumed all difference, then it will, in effect, run out of gas. But the alternative Marxian formulation as well as the theories of radical geography suggest instead that capitalism engages in a constant self-refueling. As it consumes difference in one place, it regenerates it elsewhere. Michael Speaks calls this an "injective imperative" and it bears a striking resemblance to Marx's original formulations of capital's dialectic of expansion and barrier. Speaks writes:

> Contemporary capital functions, then, not by modulating the differences within its simulational matrix (by the orbital recurrences of the same), but by modulating the differential between second and third order simulation . . . Without the ability to differentiate or modulate, late capital fails the "injective imperative": new products, market segments, and consumers can only be sold/created to the extent that capital is not a completely deterministic system, to the extent that it still has the capacity to either open up new "third world" markets and consumers (excavating the real), or create new consumers and products in the "first world" (insinuating the hyperreal).[25]

Compare this with Marx's description:

> It is the tendency of capital to remove the natural ground from the foundation of every industry, and to transfer the conditions of its production outside it to a

general context. Hence the conversion of what previously appeared super-fluous into necessities, things whose necessity is a product of history. Universal exchange itself, i.e. the world market and hence the totality of activity, inter-course, needs, etc., of which it consists becomes the universal foundation of all industries.[26]

But Speaks continues: "Without a differential register to keep 'in play' capital would implode onto the horizon that it projects as utopian . . . yet, without the presage of a fully cybernetic capitalist utopia . . . it has no claims to global dominance. . . . It must simultaneously organize and resist this pure flow."[27] Speaks is arguing that contemporary capital survives by simultaneously abolishing and reestablishing an effective illusion of differ-ence. In other words, late capitalism markets global, geographical, differ-ence. One consequence of this reformulation of capital's logic is political. Marxist politics used to depend upon capital's eventual self-destruction. The proletariat would then take over and inaugurate the new society.[28] Now, contemporary Marxism must contend with a capitalism that seem-ingly not only will not go away but also actively and continually shifts the boundaries separating "inside capitalism" or "reformism" from "outside capitalism" or "revolution"; boundaries on which a Left politics could previously reassure itself regarding the purity and eventual success—on account of that purity—of its strategies for change.

Significantly, this image of dynamic heterogeneity—irreducible to older binary characterizations—as an effect of the capitalist system also crops up in Latin American discussions of postmodernity. Arturo Escobar charac-terizes the shift as follows: "It is as if the elegant discourses of the 1960s . . . had been suspended, caught in mid air as they strove toward their zenith, and, like fragile bubbles, exploded, leaving a scrambled trace of their glori-ous path behind."[29] In fact, as I suggested in my preface, the validity of the very concept of "Latin America" may be among these casualties of the shift Escobar describes. Certainly, there is a rhetoric common to the most suggestive Latin American contributions to the postmodernism debate: a rhetoric of impurity. Pure theoretical categories, supposedly referring to equally pure real entities, are contaminated by internal differences, messy hybrids, and multiple identities. Benjamín Arditi thus speaks of a "crisis" and "transformation of ways of seeing, apprehending, and making in the world."[30] Economically, politically, and culturally, stable concepts and fixed oppositions give way to more flexible, dynamic, and open-ended characterizations.

In each case, the crisis of the institutions and concepts of modernity in the United States and Europe is viewed as the possibility for a rethinking and renewal of its ideals in accordance with a changed reality. But this critique and renewal of modernity does not take place along the lines of "completing" a stunted, but still unilinear, project of modernity.[31] Rather, a more appropriate metaphor might be one of switching modern values of economic, political, and cultural democracy off the single track of Enlightenment modernity and onto the variety of new tracks—some long, some short, without necessarily having any fixed or unified end in sight—being produced by a heterogeneous group of social actors today.[32] Even within the Latin American postmodernism debate itself, these contributions move beyond the stagnant standoff between assimilationist espousal and nativist rejection of European and North American theories.[33] These antagonistic positions, based on clear demarcations of the "native" and the "foreign," are considered obsolete in the face of global flows of capital, goods, culture, and people. Instead, theorists critically engage the concepts of postmodernism theory, reorienting them toward addressing the specific economic, political, and cultural challenges of contemporary Latin American societies.

Economically, the opposing models of modernization and dependency theory give way to pragmatic but critical strategies for negotiating and reconfiguring capitalism in Latin America. Modernization theory, developed in the United States during the Cold War, advocated a tighter relationship to industrial capitalism as a solution for Latin America's "backwardness." An infusion of capital and technology, along with entrepreneurial values, would wrench Latin America out of its traditional stagnation into modernity.[34] It is important to understand that this prescriptive theory depended on a dualistic vision of "modern" and "traditional" societies. This dualism is precisely what contemporary theories problematize.[35] Dependency theory, meanwhile, despite its many advances over modernization theory and its unquestionable radical credentials, never shed this fundamental dualism. It did posit capitalism as the problem's cause rather than its solution. But it effectively did little more than give different names—"metropolis" and "satellite" or "core" and "periphery"—to Lipset's "modern" and "traditional."[36] Otherwise, the broader polemic between modernization theory and dependency theory generated accordingly antagonistic and predictably one-tracked prescriptions for development. Modernization theory advocated "free-market" capitalism and dependency theory championed "state-planned" socialism. Both models characterized the problems of

Latin American society in totalizing, black-and-white terms and offered only violently sweeping proposals for change.

The distinctions between "metropolis" and "satellite" are not irrelevant today, but their explanatory power is severely taxed by the recent intensification of certain phenomena such as global flows of finance capital (the debt crisis), deindustrialization in certain previous industrial centers of the metropolis (the American Ohio Valley), the rise of the drug trade (Peru, Colombia, and Bolivia, but also inner cities in the United States) and so-called informal economies, the exportation of manufacturing to previously nonindustrialized "satellite" regions (the U.S.-Mexican border), the movement of large numbers of people displaced by material necessity (former peasants squatting on the outskirts of Latin American cities such as Lima, Buenos Aires, and Rio, and undocumented workers in the United States), and the increased "deterritorialization" of the corporation as national entity ("Japanese" auto manufacturers, IBM, Coca-Cola).[37] Add, as a consequence of these changes, the fact that numerous large areas with periphery-like social conditions exist within areas conventionally designated as metropolitan, and vice-versa, and one begins to grasp the magnitude of the conceptual crisis of dependency theory and its categories. It is important to discuss the specific impact of these changes on Latin America, but for now, I only want to point out that many Latin American political and cultural theorists of postmodernity depart from the observation—noted also, recall, by the radical geographers cited above—that capitalist development produces neither uniform modernization nor neatly demarcated regions of industrialization and underdevelopment, but, rather, heterogeneity and differences.[38] They insist, furthermore, that any transformative politics must take this new conception of capitalist development as its basis.

At the same time, the real operation of those economies misleadingly designated—within the rhetoric of the cold war—as "free market" or "state planned" has been freshly examined to reveal that no such pure economies have existed in the postwar era.[39] The acceptance of this reality, and the abandonment of severe programs to realize these impossible economic myths, are fundamental to successfully renegotiating Latin American modernity.[40] Finally, the very goal of "development," shared by modernization and dependency theorists, has been reexamined. Escobar's study of its history reveals that "development" served U.S. and European governments, as well as Latin American elites and intellectuals, more than the impoverished "masses" of Latin Americans it was ostensibly promoted to aid.[41] Although both the radical geographers and Latin American theorists of postmodernity depart from the description of economic phenomena, both show an increasing valorization of political and cultural practices—as opposed to the seizing of the economic means of production—as fundamental to social transformation.[42]

Politically, revolution and authoritarianism have all but broken up into multiple and antagonistic versions of democracy and new social movements. Within this shifting political field, Latin American theorists, drawing on European and North American concepts of postmodernity, have made especially provocative contributions to postmodernism theory and to social transformation in Latin America. These writers begin by defining several features of modern politics.[43] First, modern politics rise up out of a need to stabilize the chaotic elements of societies shaken by the reformation, the discovery of "new worlds," and the rise of capitalism and industrialization. Bereft of traditional moorings, modern politics seeks to reground order on a human scale.[44] Second, modern politics base themselves on the assumption that a single key can decipher the code in which modern society "is written" and thus render it transparently legible.[45] Third, the actual "subject" of what I have been calling "modern politics" is a self-anointed vanguard (military, cultural, intellectual, or political) that masks its particular interpretations and interests as those of society as a whole.[46] Finally, their programs for social transformation are utopian in sharing two characteristics. First, they are future oriented, meaning that they are based in a disavowal of the past and present in favor of a future society valorized just because it is new. And second, they are total or final, meaning that the solution promised will solve *all* the problems of present society once and for *all*.[47]

With their equal suspicion of the utopian "metanarratives" offered by liberalism, Marxism, and fascism—to say nothing of the recent authoritarianism of Latin America (considered a neo-liberal/fascist fusion by Hinkelammert)—these writers may seem merely to be echoing Jean-François Lyotard's own definition of postmodernity as "incredulity toward metanarratives."[48] However, their appropriation of Lyotard's critique of modernity's metanarratives actually exemplifies the *critical* dimension of their engagement with European and North American theories of postmodernism.[49] For Lyotard's critique implies political consequences that are all too familiar in contemporary Latin American societies suffering under the austerity measures dictated by its reintegration into "anarchocapitalism."[50] Therefore, the writers, with their ears to the tracks of popular social initiatives, produce various, different but fundamentally related, alternative analyses and strategies for the reworking of modernity's egalitarian goals on the concrete terrain of contemporary Latin America. If Jameson seeks to maintain a concept of utopia alive, these theorists trace the attempts by Latin Americans to concretely redefine utopia.

The literature on the so-called new social movements within Latin America alone since the mid-1980s is already too vast to be reviewed properly here.[51] However, Benjamín Arditi offers a useful theoretical reflection—accompanied by concrete examples—on the challenges these movements pose to the modern social sciences and proposes a "new grammar" to make the initiatives more visible and their practices more highly valorized. Departing from an image of modernity and modernization similar to that sketched above, Arditi begins his proposal with a distinction between society and the social. *Society* refers to the imperfect realization (through institutions, laws, culture, etc.) of a particular—modern—dream of homogenizing the social in the name of a single "rationality" or interpretation of reality. Yet all such realizations, however totalitarian and apparently successful, must be imperfect. Arditi therefore calls "the social" that which exceeds the "nets" of "society." "Political" examples might include homeless or squatter initiatives; undocumented workers and even informal economies; greens; and women's, gays', and minorities' rights movements. But Arditi also offers a sampling of more narrowly "cultural" examples: artistic vanguards, alternative families, feminist and punk subcultures, gangs and the drug culture, prostitution, and premarital sex. All these exceed the visibility of the law and its grid of surveillance and registering apparatuses like the church, work, business, or construction permits, museums, etc. But it is not only a matter of rigorously distinguishing between two separate realms of human practices. Rather, society must be understood as the "crystallization" of social practices, some of which continue to exist uncrystallized as "the social" itself. Thus *the social* ultimately suggests practices in constant flux, some of which succeed temporarily in institutionalizing themselves in a dominant way via interconnections—"archipelagos," Arditi calls them—to form a society.[52]

In strategic terms, Arditi's account dictates a "politics of space." Social practices "surprise" society by contesting it at those sites it has overlooked as it focused on the conventional, official terrains of struggle. In Arditi's words, "some transformations can be forged by way of a permanent nomadism on the plane of the 'social,' particularly in relation to the culture and common sense of society; but to achieve the permanence of 'colonies' of the alternative, at some point these rebellious drives should shape strategic knowledges that animate new wills to power to take over marked off spaces, to modify segments of society."[53] Far from the utopian dream of a totally new, transcendent society freed of power relations, the "politics of space" seeks to work via power. It forms new identities and temporarily crystallizes new institutions for the partial transformation of society.

In this, Arditi's strategy proposal resembles those proposed by others. Hopenhayn writes of "new logics of social dynamics" generated by the new social movements. These displace politics from conventional avenues to locally based organizations and practices, and economics from the discourse of macrodevelopment to that of economic human rights and needs satisfaction. Lechner advocates a politics that values existing social initiatives without completely renouncing visions of the future. He also proposes a reconception of social reform that does not devalue it in relation to a glorified total revolution.[54] At the same time, the concrete case of the Sandinista revolution in Nicaragua suggests that the concept of revolution may also be transformed to accommodate increased flexibility, a renunciation of the discourse of total rupture, and greater democratization. For, despite the tragic consequences of U.S. intervention in terms of lost lives, the legacy of the Sandinista revolution—if we can speak of a legacy as though the revolution were over when precisely its "end" is at issue—is the *institution* or *crystallization* of a redefined, pluralized, democratic process in Nicaragua. Perhaps most importantly, this legacy leaves open the possibility of a Sandinista return to power, giving new meaning to the notion of "permanent revolution."[55]

Arditi's account, as well as Hopenhayn's, also assigns a constitutive role to cultural practices in the transformation of the social.[56] José Joaquín Brunner, argues that the exports of the U.S. culture industry—which for a previous generation were seen as homogeneous and imposed violently on Latin America—are instead received and creatively reinterpreted in accordance with local needs, much like the Catholic religion in the Christian base communities.[57] Because modernization has produced heterogeneity and a multiplicity of "cultural logics" in Latin America, Brunner insists that this heterogeneous cultural medium must be the condition of possibility for any strategy for development, modernization, or progress in the realm of social justice.[58] Similarly, Nestor García Canclini observes that modernization in Latin America has produced a "massification" of previously exclusive high culture and a commodification of popular culture.[59] But this is not necessarily a bad thing, because the "purity" of those realms in the past functioned more to oppress than to liberate; for example, by employing a "national" high culture to oppress native cultures, or by mythologizing "popular cultures" as a national heritage to mask the assault on the social groups and relations from which they emerge. Thus, for Canclini, postmodernity is a "peculiar kind of work being done on the ruins of modernity." The "hybrid cultures" of postmodernity in Latin America redefine the meaning of popular culture—rejecting ahistorical essentialisms and myths of authenticity—in terms of "sociocultural representativity."[60] This means accepting a new inclusiveness. It means not prescribing or circumscribing, but "permitting" genuinely popular culture to draw on even the most "tainted" of mediums in its attempts to combat political and economic marginalization.[61]

These discourses and concrete instances of a newly appreciated economic, political, and cultural impurity in Latin America—together with the observations of radical geographers and some theorists of mass culture (such as Huyssen) in Europe and North America—helped lay the foundation for my critiques of Hutcheon's and Jameson's theories of postmodernity. Only from a perspective rooted in heterogeneity can one obtain a critical purchase on theories that reduce it. They also suggest the contours a positive working concept of Latin American postmodernity, as a grammatical and material modification of postmodernity, might take. Latin American postmodernity demands that attention be given to the heterogeneity that exists (and that continually reproduces and displaces itself) among the various artifacts produced under a variety of local social conditions and aesthetic traditions. But second, Latin American postmodernity demands that the "original," "native," or "unique" elements identified in those artifacts not be interpreted only in light of those local phenomena. They must simultaneously be interpreted in light of differentiating global economic, political, and cultural processes that, although not immediately present, exert an ineluctable pressure on them. In critical practice, this means tracing the various local and global, social and political, cultural and aesthetic strands that are incorporated and transformed through the formal and technical activity of a text.

The fact that global structures of domination survive on differentiation requires us to grasp the various, local postmodernities as related, but not therefore homogeneous or identical. As critics, we must retain, not pretend to resolve, a tension between what will remain an unsatisfactorily homogenizing term: postmodernism, and the heterogeneous local forms produced within and sometimes against its logic. Something of this motivates Jameson's own seemingly totalizing argument: "At any rate, this has been the political spirit in which the following analysis was devised: to project some concept of a new systematic cultural norm and its reproduction in order to reflect more adequately on the most effective forms of any radical cultural politics today."[62] Perhaps if Jameson successfully projected the "concept of a new systematic cultural norm," it remains for others to "reflect more adequately on the most effective forms of any radical cultural politics today." Perhaps the formal articulation of this tension between local difference and global totality constitutes a postmodern politics. One response to Jameson's work might then be to confront his projected concept of global totality with the details of various local forms of cultural politics. In this way, certain global categories operative within Jameson's model (or other global models of postmodernity) can be provisionally rewritten with greater flexibility to assist us in understanding and articulating the heterogeneous forms of resistance culture functioning around the world today.

The following pages have been written with this in mind. I track the general shifts outlined by Latin American theorists of postmodernity as they occurred in Argentina from 1960 through the mid-1980s. My readings of four novels will be oriented around the shifting status of utopias and the emergence of historical representation as a site of social struggle. The Latin American postmodernity of these texts might also be considered "resisting postmodernity" in several senses. Of course, they "resist" assimilation into European and North American theories of postmodernism, such as those of Hutcheon and Jameson, but more specifically, they resist Hutcheon's theory because they resist local and international forms of domination. This social and political resisting is what Hutcheon cannot incorporate into her theory. They resist Jameson's theory by being postmodern in their resistance. This postmodernism within a Third-World resistance text is what Jameson cannot account for. Thus, by *being* a "resisting postmodernism," these narratives *are* "resisting postmodernism."

Of course, it would be ludicrous to claim that the transition from modernity to postmodernity in Argentina is reproduced identically throughout Latin America. Nor would it even be possible to suggest that the transition in the same nation—if tracked through popular music, or journalism for example—would look the same. Indeed, the reason in both cases is itself historical and very much bound up with the shift to postmodernity.

For the credibility of the term *Latin America*, the faith in the fullness of that term that characterized, as we will see, the revolutionary unity of the 1960s has in the meantime passed over to the free-market apologists for whom the term promises a unified Latin American market. Thus, the need to negotiate the tension between the tenuous conceptual validity of "Latin America" and the concrete particular case of Argentina is itself a symptom of the postmodern situation of both myself and my object of study. There could therefore be a *Latin American* modernity (as an effect of that modernity) but perhaps no *Latin American* postmodernity (except as a critical concept). Instead one of the effects of the crisis of that earlier modernity is that we must, for the moment, speak only an *Argentine* or *Brazilian* or *Nicaraguan* postmodernity. Beyond this, the shift in paradigm away from high culture, described by Brunner, García Canclini, and others, defines the postmodern and marks one of the limitations of the present work, which continues to emphasize literature, albeit recognizing its imbrocation with other forms of cultural and political practice.[63]

The very critiques of Hutcheon and Jameson I offered above preclude such generalizing gestures. On the other hand, the impulse to catalogue all these shifts, as though one could exhaust them and thus "fill" the concept of a Latin American postmodernity, must also be resisted. For this too goes against the spirit of the theories and practices just reviewed. Both these strategies, universalism and encyclopedism, remain caught within a logic of "final solutions" more proper to modernity. Instead, I must remain somewhat content with the tension between the very specific image I will produce of the shift from modernity to postmodernity in Argentine politics and narrative fiction—a close analysis of which will begin in the next chapter—and a more abstract, and shadowy, background of a general and uneven shift from modernity to postmodernity throughout the region. Much can be gained by retaining this uncomfortable tension: not least the possibility of linking, over the course of many different works and practices, the various heterogeneous Latin American postmodernities into an "archipelago" of initiatives toward renegotiating and transforming the region's violent encounter with Western modernity.

1

Latin American Modernity

2

Beyond Western Modernity?

Rayuela as Critique

> For Che there could and can only be one homage: that of
> launching oneself, as he did, against the alienation of man, against his
> physical and moral colonization.—Julio Cortázar

The concept of Latin American postmodernity as I have so far described it modifies an already existing body of European and North American *post*modernism. This concept also critically reviews economic modern*iza-tion* and the politics of Western modern*ity*. These relations all refer Latin American postmodernity to an international, Western framework. However, if Latin American postmodernity is to have a historical meaning specific to Latin America, it is important to grasp its relation to Latin American modernity.

Latin American modernity, meanwhile, really exists only as a retrospective construction. Its content and shape are inevitably determined by the concerns of our own postmodern situation. Certainly we strive to be faithful to the concerns and forces that shaped the culture of the earlier period, but we cannot somehow slip out of our own historical skins. We cannot shed the constraints imposed on our vision by contemporary history and thus reach some clear and pure concept of Latin American modernity-as-it-really-was, unobstructed by the passage of time. Jorge Luis Borges taught this lesson in the tricks of historical optics more than once.[1] Borges found that Kafka generated a retrospective rereading of previous writers in whom Kafkaesque themes could now be found and who were now realigned as Kafka's "precursors." Similarly, when Borges has the imaginary, fringe-symbolist poet Pierre Menard rewrite the text of *Don Quixote*—word for word—three hundred years after Cervantes, the unforgettable developments of the intervening three centuries force a different interpretation of the original text. The point is that although the past may have happened a certain way, we can only *remember* it with all the distortions that we know memory to involve, as well as with all its empowering and enabling creativity.[2] At the same time, we must be clear to historicize this distortion, to make its particular conditions of possibility visible, to ask what in our time contributes to the particular distortion. So here, my construction of Latin American modernity does not only reflect my own particular political and interpretive agenda, it is guided especially by those issues of central concern to theorists of Latin American post-modernity: namely, issues of political and cultural purity and impurity. In politics, these consist of questions of revolution, utopia, subversion, and democracy; in culture, of high and mass culture, of vanguardism and the role of the writer, and of historical knowledge and representation.

Latin American modernity is consolidated and reaches its highest expression in the 1960s. Social and cultural forces that had meandered, occasionally intersecting, through Latin America in the earlier part of the century came together in the 1960s. This convergence constituted a second Latin American declaration of independence from Europe (and a first from the United States). Specifically, the triumph of the Cuban revolution and the critical and commercial success of the so-called boom narratives represent the cornerstones of what I call Latin American modernity. These events drew sustenance from previous Latin American social and cultural movements. But they were also driven by the inadequacy of European (and North American) political, economic, aesthetic, and philosophical prescriptions for overcoming the alienating effects of modernity and modernization on peripheral societies like those of Latin America.[3]

"The most important events in the international socialist movement in 1960 took place in Cuba." Thus began a brief report by Stuart Hall and others in only the seventh issue of the British journal *New Left Review*.[4] François Maspero recalls that for European activists at the time, Cuba represented "a new youth in the world" that "threw down an open challenge to U.S. economic domination and dependence," and that "revenge was taken for a century of humiliations and bulldozer intervention. What had seemed impossible only yesterday was now there. . . . A new era was beginning. One where people could speak loud and strong." Meanwhile, for other Third-World countries, "the Cuban revolution meant that emancipation was possible."[5] C. L. R. James, for example, by this time an eminent Pan-Africanist, saw the Cuban revolution as "the ultimate stage of a Caribbean quest for identity."[6] Even for foreigners unsympathetic to the revolution, the potential magnitude of its effects, both real and symbolic, was not lost as U.S. counterrevolutionary interventions assaulted the revolution nearly from its first moments.[7] Within Latin America itself, the euphoria extended from insurgents and students to intellectuals. The left wing of the Argentine resistance patterned itself after Castro's successful 26 of July Movement as early as December 1959, when the first rural *foco* was launched by John William Cooke's *Uturunco* group.[8] Among intellectuals in Argentina at the time, the Cuban revolution provoked "the conviction that a new epoch had been entered, a new world shaken-up by the incorporation into history of millions of hitherto marginalized human beings."[9]

Meanwhile, the self-exiled Argentine writer Julio Cortázar (living in Paris since 1951) would write in 1967 that Cuba represented

> the incarnation of the cause of man as I had finally [Cortázar speaks of 1959, four years *before* the publication of *Rayuela*, his major work] come to conceive and desire it. I understood that socialism, which until then had seemed to me an acceptable, even necessary, historical current, was the only current of modern times that based itself on the basic human fact, on that *ethos,* as elemental as it is ignored by those societies in which I have had the fortune to live, on the simple, inconceivably difficult and simple principal that humanity would begin to truly merit its name on that day when the exploitation of man by man ceased.[10]

Cortázar, like the other major figures of the boom—Carlos Fuentes, Gabriel García Márquez, and Mario Vargas Llosa—expressed explicit support of the revolution in its early years through visits to the island. Throughout the decade, Cortázar insisted on the importance of the revolution, refused to judge its possible excesses, and argued for a certain "revolution in literature" to accompany it. "Few will doubt my conviction that Fidel Castro and Che Guevara have set the model for our authentic Latin American destiny," Cortázar wrote in 1969, "but I am in no way prepared to admit that the *Poemas humanos* [of César Vallejo, published posthumously in 1961] or *Cien años de Soledad* [1967 novel by Gabriel García Márquez] are lesser responses, on the cultural level, to those political responses."[11]

Since the early 1970s, however, the boom, including *Rayuela,* has come to be seen as the elitist aesthetic expression of a petit-bourgeois liberalism wedded more to the foreign values of modernization than to those of the revolution. Recent trends in narrative—such as the *testimonio,* or "testimonial novel"—are proffered as counterexamples of a genuinely popular and native expression. Miguel Barnet writes of the elite writers of Latin America that "without wishing to, perhaps, their works come to our continent from outside. . . . With a foreign lens, of the most rancid European, the exoticist, the paternalistic, the colonizing." In its place he offers the *testimonio* as "the gaze from within, from the Latin American *I,* from the Latin American *we.*"[12] Already in 1971, the Cuban critic and poet Roberto

Fernández Retamar would characterize the supposedly culturally revolutionary innovations of the boom writers as "anti-[Latin] American." He would look to the culture produced "within" the revolution and conclude that what had been foreseeable, but not yet possible in 1961, had finally been realized by 1971, namely, "a leap in the development of that [revolutionary] culture."[13] Fernández Retamar composed *Caliban*, he stated, as a response to the harsh criticism by Latin American novelists abroad of Castro's handling of the so-called Padilla affair in which the Cuban poet Heberto Padilla was forced to publicly disavow a book of poems expressing views critical of the revolution.[14]

An interesting component of this revision of the ideological character of the boom includes a critique of its break with the past. Doris Sommer has brilliantly highlighted the boom's nearly pathological disavowal of its Latin American literary past.[15] Carlos Fuentes, for example, spoke of a "new language" forged by boom novelists as a response to the new reality ushered in by the revolution.[16] Mario Vargas Llosa was less ambiguous when he compared the relationship between the boom's new novels and Latin America's earlier "primitive" narrative to that between the "skyscrapers and tribes, poverty and opulence."[17] Jean Franco argued that the boom novelists' vanguardist self-characterizations betrayed their complicity with the language of modernization theorists intent on eradicating the stagnating traditions of Latin American history in favor of the dynamic "new technologies" of Europe and the United States.[18] All these values are seen as, in fact, antagonistic to those of the Cuban revolution. Of course, this view ignores the extent to which the Cuban revolution itself was modernizing and vanguardist, and searching, in the disparaging words Franco applies to the boom novelists, "for new areas of experience." As Sommer writes, "The impression [that nothing really notable preceded them in Latin America] was reinforced at home by a regional euphoria created, in part, by Castro's triumph in 1959. Revolution promised immediate liberation after the frustrations and disappointments with the gradual evolutionism of older liberal projects."[19] Sommer reveals that precisely because it was a sometimes violently modernizing, utopian, and totalizing aesthetic, the boom epics were the perfect accompaniment to that revolution that intended to carve a new society and a "new man" out of a past marked by dependency and misery.[20]

Ultimately, however, the feeling of Latin America's "coming of age" generated by Cuba and the boom, as two commentators have phrased it, turned out to be "inflated."[21] But not merely inflated, for these hopes were sown on shaky ground to begin with. At the very least, they were sown on that same Western philosophical and political soil they had intended—in a momentous gesture of liberation—finally to cast off from. But they constituted and represented themselves as *departures* from existing European or North American models for solving related sets of problems. And both certainly appeared during the decade as successful ruptures with various modes of colonization and as the euphoric starting points for the construction of a new society and a new human being. Both also raised important concerns taken up by their postmodern counterparts in Latin America, particularly regarding the region's unsatisfactory insertion into the process of European and North American modernity. Nevertheless, both ultimately floundered. This was *not* due to their desire to change the world. To be sure, that, above all, is carried forth in the social, intellectual, and cultural postmodernities I am concerned with. Rather, they unraveled for different reasons. Both eventually generated an internal contradiction between, on the one hand, the *purity* each required and declared realized of its new social space, of its new man, the *totality* each demanded and proclaimed of its break with a materially and spiritually impoverished past, and, on the other hand, the *partiality* of what they actually realized. Neither survived this tension intact. Again, this contradiction was not in and of itself necessarily fatal. However, it became fatal to the degree that it was ignored or repressed, and consequently "returned" with significantly more violent energy. This inability to acknowledge and to live with contradiction, this intolerance for impurity, this radical utopian impulse, more than anything else, marks Latin American modernity. And, more than anything, the realization that such impurities are not only inevitable but can also be fruitful marks the Latin American postmodern.

Rayuela (1963; *Hopscotch*, 1966) always figures—along with Fuentes's *Muerte de Artemio Cruz* (1962; *Death of Artemio Cruz*, 1964), Vargas Llosa's *La ciudad y los perros* (1963; *The Time of the Hero*, 1966), and García Márquez's *Cien años de Soledad* (1967; *One Hundred Years of Solitude*, 1970)—among the major novels of the boom, and as probably the Southern Cone's major contribution to that movement and to the Latin American modernity that the boom, in my view, represents. The novel follows the physical and intellectual wanderings of a thirty-nine-year-old Argentine named Horacio Oliveira, his lover la Maga, and his group of friends, first in Paris and then in Buenos Aires.[22] To some extent, the narrative's trajectory depends on the novel's form. The text includes 155 chapters divided into three sections. Chapters 1 to 36 comprise a section entitled "Del lado de alla" (From/Of the side over there), chapters 37 to 56 are entitled "Del lado de aca" (From/Of the side over here), and chapters 57 to 155 form the third section, called simply "De otros lados" (From/Of other sides) with the parenthetical subtitle "Capítulos prescindibles" (Disposable chapters). The importance of *Rayuela*'s form, however, lay also in the "Tablero de dirección" (Instruction table) included prior to chapter 1. Through this innovation, the novel's form partially determines the content. The *tablero* directs the reader that *Rayuela* is "above all, two books":

> The first may be read in the ordinary form, and ends with Chapter 56, at the close of which there are three garish little stars that equal the word *End*. Consequently the reader will ignore, without remorse, what follows.
>
> The second may be read beginning with Chapter 73 and following then the order indicated at the close of each chapter. In case of confusion or forgetting, it will suffice to consult the following list.

The *tablero* then lists the order of the chapters to be read in the second book. They include all 155 chapters (except chapter 55, whose contents are nevertheless divided and reproduced in chapters 129 and 133). Chapters 1 to 56 (comprising the first two sections of the novel, remember) still appear in numerical order. But they are also chopped up, separated from one another by the interspersing, in seemingly random order, of chapters 57 to 155 (from the third section).

The first book (only chapters 1 to 56, read straight through) recalls the story of Horacio and la Maga's tumultous relationship in Paris. It climaxes in chapter 28 with the death of her baby, Rocamadour, during a party. Horacio and all their friends at the party know of the baby's death but keep it from the mother. After she discovers the baby's death, he and la Maga split up and he wanders around Paris looking for her until he is arrested and leaves for Buenos Aires. This closes the section entitled "Del lado de alla." In Buenos Aires, he meets up with an old friend, Traveler, and his wife Talita. There, still consumed by his bizarre and tragic affair with la Maga, Horacio first works for a circus and then in an insane asylum that has been purchased by the circus owner. He remains unable to establish a satisfactory relationship with the pair, and, finally, he seems to jump out the third-story window of his room onto a hopscotch board in the courtyard below. With this apparent suicide, the first book ends. The second book tells the same essential story, of course, but it is broken up by the fragmentary narratives and quotations (found in what are generally very brief, one- to five-page, chapters) of the third section. The basic structural effect of their incorporation into the narrative of the first book is to continue the book after Horacio's leap from the window in chapter 56. Seven chapters from the third section follow chapter 56. The last two—chapters 131 and 58—send the reader back and forth from one to the other on an apparently endless feedback loop. In terms of content, these fragments contain quotations from an author named Morelli that is studied by Horacio and his friends in what they call the "Club de la serpiente," as well as quotes from various other European authors. In this sense, the second book gives a more explicit metatextual effect than the first book. They also include short narrative accounts of the discussions of the friends, or between Horacio and two female lovers, one in Paris and another in Buenos Aires. Although these fragments do not alter the fundamental nature of the basic narrative, they do open that narrative—of Horacio's journeys in Paris and Buenos Aires—to a different, more philosophical perspective as well as rewrite the ending of book one, an apparent suicide, as what has most often been interpreted as Horacio's leap into madness.[23]

If Horacio does go mad, or if he kills himself, perhaps it is because he can't find what he is looking for. After all, "searching," he tells us near the beginning of both books, "was [his] symbol" (1:12/7). And if beginnings count for anything, searching seems to govern both the first and second books.[24] For chapter 1 (the beginning of the first book) begins with the question, "Would I/he find la Maga?" (1:9/3). Meanwhile, chapter 73 (the beginning of the second book) begins with the long, interrogative search for some kind of healer "who will cure us of the dull fire, the colorless fire" (73:325/383).

The objects of these two searches are related because they both appear to Horacio, at different points, to offer solutions to his fundamental problem: alienation. Both la Maga and this initially unidentified healer (which turns out to be culture—or -tura as in cul-tura, pin-tura, escri-tura—or invention) seem to promise a passage to an existence free of alienating, distancing, or mediating structures—an apparent utopia of immediacy. But Horacio will ultimately reject both, and this may be partially responsible for the sense of futility that marks both endings. At the same time, Horacio may have rejected both solutions because he felt them to be inextricably and irretrievably bound up with mediating and alienating structures from which he sought refuge. Perhaps Horacio imagines a third possibility beyond the partial satisfactions represented by erotic love (la Maga) and intellectual enrichment (culture).

We may also view the relationship between these two searched-for persons in another way. They might follow a centuries-old trope in writing about Latin America in which it is associated with the body and materiality or immanence and Europe with the mind and spirituality or transcendence. The foundational moments in this trajectory would include, besides the various chronicles of the discovery, Montaigne's "Of Cannibals" (1580) and Shakespeare's *Tempest* (1611). Within Latin American literature in the nineteenth century, the regional essence was defined, in the poetry of Andrés Bello (1820s), for example, in terms of its exotic physical features. José Martí in the 1880s and 1890s made this physical nature the basis for the identity of "Our America" and for good government. This figural alignment was temporarily reversed by José Enrique Rodó's famous *Ariel* (1900), which opposed the poetic spirituality of Latin America to the prosaic and crass materialism of North America. However, the *novela de la tierra,* or "novel of the earth," in the 1920s refigured an essentially exotic or bountiful nineteenth-century nature in more savage, though no less essentialist, terms. Finally the figure was reappropriated and reoriented by Brazilian modernism (1920s) in which cannibalism was inaugurated as a metaphor for cultural nationalism that persisted through the 1960s.[25] Retamar's *Caliban,* of course, is a similar reappropriation that valorizes the creativity of the Latin American body-culture while leaving the terms of the opposition intact. Finally, the very terms of the figural opposition were deconstructed by the Cuban novelist Alejo Carpentier in his 1974 novel *El recurso del metodo* (*Reasons of State,* 1977).[26] In this tradition, la Maga might represent an American solution, and culture a European solution to the same problem of alienation. In la Maga's case, this would reinforce the gendering of that nature/body as female throughout the trajectory outlined above.[27] This seems especially appropriate considering the respective "sides" of the novel that each dominates. La Maga occupies the central role in the side entitled "Del lado de allá." That is, in Paris, immersed in culture, Horacio seeks as his remedy la Maga, distinguished by her "lack" of culture and, precisely, by her body. On the other hand, the desire for *cultura* springs from existence on "this side," that is, from Buenos Aires. There, European "civilization" has always seemed to hold the cure for what ails Argentina.[28]

Yet we can complicate this arrangement still further. For the question that begins chapter 73 is actually preceded by the word *yes*: "Yes, but who will cure us . . . ?" To what unseen interlocutor does this yes refer? To what prior discourse? Perhaps to Molly Bloom who, at the end of James Joyce's *Ulysses,* closes her famous monologue by exclaiming, "Yes I said yes

I will Yes." This ending may mean, as one Joyce scholar has argued, "yes" to love—the "word known to all men"—as the solution to Leopold Bloom's own problems of alienation.[29] In that case, *Rayuela* begins by simultaneously reaffirming Joyce (and the Horacio who opens the first book searching for *his* lover) and pointing up the insufficiency of his (European—or is Joyce, the Irishman, a colonial writer?) solution. *Rayuela* says, in effect, "Yes [love is fine], but who will cure us of the dull fire, the colorless fire . . . ?"[30] If nothing else, this speculation offers a dramatic image of Latin American modernity's critical engagement with European high-modernism.

But the novel finally frustrates the attempt to definitively establish neat schemata, especially dualistic oppositions, and particularly ones based on beginnings.[31] So, short of asserting the priority of this or that precise alignment, I should argue only that this combination of beginnings puts in play the themes that organize *Rayuela*: alienation and immediacy, love and culture, the body and the mind. To this we may add the proviso that, in many places, the text views these very oppositions as signs of alienation. Thus, for a properly liberated human, these choices themselves would be false, remnants of a superseded historical age.

At the same time, it is most important—in the historicizing spirit of the present approach—to give these rarefied "universal" or "eternal" thematics the volume of concrete temporal and spatial dimensions. The discourse of contemporary Latin American literature, particularly the "boom" industry of critics and writers, has played a central role in de-temporalizing and de-spatializing these questions. Fueled by the desire to see Latin American narrative awarded its rightful place in a canon of international literature, this industry has purchased its entry ticket at the expense of downplaying the transitory, or historically and regionally specific, aspects of these works.[32] Kristin Ross has pointed to a similar phenomenon in studies of the poetic production of Arthur Rimbaud. In that case, critics have speculated about what Rimbaud might have produced if he had matured, what his never undertaken "masterpiece" might have looked like. Such speculations are governed by a teleological, or predetermined, view of historical development. This view rests, in turn, on an organicist metaphor of the living body—birth, youth, maturity, death—as the development model for all entities. Ross instead values Rimbaud's poetic production (and the Paris commune of 1871) precisely because of its explosive and transitory, non-developmental, character. Rimbaud and the Paris commune resisted the codification, crystallization, or "reterritorialization"—in short, the institutionalization—that plagued their twentieth-century revolutionary, political and cultural, successors: communism and surrealism.[33] The critical discourse Ross refers to, like that of the boom industry, fears historical change and discontinuity. For this may mark an event or work as historically interesting, but also as superseded in terms of the solutions it offers to contemporary problems—as timed rather than timeless. Resisting the pull of this discourse means situating *Rayuela* in its time and place.

The question of alienation and immediacy by which we may situate *Rayuela,* then, necessarily has multiple dimensions. First, if alienation is Horacio's problem, if searching is his symbol, what does *Rayuela* posit as the source(s) of that alienation and what remedies does it propose? But beyond this, we must inquire into the history or histories of this problem and its possible solutions, as well as into their geography. How is the problem specific to *Rayuela*'s time and places? How are the imagined solutions constrained by these dimensions? What pressure do the specific politics of those times and places exert on the text? Cortázar was a Latin American— more specifically a white, educated, middle-class, Argentine, heterosexual male. He was in Paris writing and reflecting on these questions throughout the late 1950s and early 1960s. We should inquire into the relationship between the problems and the possible solutions and the world of social and cultural possibilities that shaped Cortázar's imagination of what appear like timeless and spaceless themes.

I did not intend, by mentioning Ross's treatment of Rimbaud, similarly to universalize or eternalize Cortázar's work. On the contrary, I meant to suggest, however speculatively, that as Rimbaud's poetry is quite fruitfully understood in relation to the set of concrete spatial and historical coordinates in which he lived and worked, so this would be the case with Cortázar and his coordinates, especially the Cuban revolution and the New Left in general. But we should not rest this speculation on the establishment—as in my quote from Cortázar's letter on the Latin American intellectual—of biographical links. On this problem, Ross instructively writes that in the case of Rimbaud and the Paris commune, one should instead consider "Rimbaud's poetry, produced at least in part within the rarefied situation of his isolation in Charleville, *as one creative response to the same objective situation to which the insurrection in Paris was another.* In what way does Rimbaud figure or prefigure a social space adjacent . . . to the one activated by the insurgents in the heart of Paris?"[34] May we substitute Cortázar for Rimbaud, Paris or Saignon (where Cortázar had a farmhouse) for Charleville, and the revolution in Cuba for the insurrection in Paris? If so, then on what grounds? There may be a formal link between Rimbaud and Cortázar: both share the abstract problem of the relationship of writing to modern society. This formal link, in turn, gives rise to a certain shared abstract content: the response formulated by each to that problem. This response is an absolute and non-predetermined flight from alienation into the material ethos of a genuinely lived experience. But this abstract content, this response, will be concretized in each case by its specific place, time, and "objective" conditions. Perhaps I could go so far as to say that if Rimbaud and Cortázar mark its two cultural endpoints, figures like Antonin Artaud—of whom, if I may yield to the lure of biographical links, Cortázar wrote a moving obituary for the Argentine literary journal *Sur*— or Franz Kafka stand in between.[35] Again, the important point is not to write here the full history of this gesture—an approximation might be found in the collaborative works of Gilles Deleuze and the late Félix Guattari. Instead our task will be to understand the specifics of how *Rayuela* narrativizes this gesture, adjacently to the social dilemmas and solutions of its times and places (and it does have more than one time and place).

However, this "flight into the concrete" already presupposes an endpoint that here, at least, we have not yet reached. We left Horacio with his searching. Searching, then, may be the futile and maddening project that fuels this narrative. But Horacio's search itself presupposes that problem of alienation to which it, the search, is a response. The concept of alienation, for that matter, opens up another route by which potentially to see the connection between *Rayuela* and the major social event of its time, the Cuban revolution. Alienation, of course, is not in and of itself limited to the experience of Latin Americans peripherally incorporated into modernity. It has, however, taken specific forms since the advent of capitalism. And these forms are further determined by the experience of colonialism.

In his *Economic and Philosophic Manuscripts* of 1844 as well as in one of his drafts of *Capital* (called the *Grundrisse* and written in 1857 and 1858), Marx characterized labor under capital as "estranged," because the product of the worker's labor is alienated from him or her. Marx thus gave more specific historical and social dimensions to earlier metaphysical conceptions of human alienation, such as those found in early Christianity or in Hegel's philosophy.[36] The product of human labor under capitalism appears not as something for the enrichment of the laborer's experience, but, on the contrary, as an "*alien* object" to which he or she is subject.[37] For that matter, external nature itself comes to appear as an alien force to be conquered in the process of production. Not only is an external world of nature and the product of capitalist labor alien, but also the process of labor itself, the activity, the production is alienated because the worker works not "to affirm himself" but to deny himself. The capitalist worker does not immediately satisfy his own physical and spiritual needs in his labor but labors out of the need to obtain subsistence wages and toward the goal of producing an alien object. Even the very time spent laboring does not belong to the worker—it is itself an alien object (or commodity) that he or she has been obliged to sell to the capitalist.[38]

But, crucially, Marx also defined several other aspects of human alienation under modern capitalism. For Marx, human beings were distinguishable from animals, among other ways, by the fact that whereas the animal is nothing more than the activity of continually reproducing its own life and its species, human beings have a consciousness of this activity above and beyond it. For the modern worker, already alienated, animal-like labor also alienates "the *species* from man."[39] If it were possible for the laborer to have an experience of the process (though precisely this possibility is diminished by alienated labor), he or she would sense that the essence of their humanity—that which makes them human—lay elsewhere, literally and figuratively beyond their grasp. In the countercultural idiom of the sixties the worker is "dehumanized" as his life becomes more and more consumed with an animal-like, unselfconscious reproduction of self and species.[40] Ultimately, alienated labor implies the alienation of human beings from each other: "If the product of labour does not belong to the worker, if it confronts him as an alien power, then this can only be because it belongs to some *other man than the worker*. If the worker's activity is a torment to him, to another it must give *satisfaction* and *pleasure*. Not the gods, not nature, but only man himself can be this alien power over man."[41] Consequently, Marx saw communism as "the complete return of man to himself" and as "the *genuine* resolution of the conflict between man and nature and between man and man—the true resolution of the strife between existence and essence, between objectification and self-confirmation, between freedom and necessity, between the individual and the species."[42]

For Marx, the fact of capitalist relations of production had alienating effects far beyond the immediate site of production. The human worker's very consciousness of him or herself as a human being is worn away, and that humanity itself becomes something distant, separate, alien. It even comes to confront that worker in the presence of some other human individual with power over the worker. Marx did not fully develop the implications of this view of alienation for colonial societies. Colonial intellectuals, however, added another dimension to Marx's four-dimensional concept of alienation. Ngugi wa Thiong'o, for example, the great Kenyan writer, defines alienation as that condition "of seeing oneself from outside oneself as if one was another self."[43] For the colonial child the very medium of self-conceptualization—language—was, literally, foreign: "This resulted in the disassociation of the sensibility of that child from his natural and social environment, what we might call colonial alienation. The alienation became reinforced in the teaching of history, geography, music, where bourgeois Europe was always the centre of the universe."[44] It may be argued that this process of colonial alienation is more dramatic for Africans than for Latin Americans—at least for those creole Latin Americans without the memory of an indigenous or tribal language. But even this distinction relies on a prior "alienation" of other Latin Americans, of earlier generations or other races and classes. And moreover, even if it is not directly a question of an imposed *foreign* language, the disjuncture of European modes of thought and social organization with the Latin American realities onto which they were applied has been *implicit* in the region's cultural production from the first moments of the conquest. Was not Fidel Castro attempting to address such colonial alienation when, in the summer of 1959, he rejected both of the "political and economic ideologies being debated in the world"? Castro asserted that "we do not agree with any of them. Each people must develop its own political organization, out of its own needs, not forced upon them or copied; and ours is an autonomous Cuban revolution. It is as Cuban as our music. Can we conceive of all peoples listening to the same music?"[45] But this has been an *explicit* theme in Latin American culture since the early nineteenth century, as Castro's own analogy shows. In fact, it is the central theme of Martí's "Nuestra américa" essay, written in 1891: "The government should be born of the nation. The spirit of the government should be that of the nation. The form of the government should come from the constitution of the nation itself."[46] Martí's proposal responds to the problem of Latin American elites searching for answers to its problems abroad. Indeed, Djelal Kadir's brilliant *Questing Fictions* departs from the fact of Latin America's "colonial alienation" to trace a history of searching for identity in Latin American letters.[47] Finally even the problem of specifying the appropriateness of a concept like "postmodernism" for Latin American culture should be inscribed within this history of colonial alienation. Though it is also true, as I argued in the first chapter, that Latin American postmodernism itself restates the problem in terms other than those furnished by the basic opposition of "indigenous" and "foreign."

As we now reopen *Rayuela,* alienation presents numerous, interrelated faces and figures, all of which we would do well to read with these historically specific (to modernity and capitalism) and geographically specific (to colonization) senses of alienation in mind. Of course, the first lines of the first book suggest a concrete, physical alienation—that is, separation—from la Maga. This turns out, on closer inspection, to dramatize an alienation that already existed even when the couple was living together. But what separates them? The various answers to this already refer us to other forms of alienation. On one level, for example, they are separated by those cultural conditions peculiar first to modernity, and second, to the Latin American—and more generally colonial—experience of that modernity that I introduced above. I mean, namely, their respective relationships to culture and nature and to the cleavage between the two that modernity institutes.[48] For while la Maga hungrily devours cultural artifacts, notions, and discussions, Horacio seeks, with equal desperation, to escape the prison-house of culture he laboriously constructed for himself. In their parallel and sometimes shared searches for meaning in life, la Maga and Horacio head in opposite directions. But, moreover, each sees the other as the possessor of that secret understanding each seeks. The subsequent resentment and incompatibility of their goals drive an alienating wedge between them.

Their problem (and I say "their" problem because la Maga's blind desire for culture was also, at one time, Horacio's—that is part of what he cannot tolerate in her) has been the problem of an educated class of Latin Americans at least since Andrés Bello wrote his famous "silvas americanas" from an industrializing London in the early nineteenth century, as the wars of independence from Spain drew to a close.[49] Bello's poems registered the tension of the colonial intellectual, a tension that he, like Martí, also articulated in essay form in 1848.[50] On the one hand, he wished to produce a cultural glue through which to cement the newly independent republics of Latin America into a coherent, sovereign, and self-recognizing entity.[51] He even apparently recognized that existing European culture alone would be an ill-fitting cloak on the Latin American body. On the other hand, the economics of a world market centered in Northern Europe, especially in England, exerted an ineluctable force on Bello and the succeeding generation of liberal elites throughout Latin America who saw no other road out of the economic debt and impoverishment and civil disorder left in the wake of the wars of independence than that paved by French philosophy and British capital.[52] Bello must assert independence, but on what grounds? This problem of grounding new beginnings that beset modernity in Europe was felt as a double-bind for a nineteenth-century postcolonial intellectual like Bello.[53]

Torn by these tensions, Bello pursues contradictory paths in his canonical poems "Alocución a la Poesía" (1823) and "La agricultura de la zona torrida" (1826), both of which were written in London.[54] He both catalogues and celebrates the uniqueness of American nature *and* primes that nature for European appropriation in the philosophic, aesthetic, and economic sense of the term. He holds a mirror of American nature up to a newly self-constituting lettered elite in Latin America. But that mirror doubles as a window through which Bello's European audience can consume the delights of that landscape, turning *naturaleza* into *agricultura;* nature into agri*culture*. He searches simply for economic, political, and cultural sovereignty. But Bello is hamstrung by the dependency established by neocolonial economic structures, huge postwar debts, civil chaos, and cultural diversity and conflict. The response is to ground that sovereignty on the European example. He legitimizes Latin American independence and civilization by appending it to a history of Western independence and civilization. Bello, a Venezuelan who lived in Chile, may have been Latin America's first postcolonial intellectual as the term is understood, with modifications, by K. Anthony Appiah: "A *comprador* intelligentsia: a relatively small, Western-style, Western-trained group of writers and thinkers, who mediate the trade in cultural commodities of world capitalism at the periphery. In the West they are known through the [Latin America] they offer: their compatriots know them both through the West they present to [Latin America] and through a [Latin America] they have invented for the world, for each other, and for [Latin America]."[55] In Argentina, this stance becomes virtually a cultural institution in its own right: "la mirada a europa."[56] And so the Faustian price of Latin American formal independence, already at this moment in the nineteenth century and arguably from the first minute of the conquest, is an alienation from a Latin American nature that is first cancelled out in reality, and then preserved as an effective, but symbolic, image of Latin American identity.

La Maga seeks to turn her back on the stereotyped violence of Latin American nature—her memory of Montevideo is of a rape by a black neighbor on a sultry summer night in the courtyard of her tenement building (15:58–59/60–61)—and goes to Paris to uplift herself by consuming European culture. But once there, she meets her own possible future, a disenchanted Horacio who has made the same journey, "has" culture, and now longs nostalgically for a lost immediacy whose original source is no longer even localizable for him. His position reminds us of the protagonist of Carpentier's *Los pasos perdidos* (1953; *The Lost Steps,* 1957) who also flees modern culture in search of a perceived lost immediacy only to find, quite literally, that he can't find his way back.[57] But it may have even a longer history dating back, arguably to Martí, and certainly including Argentine Ricardo Güiraldes, *Don Segundo Sombra* (1929) and Borges own story, "El Sur" (1944). For that matter, Pablo Neruda's *Canto General* (1950), with its elegaic celebration of Latin American nature, is nevertheless far from blind to the complications involved in finding one's voice there. As for Horacio, he can never forgive her for appearing to possess innately what he has sought so desperately, but with such futility (21:88/96 and 26:119/133). In this sense, what alienates Horacio and la Maga from each other is their respective, and contradictory, alienating relationships to culture and nature. "You're looking for something you don't know," la Maga tells him at one point. "I've been doing the same thing and I don't know what it is either. But they're two different things" (19:72/76). For each of them, but at exactly opposite times, both nature and culture come to be seen as alienating obstacles toward the fullness of a meaningful existence for which they then search via the opposite term. And the nonsynchronicity of their searches, their perfect noncoincidence, alienates them from each other. It is difficult to see how, within the framework of postcolonial cultural dependency established in the nineteenth century, especially in the Southern Cone, it could be otherwise.

Consider now this problem as it manifests itself in the example of language. A particular, but also all-encompassing, form of culture, language confronts Horacio as a mediating structure, estranging us from genuine experience. Language is the tool by which we parcel out and distance an undifferentiated and immediate reality the better to identify and dominate it. Morelli, the writer much admired and discussed by Horacio and his friends in Paris, cites a favorite passage to this effect: "Language, just like thought, proceeds from the binary arithmetical functioning of the brain. We classify by yes and no, by positive and negative. [. . .] The only thing that my language proves is the slowness of a world vision limited to the binary. This insufficiency of language is obvious, and is strongly deplored" (86:347/410). This view of language can also be found in surrealism.[58]

And the metaphor of velocity, through which language is devalued as slow, can be traced at least to Italian futurism and even, according to one interpretation, to Rimbaud.[59] In any case, although the desire for speed is merely a metaphor for an unfrozen language as fluid as material reality in general, it also expresses the very specific need for a language that can represent and keep pace with the speed characteristic of material modernization under capitalism.

La Maga, thought by Horacio to have the kind of extracultural, immediate experience of reality that he desires, at one point states that "I don't know how to talk about happiness, but that doesn't mean that I haven't had it" (24:112–13/152). Opposing "talking" about happiness to "having it," la Maga establishes the possibility of a space of happiness beyond language. Horacio seems to confirm this when he speaks of "what she understands and which has no name" (21:88/95). Furthermore, language is a large part of his difficulty in establishing the intimacy with her that he seeks as a means of transcendence: "A whole canefield of words has grown up between la Maga and me" (21:87/95). Language is a vehicle for culture, but it is also a vehicle for that specific historical form of culture called Western reason or science. In the midst of an intense philosophical discussion, itself embedded in one of the most haunting and horrifying episodes of the novel, Horacio argues that humankind has taken a wrong turn. It "has grabbed onto science like an anchor of salvation . . . Reason with its use of language has set up a satisfactory architecture . . . and it has stuck us in the center. In spite of all its curiosity and dissatisfaction, science, that is to say reason, begins by calming us down" (28:142/162). And Horacio, at least one part of him, is restless within the structure of Western reason, culture, and language.

Now let us return to those beginnings for just another moment. Recall that the narrator in chapter 73 searches for a cure. That narrator associates the fire that pursues "us" with "this side." The subsequent corollary question or search involves "how to find the *other* side of habit" (emphasis added). "Habit," for its part, is given more concrete shape as "infallible equations and conformity machines." But habit, also crucially, is exemplified by the very question "how to find the other side of habit." In that case, invention (-*turas*) must be "our possible truth," suggests the narrator. And yet, he goes on to conclude, "one can choose his ture, his invention . . . That is how Paris destroys us slowly, delightfully . . . with its colorless fire that comes running out of crumbling doorways at nightfall. An invented fire burns in us, an incandescent ture. . . . We burn within our work . . .

No one will cure us . . . we invent our conflagration, we burn outwardly from within" (73:326/384–85). Initially, culture as invention appears as the way beyond the one-dimensional society of cybernetics and rationality. But ultimately, it is unmasked as that society's twin; all, it turns out, part of the same mediating, alienating "dull fire" that chains us to "this side" of habit. The speed of the avant-garde becomes difficult to distinguish from that of the capitalist.

Horacio responds to the alienating rationality of language by speaking nonsense and to the alienating materiality of the body—which separates his "self" from la Maga's "other"—through eroticism. He pronounces the silent *H* before his name and before other vocalized words in Spanish as a way of deforming the most natural uses of language (90:352/416). Similarly he and la Maga speak a nonsense language of "gliglico" in an offhanded tone, replacing the everyday form of language with a subversive, nonrational content. "Gliglico" is often spoken by the couple as a language of eroticism (in chapter 68, for example). And eroticism, in turn, apparently serves, for Horacio, as a means of self-transcendence, of blurring the boundaries—on which reason is founded and which it preserves—between subjective self and objective other. Gilles Deleuze, writing of Cortázar's contemporary Pierre Klossowski in the context of a history of nonsense, connects the three arenas of the body (eroticism), the self (alienation), and language (nonsense): "At the same time that bodies lose their unity and the self its identity, language loses its denoting function."[60] Horacio, however, recognizes that his remedies are homeopathic. That is, he knows that, as with culture in general, his project is the risky one of attempting to turn language and the body against themselves.

With eroticism, if the problem is the cleavage between self and other, between subject and object, the solution only re-objectifies the other. He turns la Maga into a raw material or catalyst to be consumed in the process of Horacio's subjective expansion, or self-transcendence. Rather than a genuine blurring or merging of self and other, the other winds up depleted, inert, and discarded after the reaction. And Horacio is left back where he started, needing a new fix but without a supply line. In this, a feminist-inspired reading of *Rayuela* might trace this reaction back through Latin American culture to the feminization of that same nature that is so problematically refined. Literary moments in this genealogy might include Carpentier's protagonist's relationship to his Mestiza companion Rosario in *Los pasos perdidos,* Doña Barbara in the novel of the same name (1928), the various women in Bolívar's life as recounted in Ricardo Palma's *Tradiciones*

Peruanas of the 1870s, and, of course, Jorge Isaacs's María or José Marmól's Amalia in the eponymously titled romantic novels of 1867 and 1852, respectively.[61]

In all these cases, Horacio certainly recognizes the paradox of using the body to get beyond it, or language to get beyond it. But he also presumes that the *content* of language or the body is the problem, *the uses* to which they are put within a rational, bourgeois society. Obversely, the proposed solution is that language or the body, put to different uses, can lead one to a rupture with that society, into a beyond—"the other side of habit"—characterized as immediacy and plenitude. But Horacio fails to recognize, at least initially, that even this proposal fails to escape the utilitarian, means-end, logic of Western reason. Thus Horacio conceives la Maga as a means toward the end of self-transcendence, subversions of language as means toward the end of a realm beyond language. It is this form as much as the contents of bodies or words that alienates Horacio. As Georges Bataille, like Artaud, asked: *"How can man find himself—or regain himself—seeing that the action to which the search commits him in one way or another is precisely what estranges him from himself?"*[62] Horacio's failure to recognize this leads him to formulate these paradoxical solutions and dooms him to failure and death and/or madness. These last, then, might be read as the only genuine escapes from reason and only then when they either conclude definitively or are "end-less" and cannot be recuperated as an object of rational contemplation in their own right.[63]

Aside from their internal contradictions, all of Horacio's strategies to get beyond Western culture have already, by this time, a history of their own *in* Western culture. Boccaccio, Cervantes, Rabelais, Sterne, Sade, Carroll, Rimbaud, Joyce, Artaud, Bataille, and even Deleuze might form one genealogy of this strategy. In this, Cortázar might appear stuck in the mode of the colonial intellectual who, like Bello, seeking refuge from an alienated colonial existence—in which meaning or referent is always elsewhere; namely, at the metropolis—goes to the metropolis, literally and figuratively. Upon his return, he rehearses for his native audience a warmed-over routine of metropolitan cultural leftovers. Thus to the contradictions inherent in these strategies when they are applied in European culture, we must add the apparent (and not necessarily fatal) contradiction involved in grounding a decolonizing strategy on models furnished by the colonizer.

This, indeed, was the view of many critics on the Left in Latin America. For them, Cortázar's early work represented a flight from political writing and symptomatized a certain Latin American intellectual, and especially a certain Buenos Aires, dependence on Europe.[64] On the one hand, these criticisms usefully corrected the celebratory excesses of many boom apologists. But their criticisms were constrained by a certain view of what constitutes politics. Gerald Martin's otherwise excellent work succinctly epitomizes these limitations. Martin writes that although *Rayuela* "considers the state of the world today, the condition of being a Latin American, and the relation between Latin America and Europe . . . Cortazar's . . . analysis largely excluded politics."[65] Unless "politics" refers, in the bourgeois sense, to running countries or to the struggle to run countries, it is difficult to imagine how it can be said, given all that Cortázar is said to consider, that he excludes politics. Martin's rather offhand remark actually reveals that what is at stake in these critiques of *Rayuela* is the meaning of politics in Latin America, a debate over which dominated the Latin American, and indeed the global Left, in the 1960s. Did social change have to begin with the seizure of power of an economic base, followed by control of state power and, only after a period of time, the production of a genuinely decolonized revolutionary culture? Or could the catalyst, on the other hand, be cultural—or in the terms of the first view "ideological"—transformation?

By appearing to address, in his early work, the second kind of question, Cortázar seemed to have cast his lot with that New Left that would develop into the American countercultural movement and, especially, the movements in Paris in 1968. This implied, within the logic of these critiques, that he apparently had turned his back on the materialism of the Cuban revolution. This last, meanwhile, had itself, by the late 1960s and early 1970s, already committed to a fairly orthodox Soviet-line communism opposed, needless to say, to certain spontaneist, voluntarist, or irrationalist uprisings like those in Prague or Paris. Thus, what is lamented as Cortázar's *successful* flight into irrationality in *Rayuela* is opposed to the highly valued rationality of the Cuban revolution. The fictional Horacio certainly takes his place in a line of subversive European artists and intellectuals engaged in the search for a way out of the false reality of the alienating modern, rational, and rationalized Western world. However, as an emblem of these strategies or even of Argentine cultural postcolonial dependency, Horacio *fails*. This fact seems to be overlooked in most critiques. If it is acknowledged, it is gloated over as evidence of the superiority of a more measured rationality embodied in the Cuban revolution. But such a view ignores the possible critical effect of representing such a failure. Horacio not only fails in his attempts to overcome the alienated experience of modernity, he fails to escape the logic of rationality altogether. Rationality and irrationality, modernization and modernism or the avant-garde are all, *Rayuela* seems to suggest, part of the same project of Western culture. And this whole project, not simply rationality or irrationality, this or that strategy, but the whole project, is what has failed.

The novel's representation of the project of European modernity as fruitlessly paradoxical and therefore failed is perhaps the central dimension of *Rayuela*'s critique of that modernity. It is as if the narrator who addressed the insufficiency of Joyce in the first lines of the second book glimpses the problem that the culture of modernism springs from the same font of Western knowledge as the material modernization to which it critically responds. The development of Western sciences as a result of the Enlightenment and the Renaissance—not to mention the "discovery" of Cortázar's homeland, the appearance of capitalism, together with the passionate desire for the new—serves as the common wellspring for the technological advances that fuel modernization and the technical innovations that mark the high modernism of, say, a James Joyce. And furthermore, the very process of social and economic modernization brings with it a concomitant change in the status of the writer with respect to society that is as much a marker of modern literature as any particular technical innovation.[66]

Andreas Huyssen, in an essay first published in 1984, argued that "the larger problem we recognize today . . . is the closeness of various forms of modernism in its own time to the mindset of modernization, whether in its capitalist or communist version."[67] Huyssen even suggests that this recognition—the critique of modernization in society in culture—marks a space of possible coincidence for Western postmodernism and Third-World culture. Yet this sort of observation, taken out of context, may authorize the postmodernization of a work like *Rayuela* in European and North American literary criticism. For Horacio's fortunes in *Rayuela* certainly reveal the complicity of modern culture with modernization. Perhaps this critique of modernity, this refusal to bestow success of any sort on Horacio as either the strategist of modernism and the avant-garde or the postcolonial Argentine intellectual, launches *Rayuela* into the orbit of transnational postmodernity. Is it then the case, as Hanns-Josef Orthel has neatly asserted, that [postmodern literature's] "central example is *Hopscotch,* that great work by Julio Cortázar"?[68]

But the mere positing of this problem of the modernism/modernization association alone does not make *Rayuela* a postmodernist work. It does seem to position *Rayuela* "peripherally" and critically with respect to European aesthetic modernism. But recent critical work has already shown how many different modernisms of European provenance were already "peripheral" or "critical" with respect to European aesthetic modernism, depending on how one constructs the category.[69] Moreover, in our case, two crucial considerations are still lacking: first, an examination of the alternatives the novel proposes, and second, a consideration of the concrete historical and geographical circumstances out of which these alternatives emerged. Short of this, we could only reproduce the gestures of earlier critics by either, on the one hand, falsely and prematurely assimilating *Rayuela* to currents in either *European and North American* modernism or postmodernism, or, on the other, naïvely repudiating its relationship to these two trends.

It may be helpful, therefore, to pause and observe that the novel also carries this drama of alienation, modernist solution, and failure/critique of modernism within its formal structure. Recall that Cortázar offers the reader two books in the "Tablero de dirección." The first is a more or less conventional narrative, including fifty-six chapters numbered in cardinal sequence and divided into two sections and finishing with the word "END." The second book is ostensibly the more innovative because it includes some 150 chapters in a relatively scattered order (certainly not in cardinal sequence) divided into three sections and ending (or not) with the directive to go back and forth from chapter 131 to chapter 58.

Critics have often read this formal drama as an expression of the intent of Cortázar as presented in the words of the invented author within *Rayuela*, Morelli. Morelli asks himself "whether someday I will ever succeed in making it felt that the true character and the only one which interests me is the reader, to the degree in which something of what I write ought to contribute to his mutation, displacement, alienation, transportation" (97:370/437). He wants to make "an accomplice of the reader, a traveling companion. Simultaneanize him, since/provided that [*puesto que*] the reading will abolish reader's time and substitute author's time. Thus the reader would be able to become a coparticipant and cosufferer of the experience through which the novelist is passing, *at the same moment and in the same form*" (79:337/397; translation modified). The reader comes to share in the experience of aesthetic production, so that finally, Morelli hopes, "what the author of this novel might have succeeded in for himself, will be repeated (becoming gigantic, perhaps, and that would be marvelous) in the reader-accomplice" (79:337/398).

Morelli also suggests the form through which this kind of reader might be elicited or evoked. This new novel should present to the reader "something like a façade, with doors and windows behind which there operates a mystery which the reader-accomplice will have to look for" (79:337/398). He opposes this active reader-accomplice with a "female-reader" who passively lets herself be carried along by an author-itative narrative, the (male) reader-accomplice aggressively participates in the construction of the narrative. Let us leave aside what today appears as the unacceptable gendering of the distinction even though its roots are nonetheless quite specific regionally and historically, and hardly irrelevant to a discussion of the distance between the aims and claims of a revolution relative to its actual accomplishments.[70] Cortázar does indeed seem to have constructed *Rayuela* around this opposition. He invites, but really much more aggressively challenges, the reader to take up the "masculine" position of the accomplice and read the obviously privileged second book. This choice pretends to lead to a liberation of both reader and author from the alienating constraints of their conventional roles. And overcoming alienation, is, after all, what this is all about. The conventions of realism (as perceived, of course, by modernism) are bound with rationality, linearity, and an *author*-itarian logic that positions *author* over reader. Cortázar and Morelli confront these conventions and the order they emblematize by trying to undermine themselves and their practice as it has come to be institutionalized in bourgeois aesthetics. From an avant-garde position, they practically force the reader to assume an uncomfortable, but ultimately self-realizing position as a coauthor. The text ceases to function as an alienating screen between author and reader and becomes instead the site of their immediate reunion.

Reviewing one such account of *Rayuela* in the mid-1970s, Lucille Kerr questioned the oppositional logic of the *tablero*.[71] According to Kerr, the apparent opposition between two modes of reading, one repressive and one liberating, is spurious. To begin with, essentially the same story is told, though with a different ending. But, more important, the arrangement of the second book's chapters, although not cardinally sequential, is nevertheless tightly organized. And, for that matter, the illusion of reader participation is counterbalanced by the authority of the writer who has organized the chapters in the second book. Thus rationality and authority, the deplored qualities of the first (realist) book and the mode of existence with which it is associated, reassert themselves in the second (modernist or avant-garde) book.[72] But there is an even more striking flaw in this attempt to transcend the alienation of aesthetic form. I mean that its intended function—to liberate the reader from the structures of bourgeois rationality and utility—*as function* negates its ability to achieve the intended effect.

We are once again before one of Horacio's paradoxical formulations: get beyond language through language, beyond bodies through bodies, beyond the fire through the fire. All, as we said, are caught within the same logic of rational utility, all are still means to an end. But Horacio's failures, we said, were the failures of modernism and the avant-garde as well as the failures of the postcolonial intellectual embracing the iron maiden of metropolitan forms. This is true also of the contradictions within and the failure of the *tablero*. For a staple of modernist and avant-garde aesthetics has been its self-positioning in opposition to a caricatured straw man of realism. The essential strategy of modernism, even beginning with Flaubert and on through such otherwise diverse figures as Baudelaire, Darío, Breton, Adorno, Sontag, boom writers such as Vargas Llosa, Fuentes, or García Márquez, Eco ("the open work"), and poststructuralists such as Roland Barthes ("readerly" vs. "writerly" and "work" vs. "text"), has involved "the division of literature into these two starkly antithetical tendencies (form oriented vs. content oriented, artistic play vs. imitation of the real)."[73] Thus, Kerr's reading suggests, though nowhere explicitly, that consciously or unconsciously, the failure of the *tablero* echoes the other modernist failures in the novel's narrative unfolding and thus reveals another dimension of *Rayuela*'s critique of European modernity.

Rayuela's critical engagement with European modernity should be read within a long Latin American tradition of such critical engagements in relation to metropolitan culture. Many of these come from precisely the difficult space of the postcolonial intellectual. And their paradigmatic form might be the false or deforming citation. As Julio Ramos has convincingly argued, the quote from Europe need not only be considered the cultural counterpart to material dependency or debt.[74] Citing does not spring only from impoverishment, and it need not signify only the enrichment of the source and the dependent consumerism of the ultimate audience. On the contrary, by its very nature, citing is a violence done to an original, an excision. Not the economic metaphors drawn from dependency theory, in which any engagement with the metropolis must degrade the periphery, but rather that of a guerrilla raid—or of Caliban, the *bricoleur*—reworking the stolen tools of the enemy seems best to express this notion of citing. Of course, depending on the concrete circumstances, what may really be involved is the enrichment of the middle-man, the avant-garde mediator—Appiah's postcolonial intellectual—between two cultures whose cultural capital is that neither his source nor his audience has access to the other except through him. In the Argentine tradition, beginning with the falsely attributed epigrammatic citation that opens the pages of Sarmiento's *Facundo*, the *cita* is, at the very least, a way of purchasing and securing the authority of the writer at the expense of the authority of the source. In either case, the *cita* marks the space of an encounter or—as Ramos writes, a *desencuentro*, or "dis-encounter." I don't mean that every mode of citation in Latin American literature is a kind of politically radical cultural raid, only that it has always the potential to be this given certain concrete social conditions.

This view draws on the work of Cuban anthropologist Fernando Ortíz, who, in 1940, proposed the term *transculturación*, "transculturation," to replace "acculturation" in reference to process initiated by the violent clash between two cultures such as we find in colonization. Ortíz felt that "acculturation" implied simply the acquisition of the new culture. Colonization however involved also a destruction of the old culture (with varying degrees of effectiveness: *desculturación*) as well as the creation of new cultural elements through the mixing of the old and the new, the native and the foreign: *neoculturación*.[75] Michel de Certeau, viewing colonization through the lens of everyday life practices, observed a similarly complex process. He was concerned with the difference between the production of a representation, perhaps in a metropolitan center, and the ends to which it is put by its consumers, perhaps in the colony. Certeau speaks of this consumption as a "second production" and draws an example of its subversive potential from the manipulations of the Catholic religion and its symbols and architecture by indigenous labor during the colonization.[76] This particular practice, I might add, continues today in the form of Christian base communities and liberation theology. Ortíz's concept of transculturation has been disseminated by the work of the late Uruguayan literary critic Angel Rama, who applied it to Latin American narrative as a means of problematizing polemical terms such as *native* and *foreign, regionalist* and *modernizing*. For Rama, Latin American writing could be characterized as just such a process with the addition that in the twentieth century, Latin American writers had the additional choice of adopting elements from the metropolitan culture that it never intended for export to Latin America— Marxism, for example.[77]

If I dwell here on the *cita* it is because it will function centrally in what is perhaps, for me, the principal work of Argentine *post*modernism: Ricardo Piglia's *Respiración artificial*. The *cita*, and a certain radically oriented mode of employing it, persists from the Latin American modernism of *Rayuela* into the postmodernism of Piglia's work.[78] Borges, perhaps, may be the most conspicuous of citers in Latin American letters, but for Borges the *cita* refers to a "universal library," sealed off from other social practices. The concrete implications of a Latin American writer marginalized from European culture and thereby more free to pilfer from it—this is Borges's characterization from an early essay—are completely absent in Borges.[79] On the other hand, for Cortázar—as for Carpentier, for some Brazilian writers also connected with surrealism, and of course, for Fernández Retamar—the *cita* is a raid into enemy territory. Of course, the very mobilization of Caliban, from Shakespeare's *Tempest,* as a figure for this sort of citing is itself an example of the practice. The heart of the Western canon has ironically furnished one of the most potent emblems of cultural decolonization—the citing, cursing, Caliban—mobilized by Third-World writers.

But the citation does not only, on this view, negate the source (and it is, of course, also still a preservation of the source—but that is a question of strategic and exclusively situationally determined emphasis). It also opens up a space in which something new can be said or made. We thus return to the crucial question of the alternatives, the new spaces *Rayuela* opens up in the wake of its critical, formal and thematic, citing of European modernization, modernity, and modernism. A last look at the *tablero* in *Rayuela* and at Kerr's critique of it in particular illustrates this. Kerr observes that the choice between two books (spurious as it may be) is, moreover, a reduction from a postulated many: "This book is many books, but above all it is two." The possible permutations and sequences boggle the mind and could not properly be taken up other than to signal their existence. But Kerr, strangely, glosses over what she calls the "possibly most obvious" of the "many" other possible readings, namely, reading the book straight through from chapter 1 to chapter 155, characterizing it as being "narratively non-sequential."[80] And yet, by fastening on the slippage in *Rayuela's tablero,* whereby an author-itative reduction of freedom is effected, and by challenging Kerr's own presumably unwitting reproduction of that reduction, we may indeed choose to read that "third" book.

Now, we should dismiss certain illusions at once. This choice does not constitute some absolutely radical innovation. We are, after all, still choosing to read the book. We are essentially reading the same narrative. And we are certainly reading the same chapters as in the second book, just in a different order. Nevertheless, perhaps some continuum of initiative or agency may be admitted here. We might cautiously suggest that reading the text in a way other than the two encouraged by the *tablero* involves a greater (though in no way some utopian total) degree of reader participation. This may be so especially to the extent that it overtly frustrates the ostensible binary oppositions organizing the *tablero*. The *tablero* opposed numerical sequence and partiality to numerical nonsequentiality and completion. The mythical complete text, a whole coherent text—suggesting a reality comprehended fully in both appearance and essence—is *valued*. It contrasts with a degraded partial text, comprehending only appearance, and damned all the more for its false, absurd claims to "realism." In our third book, numerical sequence need not be purchased at the expense of completion. Thus, this third reading pragmatically deconstructs the organizing logic of the *tablero* that Kerr theoretically deconstructed. At the same time, however, this is not a text beyond such oppositions. Like any identity, it is founded by exclusion, by what it is not. We can read and study this text in a certain light only at the expense of all the other possible texts and interpretations. And we may, moreover, make this choice on our part appear natural only by mythologizing this text as, for example, the "most obvious." But this is one of those choices, perhaps, that my own situation within postmodernity permits me to make with a good deal less agony than might have been the case for an earlier, purer generation.

At any rate, my thesis is that this modest participatory gesture on our part as readers is echoed in the narrative that unfolds on a reading of the third book. We reject, by choosing another book, the equally alienating alternatives offered us by modern life: to either passively obey rationality or falsely pretend to elude it through cultural innovation. Instead, we make an affirmative leap into literally uncharted territory. This is the alternative *Rayuela* offers amid the ruins of European modernity. And this utopian formal gesture, together with the content it releases I wish to characterize at length as a positive *Latin American modernity,* with its own, specifically Latin American, social conditions of possibility.

3

Toward a Latin American Modernity

Rayuela, the Cuban Revolution,

and the Leap

> The true revolutionary is guided
> by profound feelings of love.—Che Guevara

> All love goes beyond the couple, if it is love.—Julio Cortázar

Horacio's problem in *Rayuela* is still modern and colonial alienation. He still feels that genuine human life and reality are elsewhere, in a different mode of existence. But here, Horacio's failed attempts to discover immediacy through eroticism and cultural subversions are accompanied by the more subtle unfolding of a parallel narrative. This narrative can be tracked by focusing on certain crucial—in the etymological sense of "crossroads"—episodes. Horacio, frustrated by his relationship with la Maga and by the high culture of European modernism, wanders aimlessly. For once he is *not* searching. And thus, almost in spite of himself, he reaches out a hand to another. The mystical other side is simply another human being in need of companionship and solidarity. But this third narrative takes Horacio from this intensely joyful discovery (figured as a kind of physical materiality beyond reason) and its painful loss, to the repression of the whole episode (figured, within a hyper-rational discourse, as a kind of idiotic pity), to its eventual recovery in Buenos Aires, when he leaps, at the end of chapter 56, into the arms of his friends/lovers Traveler and Talita. All this said, it may be argued that this third book is really only imaginary. It merely emblematizes another possible reading of the critique of European modernism contained in either of the *tablero's* two books. In this sense, it might seem superfluous to construct an entire reading of this third book. Unlike book one, however, this book continues *after* the leap, projecting Horacio and ourselves into a utopian world that contains all ("other") spaces. There, Horacio sheds the gravity of his searches and moves instead easily and randomly from one space to another. It also departs from book two because it retains a discontinuity—which must be leapt over—between the first two sections and the third. The very experience of reading the third section changes. And many of the fragments contained in it take on a different dimension than if one follows the *tablero*.

It is important, for this reading, to establish the difference between searching and wandering. In chapter 1, Horacio tells about one of his searches. He drops a lump of sugar at a restaurant. Desperate to find it, Horacio falls to the floor, crawling and clawing frantically amid the legs and shoes of other patrons. Finally, exhausted and furious, Horacio finds the sugar. But then: "I held the sugar tightly in my palm and felt it dissolve in the sweat my hand gave off" (1:14/10). Horacio makes explicit the symbolic significance: ". . . as if it were some sort of mean sticky vengeance meant to terminate another one of those episodes that I was always getting involved in." Indeed, if both the first two books are organized around searching, this first tale of a search is a parable, the novel in miniature. But it is this also because Horacio's search is self-defeating, or rather, self-consuming. The lump of sugar—in this case the object of the search—is dissolved, or consumed, by the very energy expended in the search. But also, the search itself, like any search, is dissolved because it seeks, aside from a given object, to complete itself. We have already seen how the specific *content* of Horacio's other searches are paradoxical and self-defeating. We have also seen that the means-end logic in which each was cast was a component of that paradox. Now we see that perhaps the *form* of the search itself inevitably dooms the search to an eternity of self-consumption or a tragic exit; alternatives, of course, that the first two books reproduce formally.

This suggests that, for *Rayuela,* searching is a movement governed by an inner logic, a real or imagined endpoint, wandering that is subordinated and ordered by a guiding, master force. Its enemy is the unforeseen interruption, especially when the searcher occupies the space of interruption in and for itself. This fable of the sugar cube, somewhat hidden itself within the beginning chapter of book three, perhaps suggests that we should look away from the strategies Horacio is overtly concerned with, look beyond his futile searches. Once again, the emphasis is on our participation, now in determining the significance of certain less-obvious motifs within the text. If so, then the situation in which we find Horacio in book three is quite interesting. After leaving la Maga in a fight in chapter 20, Horacio goes out walking. Is he searching? He seems to have no purpose other than to leave the space he was occupying, no endpoint in mind. Indeed, he physically is not even looking where he's going, his head buried in a book he is reading from. But even if we want to posit the persistence of some kind of logic to his movements in chapter 21 (especially as he is still preoccupied with culture—a book), it is definitively *interrupted* at the beginning of chapter 22 by the absolute noncontingency of an automobile striking a pedestrian. Horacio leaves the scene of the accident and begins "to walk in no direction in particular [*sin rumbo*]" (22:90/98).[1] Horacio physically begins to wander, abandoning his search.

This alone marks a shift in emphasis from books one and two. But intellectually as well, Horacio, who began this chapter confronted by material chance, ends it with a review and rejection of the strategies of books one and two for overcoming the alienating solitude of modernity. He rejects "contacts made in action in tribes in work in bed" as "contacts between branches and leaves . . . while the trunks stood there disdainfully and irreconcilably parallel" (22:90/99). Believing that there is the possibility of some true otherness, Horacio nonetheless recognizes that he has come no closer than the "border of otherness," without being able to cross over. Ultimately, "that true otherness made up of delicate contacts, marvelous adjustments with the world, could not be attained from just one point; the outstretched hand had to find response in another hand stretched out from the beyond, from the other part" (22:91/99). These are the last words of this chapter. No solipsistic self-reflexive culture or reason, nor any self-serving, macho eroticism ("which lasts only as long as a woman lasts") can do more than merely lead one to the border.

Instead, three new values are invoked, which I'd like to characterize as immanence, materiality, and ethics. "That true otherness *made up* of delicate contacts": true otherness is not laying out there, a physical other realm that one reaches, it is not a *transcendent* space. Rather it is constituted through certain actions and exists only while these actions exist. In this sense, it is *immanent* in our daily lives. French New Left philosopher Henri Lefebvre wrote in 1967 that because "everyday life, the social territory and place of controlled consumption, of terror-enforced passivity, is established and programmed . . . It is therefore everyday life that must be tackled by broadcasting our policy, that of a cultural revolution with economic and political implications."[2] Now materiality intervenes as a necessary dimension: "*Contacts*," "marvelous adjustments with *the world*." Now, the emphasis is shifted from a supercharged subjectivity lifting, per force, a degraded and alienated materiality into some higher plane. This was the project, for example, of modernist architecture: "Absorb that multiplicity, reconcile the improbable through the certainty of the plan."[3] Instead, the action that will constitute otherness involves a new recognition and appreciation for the physical, especially where it requires adjustments. Finally, this physicality is figured as the hand reached out by another. This opens up the ethical dimension, where ethics refers to a shared project and set of codes that constitute a community working toward a continually renegotiated common good. Hegel distinguished between *Sittlichkeit* (ethical substance) and *Moralität* (morality). The former refers to "the moral obligations I have to an ongoing community of which I am a part. . . . [Its] crucial characteristic is that it enjoins us to bring about what already is. . . . the common life which is the basis of my *sittlich* obligation is already there in existence. . . . there is no gap between what ought to be and what is."[4] *Sittlichkeit* anticipates Marx's understanding of communism as the solution to the riddle of modern alienation. The other, in true otherness, is not a passive vehicle for the transcendence of the self, to be discarded upon completion. Instead, the self can only be realized (dealienated) through its adjustment with the already initiated action—the activity—of the other; an activity the text figures as physical, specifically as the hand reaching out.

This hand will return in the very next chapter, when Horacio, for no reason in particular, listens to a horrendous piano recital by one Berthe Trépat and then accompanies her home. First, a hand, figuratively and literally, is what Horacio offers Berthe Trépat out of "a certain sympathy." Then, it is repeated touches by Berthe Trépat along the way that keep Horacio around when he begins to hyper-rationalize the whole episode and wants to leave (23:100/110 and 102/112). Third, Horacio figures the kind of irrational, extralinguistic "joy" he feels during their walk as "a hand clasped underneath his skin like a delightful torture" (23:106/118), or "a hand underneath his skin squeezing his stomach" (23:107/119), or yet again: "The hand was clutching at his stomach so much that he was feeling nauseous. He was inconceivably happy" (23:106/118). On one level, these hands are emblems of the materiality of physical contact, as opposed to rational self-reflection. Horacio's own physical presence with Berthe Trépat on the stage after the concert is emphasized as something that defies not only his usual way of using language, but reason entirely (23:99/108). But on another level, this hand is also the hand of the other reaching out that constitutes the ethical dimension of "true otherness."

And indeed, throughout the episode we find other indicators that Horacio and Berthe Trépat's activity constitutes precisely that immanent space of "true otherness"—beyond language and reason—intimated in the previous chapter. To begin with, Horacio has abandoned his grand plans and rationalized strategies, not to mention his own will. Instead, he goes with the flow. After the concert he agrees to get a drink with Berthe Trépat, saying, "Whatever you want." A seemingly innocent statement whose significance as a departure is indicated only by the narrator's cue, "Oliveira said *incongruously*" (23:100/110). Also rationality and alienating language are both conspicuously not up to the task of domesticating this event. Horacio refers to feeling "crazy" and to "inexplicable" contentment (23:105/117) and "inconceivable" happiness (23:106/118), to not "knowing" why he is engaging the pianist (23:99/108) and to there being "no reasons" for his behavior, no way of "understanding it" (23:105/117). As for language, he resists his "usual" way of using words (23:99/108) and repeatedly refers to his joy as "pure" and "indescribable," finally figuring it as simply a "laugh" from deep within, "like a physical form of joy" (23:105/117). It is true that discerning the novelty in some of these cases depends upon the cynical presence of a still-rational third-person narrator. However, this narrator seems to be progressively losing ground to Horacio's immediate experience of the event, at least until the very end.

Then, the hand of the other—to which Horacio has necessarily submitted himself in a "marvelous adjustment with the world"—ultimately shatters Horacio's utopian journey. For when they finally arrive at the pianist's house, she does not want Horacio to come upstairs and becomes upset with him. Horacio pleads with her, but to no avail: "Strange as it seemed, he still wanted to do something for Berthe Trépat who was looking straight at him and raising her hand little by little, and suddenly she let it go full force across Oliveira's face and he drew back confused, getting out from under the worst of the slap but feeling the lash of her slender fingers, the instantaneous scratch of her nails" (23:110/122). This moment is critical. It is a test. How will Horacio react when this joyful wandering, already an interruption, is itself interrupted? Can he adjust again? Can he revel, like Rimbaud, in its transitory character? Or has he unconsciously turned the stroll into a full-blown, all-or-nothing, search?

Horacio is confused and hurt and even cries initially. But relatively quickly the whole episode becomes a repressed bitter memory. Horacio reproaches himself for what he now perceives to have been one of his usual searches and reduces the potential goal of the search to the desire to get warm and to dry his socks. But his very crying, of course, suggests the depth of his feeling as well as the novelty of the experience as la Maga earlier accused him of "not knowing how to cry" (20:80/86). Psychoanalysis tells us the basic function of repression is as a defense mechanism against painful memories. But significantly, for Horacio it will also take on Freud's other, preventive sense: repression as a means of repelling an instinct whose gratification would incur the risk of unpleasure.[5] In this way, repression, like the crying, suggests to us the depth of the experience. In this particular episode, Horacio was torn between an instinctual impulse to behave ethically and a hyper-rational critical faculty. His desire for genuine human interaction seemed to hold sway until the hitherto unseen risks of such interaction were made painfully palpable. Horacio's new found capacity to reach out and to make "marvelous adjustments with the world" clearly finds its limit when Berthe Trépat slaps him and rebuffs his own extended hand.

The force of this experience, in a form muted and distorted by repression, returns in the next long chapter. The unconscious desire to not repeat this episode determines Horacio's decidedly transcendent, metaphysical, and unethical behavior. Having returned to la Maga's apartment after the Berthe Trépat incident, Horacio, la Maga, and their mutual friend Gregorovius are awaiting the arrival of other friends. Then, "without really knowing why, he stroked his [la Maga's baby Rocamadour's] forehead with a finger" (28:130/146). This is, as before, a moment of un-reason, a physical behavior not explicable by rational knowledge. This intensifies when he discovers that the little baby is not sleeping but dead. Horacio silently argues with himself. On the one hand, he checks the baby's airway, wants to administer artificial resuscitation, feels for warmth under the sheets, and, finding only cold, thinks that he must turn on the lights and alert la Maga and Gregorovius. But, on the other hand, he squashes these impulses at every turn with a sneering discourse of extreme self-consciousness: "Artificial resuscitation [*respiración* artificial], idiocy. Another form of idiocy that his hands should be trembling so much, barefoot and wet" (28:130/147; translation modified). He characterizes his physical, or "natural" reactions as idiocy, a word suggesting a lack of reason, intelligence, or power of reflection, and the same word in which he "remembers" the Berthe Trépat episode. Horacio continues to rationalize away the possibility of a risky emotional investment, for "if I call out it will be Berthe Trépat all over again, the same stupid attempts, pity" (28:131/147).

This inverted memory of the episode with the pianist thus dictates Horacio's cruel experiment. He secretly informs each of the arriving guests of the baby's death and observes their reactions without ever telling la Maga, who shockingly discovers it when she goes to administer the child's medicine toward the end of the night. The tableau as a whole, moreover, contains some of the most intense metaphysical exchanges in the novel and displays Horacio at a self-contradictory extreme of abstract, rational anti-rationality—far from the depths of materiality, immanence, and ethics that constitute "true otherness." But this ornate philosophical veil fails to mask all traces of Horacio's now repressed desire for genuine experience. In the commotion following Maga's discovery of Rocamadour's death, Oliveira "thought of Berthe Trépat's arm on his, the walk in the rain" (28:149/171). His friend Etienne wants to know "why your mouth is quivering so much." When Horacio responds that it's just a nervous tic, Etienne replies, "Tics don't go well with the cynical air" (28:149/171). Horacio continues to repress the significance of such physical symptoms, at most scorning them as signs of his weakness.

As a result of this episode, Horacio spirals into an incongruous state of extreme self-consciousness and nearly absolute physical degradation, deepening the alienating gaps between mind and body, subject and object, that have been his central problem. The Paris section of *Rayuela* ends with a drunken Horacio in a paddy wagon with two homosexuals, having been arrested for having sex with a homeless woman. He moves back to Buenos Aires hoping to find, along the way in Montevideo, la Maga. But he does not find her and instead moves in across a courtyard from his two married friends, Traveler and Talita. In the longest episode from this section, Horacio laboriously manipulates the two in a quasi-scientific attempt to reproduce a structure of otherness. The experiment consists in running two boards end to end from the couple's window, across the courtyard, to Horacio's. While Traveler and Horacio stand in either window supporting the boards, Talita is to scoot across the boards, over the courtyard and *hand* deliver some *yerba mate* and nails to Horacio. The model for this experience, though Horacio represses it entirely, is the walk in the rain with Berthe Trépat. But he is hardly wandering aimlessly. It is as though Horacio is once again searching, not for la Maga, but for that experience that he had, lost, and then deliberately avoided. Now, he repeats it in an impossibly self-conscious form.

References of two kinds in particular measure the distance between the joy of the Berthe Trépat episode and this one. First, Horacio remains thoroughly detached throughout this episode. He establishes his detachment when he tells Traveler that "I get dizzy from heights" (41:208/243). This fear of heights perfectly figures his fear of participation. He cannot take the risk involved. He will say later, gazing up at the hole at the top of a circus tent—"that escape-hatch to a maybe contact, that center, that eye like a bridge between the earth and liberated space"—that maybe "some other [*otro*] would probably have climbed up the nearest pole to the eye up there as if it were the most natural thing to do" (43:225/264; translation modified). He cannot take the risk of the climb. That "other," he knows, is not himself. And here, with Talita perched on the bridge, Horacio does not participate, but directs. "Everything falls into place perfectly [*se encadena perfectamente*] if one really wants it to. The only false thing in this is the analysis" (41:210/246; translation modified), Horacio observes as Talita slides slowly toward the center of the bridge. His attempt to distance the "truth" of the experience from the "falseness" of analysis itself takes the form of an analytical binary opposition.

Second, Horacio conceives the experience solipsistically, as of his own making entirely. The others, far from constituting dealienation, are merely passive pieces of a puzzle to be assembled by Horacio. For instance, when Talita begins to waver from the heat and Traveler tells her just to throw the package through the window and return to their side, Horacio becomes impatient: "It had to happen, nobody can change you. You come right up to the edge of things and one gets the idea that finally you're going to understand, but it's useless, you see, you start turning them around to read the labels. You always get stuck in the planning stage, man" (41:212/248). The statement implies that someone, Horacio, was trying to change Traveler. And, even as he tries to deny having "fabricated the game," Horacio acknowledges that "all I did was create the circumstances" (41:212/248). But if Traveler feels that he has been manipulated, Talita serves as the catalyst to be consumed in Horacio's chemical reaction. She feels "another bridge" above her, "words that passed back and forth, the laughs, the hot silences," and she thinks to herself: "It's like a trial . . . Like a ritual" (41:212/248). She first feels that she is being judged, but then she recognizes that they are judging something "through her." She has become the means, the medium, through which Horacio and Traveler work out their own differences. Horacio confirms this suspicion when he tells her that "you add yourself [*vos te sumas*] somehow to the two of us to accentuate the similarity [*aumentar el parecido*], and therefore the difference" (41:216/253; translation modified). He defines her in terms of what she "adds" to the reaction between him and Traveler. Her identity depends exclusively on her function in a system of mediations constructed rationally by Horacio. Horacio reveals the importance of Talita as an object facilitating the construction of a "structure": "We had her/it there, almost perfect, like a rainbow between our thumb and our little finger." Moreover, though he claims not to pretend to know where truth is, "I only know that I liked the feel of that rainbow, like a little toad between my fingers. And this afternoon . . . we were beginning to hit upon something serious" (41:219/257).

Finally, the uncontrollable behavior of the Other—in this case, Traveler, Talita, and Horacio's lover, Gekreptken—disrupts this system and this irritates Horacio. He admonishes Traveler: "You don't seem to realize that these outbursts, pardonable when they're beautiful or at least inspired, become repulsive as soon as they start to cut into an order of things, torpedo a structure" (41:219/257). When Gekreptken interrupts, Horacio repeats, in the classical language of reason, "Quod erat demonstrandum, old buddy" (41:219/257). An interruption only appears destructive if one presupposes the presence and value of a rationally ordered structure. Only a searcher is annoyed by detours. Indeed, only when one is searching does a detour even appear as such. Authentic wandering cannot be interrupted because it presupposes no stationary endpoint.

The bridge itself figures the concept of unity through structured mediation, especially when Horacio puts someone else on it, avoiding the risk himself. By contrast, as we will see below, a "leap" between two windows might have figured the kind of committed participation that transforms experience and constitutes dealienation. The difference between alienated and unalienated practice can be gauged in terms of the difference between watching others and participating oneself. However, since his painful experience with Berthe Trépat, Horacio reverses the terms. He sees commitment as a sell-out, "leaving the game, leaving the crossroads and following any one of the roads put there by circumstance, proclaiming it to be the necessary one" (48:246/340). Instead, he believes liberation to lie in the discomfort of being pinned to a cross(roads). All his moments of participation—his relationship with Maga, his encounter with Berthe Trépat, his crisis with Rocamadour—appear to him as failures because they constitute so many exits from the game, so many *choices*.

But he also asks himself, "Must one stay in the center of the crossroads, then, like the hub of a wheel? What good is it to know or to think we know that every road is false if we don't walk" (48:247/291). The notion Horacio is contemplating here is precisely one of practice as liberation. But it quickly gives way to a rush of destructive self-consciousness: "How many times had he reached similar conclusions, felt better, thought he could begin to live in a different way; one afternoon, for example, when he had gone in to listen to an idiotic concert and afterwards . . . Afterwards it had rained so much, why think about it" (48:247/292). Again, he has inverted the experience with Berthe Trépat in his memory, where it appears only as one foolish failure among others. The ellipsis marks suggest the repressed and inexpressibly painful conclusion to that episode. He can only remember it as "pity" as "idiotic as the other time: rain, rain" (48:247/292).

In Freud's theory, the compulsion to repeat "is an ungovernable process originating in the unconscious. As a result of its action the subject deliberately places himself in distressing situations, thereby repeating an old experience. But he does not recall this prototype. On the contrary, he has the strong impression that the situation is fully determined by the circumstances of the movement."[6] But later interpretations also emphasized a "restitutive tendency" that operates as a parasite to the primary function of repetition. In this, the subject seeks, through repetition, "to re-establish the situation which had existed prior to the trauma."[7] Ultimately, Horacio's inverted memory will be righted only when Talita repeats Berthe's Trépat violent gesture with a difference. Talita and Horacio have descended into the morgue of the asylum in which they and Traveler are employed. Horacio feels drawn to Talita but holds himself back, remembering the episode with Berthe Trépat. But then Talita's "hand rose up without her feeling it rise, and she held it for an instant on Oliveira's chest" (54:271/320–21). This represents the negative image of the experience with Berthe Trépat, who raised her hand to slap Horacio and painfully terminate his first taste of freedom. And, to be sure, this transforms Horacio, for Talita sees that "he was smiling. . . . She had never seen him smile like that, faintheartedly and at the same time with his whole face open and frontward, without the usual irony, accepting something that must have come to him from the center of life. . . . approaching her in the act of accepting that unnameable thing [*esa cosa innominable*] that was making him smile" (54:271/321, translation modified). Horacio's defenses are lowered. He again accepts something "unnameable," and that precisely indicates its proximity to the kind of unalienated joy he felt with Berthe Trépat. Similarly, the unnameable cannot be represented by Horacio's abstracting self-consciousness, but only concretely described by Talita as "that thing . . . that was making him smile." When he kisses Talita it is as though they are transported, in that kiss, to another spatial and temporal realm. Indeed, it is a realm in which Horacio reunites with la Maga and sees their relationship for the genuine experience of immediacy and freedom it was, reversing his earlier, mistaken belief that the relationship obstructed his search. The instant's importance appears in the confused rendering of the subjectivity authoring these thoughts. Logically, that is, in terms of the preceding passage, they should be Talita's thoughts, but as the passage continues, the thoughts seem to be Horacio's. This confusion, however, is precisely the point. In such moments, the alienating structures of subjectivity and reason, which cordon off the self from the other dissolve, and one gives one's self over to an other.

The transformative effect of this experience nearly drives Horacio mad. Later in his room, he strives unsuccessfully to conceptualize his experience. "It was always going to pain Oliveira that he could not even get a notion of that unity that other times he called center, and which for lack of more precise dimensions was reduced to images like black shout, kibbutz of desire" (56:279/331). The impossibility of thinking—"getting a notion"— about freedom hurts him. He still wants to abstract it, to conceive it, trap it in the structure of his rational thought and his language. And yet, he knows that

> it could be felt in terms of stomach contraction, territory, deep or spasmodic breathing, sweat on the palms of his hands, lighting a cigarette, pulling in his guts, thirst, silent shout that broke like black masses in his throat . . . and enough, hey, enough please; but it was good to have felt one's self deeply there for an unmeasurable time, without thinking anything, only being that which was there with tongs caught in his stomach. *That* against the territory. (56:279/332)

The "territory" signifies the territory of reason and rationality, of mediation and alienation. And we should note the interesting anticipation of Lefebvre's use of "territory" to signify the space of a programmed daily life as well as Deleuze and Guattari's distinction between "territorialization" as in rational regimentation and "deterritorialization" as in Brownian dispersion.[8] In contrast to this, Horacio recognizes the value of all these *esos* that he can only describe concretely in terms of immediate feelings, that fully escape his rational powers.

Horacio confesses to Traveler his wish that "we could really hold out our hands instead of repeating the gesture of fear and wanting to know if the other person has a knife hidden between his fingers" (56:290/345). He says that he gets close to this freedom when "I give a push and something happens to me" or "I stick my finger into habit and it's incredible how one's finger sinks into habit and comes out the other side." He refers to those moments when he participates actively, when he risks openly. However, he feels that "five thousand years of rotten genes draw me back and I fall into the territory again" or "I get an attack, an attack of useless pity" (56:290/345). And this always happens right when "it looks as if I'm finally going to get to the last square." But only keeping his gaze fixed on what he thinks is the still-absent, still-to-be-reached "last square" prevents him from recognizing the movement of the stone from one "square" to the next, the wandering, unstructured movement that constitutes true freedom.

Horacio seems completely desperate; as is Traveler, who feels helpless and convinced that the former will kill himself. "Traveler looked at him, and Oliveira saw that his eyes were filling with tears. He made a gesture as if to stroke his hair from a distance" (56:291/346). Then, as Traveler leaves, he throws the noisy hospital staff back from the door, tells them to leave Horacio alone, and advises the latter to bolt the door if he wants to remain undisturbed. This totally selfless activity, motivated only by concern for the other, even when it comes at the expense of personal pain because he feels sure that Horacio will jump, redeems Horacio.

By himself, seated by the open window of his third floor room, Horacio looks down to the courtyard at Traveler, standing with his arm around Talita:

> After what Traveler had just done, everything had something like a marvelous feeling of conciliation and that senseless but vivid and present harmony could not be violated, could no longer be falsified, basically Traveler was . . . the man of the territory, the incurable mistake of the species gone astray, but how much beauty in the mistake and in the five thousand years of false and precarious territory, how much beauty in those eyes that had filled with tears and in that voice that had advised him: "Throw the bolt, I don't trust them," how much love in that arm that held the waist of a woman. (56:291–29/347)

This valorization of the "territory" reveals a glimmer of consciousness, an incipient understanding that there is no beyond, but only the "beauty" that one can experience in the ordinary. Notions of "mistake" and going "astray" are revalorized as a result of Horacio's discarding a specific endpoint.

"Probably," Oliveiera thought, "the only possible way to escape from the territory is to plunge into it over one's head." But he also knows that as soon as he suggests this—participation as freedom—he will recall the "image of a man taking an old woman along by the arm through rainy and freezing streets." Yet now the fullness of the experience is restored, "who can tell if maybe I haven't been staying on the edge, and that there probably was a passage. Manú [the familiar nickname for Traveler] would have found it, certainly, but the idiot thing is that Manú will never look for it and I, on the other hand . . ." (56:292/397). Exactly. Horacio begins to recognize that he did have an experience of freedom with Berthe Trépat, but that faced with the painful risks of that participation, he pulled back from "the border." At the same time, he knows that *Traveler,* who never searches, who simply lives or wanders, frequently criss-crosses but knows no such alienating boundaries. This freedom cannot be contemplated, planned, structured or otherwise rationalized. Only "the idiot thing," that which is lived and experienced in all its intensity, constitutes unalienated immediacy.

But Horacio still watches. Now he must commit himself. The opportunity arises when, as the hospital staff tries to coax him down with patronizing false promises, Talita and Traveler tell them to shut up, risking their jobs. This display of solidarity prompts Horacio to act, to participate:

> That's the way it was, the harmony lasted incredibly long, there were no words that could answer the goodness of those two down there below, looking at him and talking to him from the hopscotch . . . so that the only thing left to do was to move his right hand a little in a timid salute and stay there looking at La Maga, at Manú, telling himself that there was some meeting after all, even though it might only last just for that terribly sweet instant in which the best thing without any doubt at all would be to lean over just a little bit farther out and let himself go, paff the end. (56:348–49/404)

In my view, interpretations that dwell on whether Horacio kills himself, goes insane, or both, miss the point of the scene's open-endedness.[9] It is not that we don't know what happens, but rather that the leap itself is what happens. Horacio has learned to valorize participatory processes over meaningful endings. And we should be forced, deprived of an ending, to attend to the act itself, precisely as Horacio has learned to do. It is the leap itself, the act or experience, and not what follows it, its meaning, that we must focus on.

Horacio's "leap" realizes the participatory, material, and ethical practice that he has buried since his encounter with Berthe Trépat. We saw in his behavior with the pianist an unselfconscious enactment of the solution he proposes just before going into her concert. That solution itself was proposed in response to Horacio's feeling that he was stuck in the crossroads: the triple crisis of modern alienation, modernism's alienating responses to it, and the postcolonial's cultural alienation. When that experience seems to collapse, Horacio's next crisis experiences, his next crossroads, precipitate his desperate attempts to recover a sense of freedom and happiness that he no longer, because of his repression and distortion of the memory of Berthe Trépat, can even recognize. In this scene with Talita and

Traveler, another crossroads, the full implications of that episode are released and Horacio can once again assume the genuine, participatory practice—the leap—that in itself (and not as a means or path) constitutes freedom. Horacio escapes the paradoxical, paralyzing crossroads in which he was caught. This is the significance of the leap in the Latin American modernist *Rayuela*.

The importance of the leap, in contrast to the modernist strategies proposed in book two, lay in its nonpredetermined nature. But in book three, neither Horacio nor we, the readers, end with the leap. Horacio's leap is accompanied by our own leap out of the oppositional spaces of *allá* and *acá*—themselves figures for alienation, particularly colonial—and into *diversos lados*, "diverse sides" or "other sides." Thematically, this third section partly contains fragments that theorize narrative in general, the author-reader relationship, and even seem to provide the metatextual blueprint for *Rayuela* itself. But I do not want to reduce Horacio's narrative of liberation—of independence from the dead-end strategies of European modernism—to mere dramatization of the reader-author relationship. Indeed, the "postmodernization" of *Rayuela* is facilitated precisely by such interpretive reductions. And, for that matter, this metatextual commentary hardly exhausts the significance, thematically or formally, of the fragments in the third section.

Let us review these final fragments. Read in view of the discourse of the leap, they might appear as rehearsals in miniature of that drama of alienation and participatory ethics. For example, chapter 59 consists only of the following quote from Claude Lévi-Strauss's *Tristes Tropiques:* "Then to pass the time, they catch fish they cannot eat; to avoid the rotting of the fishes in the air, notices have been posted all along the beach telling the fisherman to bury them in the sand just as soon as they have been caught" (59:301/357). Allegorically, Horacio similarly entraps Talita and Traveler, as he caught la Maga (who elsewhere was explicitly figured as a swimming fish). But like the Brazilian fisherman, Horacio can do no more. His alienated work is not creative or generative, it merely destroys. On the other hand, such unproductive expenditure seems to defy the utilitarianism of Western capitalism and the rationality of Western modernity as embodied in Lévi-Strauss. But Horacio is also like Lévi-Strauss himself. Lévi-Strauss stands today as an emblem of the modern Western anthropologist ignoring the material conditions (of colonialism, for example) determining his possible insights. In chapter 78, Horacio laments his outsider status with respect to the intimacy of the Travelers. And, in chapter 98, he points to the paradox that "blind people are the ones who light our paths," illustrating it with the example of la Maga, who "will never know how her finger pointed towards the thin line that shatters the mirror" (98:371/438).

But the fragments from the third section do not only refigure Horacio's alienation, or the alienating effect of modernity's dealienating strategies. They also suggest the utopian dimension into which Horacio's leap has propelled him. Thus, Morelli muses that "maybe there is another world inside this one." But it won't be found in various unproductive expenditures "elevated into a system, into a key to the kingdom." In fact, "that world does not exist, one has to create it like a phoenix. That world exists in this one, but the way water exists in oxygen and hydrogen, or how pages 78, 457, 3, 271, 688, 75, and 456 of the dictionary of the Spanish Academy have all that is needed for the writing of a hendecasyllable by Garcilaso. . . . the world is a figure, it has to be read. By read let us understand generated" (71:322/379). As we found in the narrative of the leap, Morelli rejects the notion of an endpoint—the *cielo*, or goal, of the hopscotch board—and recognizes that an unalienated existence exists only as a constitutive *process*.

Even theorizing his own narrative practice and thereby suggesting to some critics the formal strategy behind *Rayuela* itself, Morelli's comments refer us to the question of a participation emergent onto some other world. What he calls "bridges" (recall the experiment with Talita in chapter 43) between fragmentary episodes serve the comforting, and therefore suspect, function of leading himself, and the reader, along by the hand. Instead, he wants to induce the reader to leap, because "sometimes the missing lines were the most important ones, the ones that really counted" (109:399/468–69). Ultimately, "Morelli had hoped that the accumulation of fragments would quickly crystallize into a total reality . . . a city, or a tapestry, or men and women in the absolute perspective of their future." But this crystallization requires the participation of a "lucid eye" that "might peep into the kaleidoscope and understand the great polychromatic rose, understand it as a figure, an *imago mundi* that outside the kaleidoscope would be dissolved into a provincial living room" (109:399/469).

The content of these fragments—often representing alienation and utopian immediacy—is certainly important. But this last fragment and the fact that the problem of alienation and immediacy is often staged in terms of the drama of aesthetic form should also turn our attention to the form of this section. Bereft of the "bridges" of traditional narrative, we are forced to leap from vignette to vignette, from quotation to quotation. Again, this section does not offer the satisfaction of a resolution. Instead, we are forced to remain on the surface of the text, skipping from chapter to chapter, and it is this process, this movement, that is formally represented. In this way, in the final section of the Latin American modernist *Rayuela* (that we arrived at only through a leap of our own in which we rejected the passivity of accepting the *tablero's* reduced binary alternatives), we mimic the participatory practice of Horacio.

What I have done is provide an extended reading of a specific textual feature of *Rayuela,* namely, its leap as a positive solution to alienation intended to replace the various negated strategies of European modernism. The question of whether this leap is modernist or postmodernist is a question of periodization. And, from my point of view, we should refer questions of periodization to the field of history.[10] If we were to trace the literary historical paths taken by particular textual features, themes, formal problems, or solutions in isolation from the social conjuncture in which they emerged, we might well gloss over important differences in the specific functions of those features. These variations in function may be specific to time and place, but also to more particular social determinants such as class, gender, sexuality, race, or ethnicity. This function is as important a component of the "text," broadly conceived, as any particular stylistic feature found "within in it." It is for this reason, for example, that although self-reflexivity may well define the novel as a genre, the self-reflexivity in *Don Quixote* (early-seventeenth-century Spain) nevertheless means something different than the self-reflexivity in André Gide's *Faux Monnayeurs* (early-twentieth-century France), owing to the different sets of social conditions that make self-reflexivity a preferred device in each and that confer on it a different social function and meaning. And it is by ignoring these variations in function and the concrete circumstances that produce them that so much postmodernism theory has expropriated Latin American culture. To adequately periodize such features means to inquire into their conditions of possibility or into their genealogies, if one prefers. It means to ask, Where did they come from? At the same time, we must restore to this question of "where" its proper dimension, namely, space or geography. "Where" means not only from what historical sources but also from what specific locale. Or, better yet, it requires us to address both these questions as well as the interrelationship between history and space. This dimension takes on particular importance when, as in the present case, we are dealing with a colonial or postcolonial literature. As for *Rayuela,* we have already explored such conditions with respect to both its thematization of alienation, as well as to its negative position with respect to European solutions to that problematic. It now remains to *historicize* Horacio's leap. What makes Horacio's leap appear as a solution within the imaginary horizon of *Rayuela?* What historical developments in thought and practice make this dramatic rupture, this flight into the concrete, into a vision of freedom through ethical solidarity, what make this legitimate and credible?

Cortázar's *Rayuela*, I observed above, has sometimes been read—negatively—as a kind of narrativization of the ideology of the New Left.[11] These interpretations presuppose an absolute disjuncture between the rationality, the scientific and materialist character, of the Cuban revolution and the irrational and cultural character of the New Left movements of the sixties. The value of Cortázar's work, then, lies in its unwitting expression of this contradiction or disjuncture. It marks the distance still to be traversed by even committed Latin American intellectuals on the path toward a decolonized revolutionary culture. The connection of Cortázar, especially early works such as *Rayuela,* to the New Left seems not only accurate but also strategically commendable in the face of so many depoliticizing and dehistoricizing readings of the novelist. Cortázar himself wrote poetry, letters, and essays establishing his explicit support of, for example, the movement in Paris in 1968.[12] However, neither the historical opposition between Cuba and the New Left nor the theoretical oppositions on which it is based bear up under scrutiny. Of course, I should point out that the very possibility of scrutiny is itself conditioned by historical developments, both social and theoretical, emerging since the sixties. Or, to put it more precisely, my perspective is informed by theoretical developments that emerged in the wake of the social collapse of the defeats dealt the New Left in Paris in 1968, of counterrevolutionary backlash around the Third World, and of the gradual ideological hardening of those revolutionary governments that were not defeated. In other words, it is the revalorization of discourses of impurity, internationally and in Latin American postmodernity, that makes possible the deconstruction of these oppositions.

The rationality of traditional Marxian science, for example, rests on the construction of an impossible position of absolute social consensus or, what amounts to the same thing, "the structural void" of an all-knowing subject free from the constraints of particular interests or relations with society.[13] A knowledge produced within such constraints, of course, constitutes ideology, a particular form of which is the irrationalist culturalism of the New Left. But if rationality or science depends on assuming this impossible position, then what is advanced under the powerful and authoritative banner of science is actually the situated, positional, and provisional knowledge afforded by a particular ideology. With the belief in the possibility of an objective science goes the devalorization of ideology as false consciousness.

But ideology has another meaning within Marxism. It also refers to the "superstructure," that amalgam of politics, culture, religion, law, and aesthetics that is determined by the economic base. Of course, for orthodox Marxism, attempting to change society by transforming one of the spheres of the superstructure was hopeless and, precisely, *ideological,* now in both senses of the term. Such attempts were not only mistaken, but mistakes with the dangerous power to distract social agents from the real task at hand, that of transforming relations of production in the base. In one version of Marx's theory of history, interventions in the base before it had developed fully into capitalism were seen as counterproductive. This strategic corollary to the theory of ideology was invoked by the Soviet government in its refusal to support Third-World revolutions in the 1950s and 1960s. They were characterized as spontaneist, voluntarist, and culturalist. This suggests that the separation, on ultimately untenable theoretical grounds, between a scientific materialist Cuban revolution and an ideological idealist New Left is a historical echo of the orthodox Communist party doctrines whose ultimate effect was to undermine the advances of both Third-World revolutions and the New Left.

But in concrete historical terms as well, the antagonistic opposition between the New Left and the Cuban revolution seems difficult to sustain. George Katsiaficas argues that "Cuba provided a powerful impetus for the New Left."[14] But, furthermore, the Cuban revolution was itself successful precisely to the extent that it, like the New Left, broke with orthodox Communist doctrines such as those that inform the leftist critique of Cortázar. Katsiaficas outlines the two dimensions of this break. On the one hand, there was a belief in voluntarism or agency and armed struggle. This rejection of the Soviet doctrine of stagism whereby the task of the Communist party was to work within the political process and to organize an avantgarde of the urban proletariat until objective conditions for revolution were "ripe." And on the other hand, there was the call for an active transformation of human beings and culture. Rather than waiting for changes in the economic base to mechanically lead or trickle up to cultural transformations, the Cuban revolution and the New Left shared a demand for a "simultaneous transformation of politics, economy, and culture, of social structure and individual subject."[15] Katsiaficas rightly implies the common value that informs both these ruptures: namely, that of action or participation. In this sense, this value itself emerges as a result of an active, participatory rejection of both U.S. imperialism (fronted by the prescriptions of modernization theorists) and Soviet communism as solutions to the problem of alienation whether felt in colonial outbacks or in metropolitan urban centers.

During the period of the Cuban revolutionary war itself, what was to be theorized as *foquismo* or *foco* theory best embodies the kind of material participation—the leap—that *Rayuela* seems to put forth. *Foco* theory, initially formulated by Che Guevara and developed further by the French activist Regis Debray, offered a strategy whereby a tremendously outnumbered and outarmed rebel guerrilla group could win a military victory over the armed forces of the state, even where "objective" conditions for revolution were not yet present. Its fundamental thesis rested on the belief that first, throughout the Third World, a repressed rural peasantry more than an urban proletariat would provide the mass support for the revolution, and second, military operations by a small vanguard could bring about such "objective" conditions. The *foco* installs itself in the "wildest and most impenetrable places."[16] Only after a "fortunate blow" is struck, does the *foco* begin to propagandize among the peasants, articulating their immediate needs and demands with the larger exigencies of the national revolution. It may be true that this image of the *foco* as a self-igniting spark that catches the entire nation on fire overnight was a mythologization of the actual process of the Cuban revolutionary struggle.[17] Nevertheless, it was a symbolic image that, especially in the early 1960s, provided for very real effects in terms of dramatizing the agency—where none had been thought to exist—of the Third-World subject. This agency, the watchword of *foquismo*, inspired groups struggling against either the alienation of colonization or that of mass society.[18]

After the triumph of the revolution, the struggle against alienation was formalized politically and economically. Politically, the alienating structure was bourgeois representative democracy. It had functioned throughout the history of Cuban independence as an exclusive instrument by which elite Cubans, excluded from the basically U.S.-owned sugar and tourist economy, gained some measure of power, always at the expense of the millions of effectively or actually disenfranchised Cuban peasants and workers.[19] Throughout his speeches in 1959, Fidel Castro describes the revolutionary government as "of the people, for the people" or as the "people governing." Cuban democracy was reminiscent of "the ancient greek democracies."[20] Che Guevara figures Fidel's rapport with his audience during such speeches in erotic terms: "At the great public convocations [*concentraciones*] one observes something almost like a dialogue of two musical pitches whose vibrations provoke new ones in the interlocutor. Fidel and the mass begin to vibrate in a dialogue of increasing intensity until achieving a climax in the abrupt conclusion, crowned by our cry of struggle and victory."[21] And Doris Sommer, in *Foundational Fictions,* has demonstrated the power of romantic rhetoric in cementing identities. Spontaneity and the identity of the Cuban people and the government repeatedly appear in early accounts of the first months of the revolution.

Having discussed earlier Marx's theoretical discussion of alienation, it hardly seems necessary to point out that the vast majority of Cubans were economically alienated prior to the revolution: separated from the land and from the products of their labor. They were also, as a result of an export oriented monocultural sugar economy, subject to a colonial alienation similar to that discussed by Ngugi. Once again, the revolution emphasized dealienation. Before the final victory, one source of the rebels' popular support among peasants was their system of ongoing land reform. As zones were occupied, large estate holdings were reparceled to landless peasants. Five months after the revolutionary triumph, in May of 1959, an agrarian reform law extended the practice. These Cuban land- and wage-reform measures implemented after the revolution were, by all scholarly accounts, hugely effective and successful.[22] Although the attempts to diversify and decolonize the economy were not ultimately as successful as the redistribution efforts, they nevertheless succeeded in reducing, at least initially, the dependency on sugar exports and certainly galvanized nationalist sentiment. And Castro equated the agrarian reform—both land redistribution and the diversification of agriculture—with the larger process of restoring the nation to itself, that is, of dealienating it.[23]

Now perhaps my own agenda may be more apparent as three central moments of my reading of *Rayuela* emerge as fundamental to the originality of both the Cuban revolution and the New Left. First, all three depart from the problem of alienation understood not only as a material problem but also as a spiritual and cultural problem, not only objective but also subjective, as in Marx's original formulations. Where capitalism alienated the worker and imperialism alienated a people from its own identity, capitalist culture alienated art from daily life and human beings from genuinely human sensibilities.[24] Then, all three share a critique of existing strategies for overcoming the problem of alienation. Cuba, of course, rejected both the political and military strategies of Soviet-style orthodox communism and the New Left rejected the alienated and elitist establishment art of high modernism. Finally, all three favored instead participation and concrete action as the central value of their new strategies or proposals. Che's *foco* theory of activating armed struggle, the revolution's style of mass, direct democracy and the New Left's political demonstrations and cultural activism in the form of happenings and a new valorization of genuinely popular (or participatory) culture both stand as historical counterparts to Horacio's leap. We may now be in a better position to see how that leap was possible, how Cortázar's understanding of a "revolution in literature" measured not his own distance from Cuba but rather the distance of both from accepted European strategies for de-alienation, and how, finally, Jean Franco, reflecting on the Latin American experience of the 1960s, could write that "*Hopscotch* by Julio Cortázar spoke directly to an iconoclastic youth for whom social change was a matter of urgency and for whom the violence of the past . . . was an evil that only immediate action could overcome."[25]

Again, the reader should bear in mind that the conditions of possibility for my speaking, on a continental level, of Latin American modernity are themselves provided by the objective and subjective conditions of the period in question. In other words, as I noted above, one measure of the transition from modernity to postmodernity in Latin America is the crisis—at once conceptual and political—suffered by the term *Latin America*. If in Latin American revolutionary ideology of the sixties, a string of countries—Cuba, Bolivia, Colombia, Argentina—could be rattled off like a chain of equivalents, they are today more likely to be named as examples of four very different types of Latin America. Or, alternatively, if they are cited in an expression of desire for continental unity, it is by free-marketeers eager for the unification of Latin America as economic unit.

Finally, though, if this account historicizes *Rayuela* in terms of its historical conditions of possibility, this whole social logic—alienation, critique, participation—must also be historicized. In a sense, we have already done so for alienation and critique. But what about participation? Where does this more general Latin American sixties discourse of the leap come from? In his *Notes on Dialectics,* the brilliant reading of Hegel, Marx, and Lenin, C. L. R. James fixes on Lenin's commentary of Hegel's *Logic* (of which Lenin once said that without an understanding of it one could not understand even the first chapter of Marx's *Capital*): "This is a passage of great importance [in Hegel's "Doctrine of Being"] and Lenin has summarized it perfectly with his LEAP LEAP LEAP LEAP. The new thing LEAPS out. You do not look and see it small and growing larger. It is there. . . . It would leap up."[26] Significantly, "the" philosopher of the sixties and the New Left, Herbert Marcuse, pointed out in his own commentary on Hegel a few years before James, writing that "the appearance of every new condition involves a leap; the birth of the new is the death of the old."[27] Thus, we might observe of *Rayuela*, Cuba, and the New Left, as James did of Hegel and Lenin, that "you can go on reading for a long time and not get the true significance of the leap. . . . But let us sit and write in large print on our notes: LEAP, SPONTANEOUS ACTIVITY, SELF-MOVEMENT."[28]

I don't mean to suggest that Cortázar was reading these Marxists and from there derived Horacio's leap. Rather, I am suggesting that this leap—in Lenin, James, and Marcuse, but also in the Cuban revolution, the New Left, and Cortázar—is a figure for the kind of utopian rupture, constituted by a spontaneous activity, that each envisioned as essential for de-alienation, for the realization of a liberated community of human beings. We must understand utopia as a kind of space just off the beaten track, just off the map, involving a defamiliarizing rearrangement of the known.[29] For Sir Thomas More in 1516—just twenty-four years after the discovery of the New World—utopia was somewhere in the New World (his guide was himself a marginal figure on Vespucci's ships), though nowhere that the major European expeditions had yet been to or known.[30] Thus, in his encounter with Berthe Trépat, Horacio's first taste of this ethic of participation, he characterizes his experience in terms of "going . . . anywhere where until that moment sit had not occurred to him to go" (23:106/117–18), "like a path suddenly opening up in the middle of the wall: all you have to do is edge one shoulder in a little bit and enter, open a path through the stones, go through their thickness and come out into something else" (23:106–7/118); or finally, as a "step forward, a real step, something without feet or legs, a step through a stone wall" (23:107/119). Horacio may repress this experience through much of the third book, but this step without feet or legs prefigures the leap he will eventually take. A leap that literally brings the reader to a place neither *acá* nor *allá*, but rather to diverse, other places. After Talita helps to reconstitute his ethical experience, Horacio seems to be looking at her with eyes from "some other place" (54:271/325). As Horacio comments to Gregorovius—in chapter 57, right after his leap—when the latter notes that he has a certain "look about him": "It's so very strange to be able to be in three places at once, but that's just what's happening to me this afternoon . . . I'm getting close to ubiquity" (57:297/353). He describes to Gregorovius the experience of "diving into washbasins": "You fall inward for a moment, until the defenses of wakeful-ness, oh pretty words, oh language, take charge and stop you." "A typical existential experience," Gregorovius says "petulantly." But Horacio dis-agrees: "Everything depends on the dosage" and, in the case of this leap—an overdose if you will—"the washbasin" has "really sucked him in" (57:298/354).

But, in view of the contributions of Latin American theorists of post-modernity, we can recognize this utopian impulse as a fundamentally mod-ern one.[31] The ills of the degraded old order are identified and reduced to their fundamental determining principle, and the avant-garde (military, political, or aesthetic) prescription is taken to be an effective cure for all of society and once and for all: "A revolution," Henri Lefebvre wrote, "cannot be other than total."[32] By definition, no further adjustments will be re-quired. As James wrote approvingly in the historical context sketched in above, gradualness is excluded from this picture. No shades of gray, no need for conflictual politicking. Politics, indeed, may be dispensed with as the homogenized will of the homogenized people is transparently embod-ied in the state. If utopia is a fundamental form of European modernity, it is also a product—in its modern form—of Europe's encounter with Latin America as its new world. But in that case, we may recall Carpentier's belief that in Latin America surrealism is real, that is to say, is realized. And we may consider that in *Rayuela,* in the Cuban revolution, and in other expres-sions of Latin American modernity, Latin America claimed to have real-ized utopia. Che explicitly formulated a version of this relationship when he said that "we, practical revolutionaries, initiating our own struggle, sim-ply fulfill laws foreseen by Marx, the scientist . . . The laws of Marxism are present in the events of the Cuban revolution."[33] And Beatriz Sarlo adds to this a cultural dimension when she writes:

> Avant-garde and revolution: for a few years, we leftist intellectuals in Argentina
> believed that unresolved tensions had found their avenues of synthesis. Havana
> offered itself from the beginning of the sixties as the space of a new American
> utopia, and Cuba did not simply translate revolution into Castillian, rather it
> converted itself into a gigantic space of mediation: there were found the intel-
> lectuals and artists, the politicians and militants relived there, in an almost
> Byronesque fashion, a romantic version of commitment.[34]

Yet in all respects sketched in above and despite its expansive modernist claims, the Cuban revolution reintroduced alienation as it sought and claimed to abolish it, and then repressed this fact.[35] The *foco's* success depends on the "impenetrability" not only of its hideouts but also of the moral character of its men. They are taken to be of a higher caliber in both character and understanding. In Morelli's vanguardist terminology, they possess the "lucid [male] eye" capable of discerning the contours of freedom buried within the muddled pattern of domination." It is also true that this vanguardist discourse masked that broader base and multiple fronts that actually secured the revolutionary victory. But in the early years, Castro's Sierra Maestra veterans affirmed their identity, not with other revolutionary leaders but with the Cuban people. And it is this identity that is contradicted by the myth of the vanguard *foco*, a myth that persists after the revolutionary victory despite overt declarations of identity.[36] Saul Landau recounted—favorably, I might add—a somewhat disturbing anecdote of his visit to Cuba in 1961. As he visited a slum in Santiago, he was approached by an old woman begging for cigarettes in English and by little children begging, also in English, for a nickel. Landau's guide, an army lieutenant, "leapt up on a box in the middle of the square and he pointed his finger at this old woman and he said, how dare you! You've got some nerve! . . . He says, are you going to be beggars all your lives, or are you going to start to be human beings. He says, *that's what this revolution is trying to do for you, make you human beings.*"[37] It is not a matter of denying the overwhelming popular support enjoyed by the revolutionary leaders in the first months, even years, after their victory. Rather, it is a question of pointing out that this popular support of a revolutionary vanguard was rhetorically transformed, by that vanguard—in speeches and writings—into absolute identity. This fusion of the identity of the Cuban people with its leaders involves the flattening out of several disjunctures, the homogenization of possibly disparate elements. Indeed, the very notion of "the people" depends entirely on such a homogenization. Whatever its commendable strategic value in the early years of the revolution, the measure of the revolution must, I believe, be taken by the degree to which it accommodates its strategy to the tensions produced within itself. In other words, when it became evident that many different, and sometimes antagonistic, groups actually composed the "people," then the rhetoric of identity, of absolute dealienation, should have been opened up.

Part of the problem in this case, and it may be generalized to other attempts to realize utopian projections, is that acknowledging the persistence of any form of alienation would amount to acknowledging the persistence of the old within the new. Whatever its political valence, the discourse of the leap was relentlessly modernizing. Horacio's need for a leap is fueled precisely by his frustration with inherited strategies for human realization, not only old tools, but impure tools often bound up with the thing they are supposed to combat. In Cuba, a vanguard of military and political leaders, realizing genuine gains in material and social terms, rhetorically absolutized these gains into a complete break with the past. Castro referred to the "limpieza pura" of Cuban democracy, to its pure cleanliness. Even dependency theory, which developed in conjunction with the example of Cuba, offered this utopian and purist discourse of the leap as modernizing rupture with a dependent past. "Underdevelopment or revolution" challenged Andre Gunder Frank in 1967. "Within the revolution: everything; against the revolution: nothing!"[38] With these words spoken to a group of intellectuals, Fidel Castro succinctly expressed this problematic discourse. What constitutes the revolution? Who defines it? How can one tell "within" from "against" or "inside" from "outside"?

The critique of this kind of thought from the postmodern perspective does not entail the disavowal of the need for fundamental social transformation in Latin America. It does however resist the belief that contemporary societies and human beings are beset by *a* condition that can be reduced to a single principle and therefore remedied by one response generated out of that single rationality. It does criticize the process by which the utopian impulse as a never realizable driving force for social change slowly blocks—in the discourse of its ideologists—our view of a conflictual, necessarily only partially achieved reality.[39] And it does criticize (and historicize as part and parcel of an ideology of modernization) the blind valorization of the vanguard as transparently representing the best interests of the people. When the vision of the utopian society comes to blind its leaders to the shortcomings in the present and when this blindness leads further to a paralyzed incapacity to mobilize, accept, or even entertain new initiatives for social change then utopia has been not realized, but reified. It becomes a frozen hardened thing weighing down on a fluid reality that would properly take utopia to be an ever-receding horizon.[40] Of course, at the moment in the early sixties on which we are focused, the moment of the Cuban revolution and of *Rayuela,* the euphoria of what had been achieved gave rise to that "inflated" belief in Latin America's coming of age. The contradiction inherent in declaring the realization of a properly unrealizable—but still quite indispensable—imaginary would not reveal consequences for several more years in Latin America. In Cuba, however, beset by continual attack from abroad and hamstrung by the persistence of neocolonial international economic relations, the persistence of these contradictions were never recognized—or if they were, the political apertures one would expect failed to materialize and were actively repressed. In this sense, the very intensity of the commitment to utopia, the unfortunate vigor with which blights on the utopian imaginary were eradicated, would ultimately destroy the revolution or disfigure it beyond recognition.

Only when the contradictions inherent in the utopian discourses of Latin American modernism tragically resurfaced, as they did in the early 1970s, did a new discourse of liberation emerge: that adopted by theorists of Latin American postmodernity and, for that matter, by the Sandinistas in Nicaragua. This discourse founds itself not on the premise of a sudden and de jure break with the past in the interests of a purified future, but on that of a continuous negotiation with the demands than an oppressive past makes on the present's desire to construct a new future. "The remaking of history," Gayatri Spivak advises, "involves a negotiation with the structures that have produced the individual as agent of history."[41] But this new discourse itself emerged from a dark and painful period of crisis and catastrophically repressive counterrevolutionary activity in which the inflexibility of earlier strategies were finally and tragically revealed in the inability to mount an adequate resistance. In the following two chapters, I want to explore the crisis of this utopian moment as it is registered in Manuel Puig's *El Beso de la Mujer Araña*. *Beso* clings to this utopia on one level, but on another level it tells the tale of that utopia's impossibility and of the tragedy of believing in its inviolable realization. In this sense, *El beso de la mujer araña* represents, in my view, a turning point in recent Latin American narrative from a Latin American modernity, critical but still within the logic of European modernity, to a Latin American postmodernity that operates from a point beyond the exhaustion of those paradigms, when hope lay not in the totalized utopia of a dramatic leap, but in the laborious critical procedure of "de-" and "re-" constructing history.

4

Latin American Modernity in Crisis

El beso de la mujer araña and the

Argentine National Left

This dream is short but this dream is happy.—Manuel Puig

Manuel Puig's *El beso de la mujer araña,*[1] like *Rayuela,* explores the construction of utopian spaces; the ways people seek to transcend the restrictive conditions—the prisons—in which they live. The prisons of *Rayuela,* though quite real, were of a less-tangible sort. In this novel, the action takes place quite literally in a prison cell in Argentina in the mid-1970s. Puig had dealt with "prisons" of different sorts in his first three novels, but *El beso de la mujer araña,* published in 1976 in Barcelona (it was banned in Argentina), was the first in which he explicitly addressed the problem of political repression. In March of that year, 1976, a military coup headed by General Videla ousted the discredited regime of Isabel Perón. The following seven years (about which more below) were known as the Process of National Reorganization or simply as the *Proceso.* The military government terrorized, tortured, disappeared, and killed tens of thousands of Argentines, and millions fled the country in exile—all in the name of a doctrine of "national purification." Puig's novel seems prophetically to confront this reality, though its publication coincided only with the beginning of the *Proceso.* This almost prophetic character perhaps owes to the fact that the narrative was composed during the no-less-fearsome period of semi-official state sanctioned terrorism from 1973–76 that caused Puig's own self-exile. The increasingly right-wing Peronist regime of Isabel Perón exterminated, via the death squads of the Argentine Anti-Communist Alliance, members of the left-wing Peronist urban guerrilla group Montoneros, as well as labor leaders, journalists, writers, intellectuals, and other political activists or suspected "subversives." The civil chaos produced by this undeclared civil war ultimately produced, at least on a domestic level, the conditions that helped make the coup of 1976 possible.

El beso de la mujer araña tells the story, through a series of starkly presented dialogues, prison-warden reports, film narrations, and interior monologues, of the relationship between two inmates in an Argentine prison from April to October of 1975. Valentín Arregui is a Marxist guerrilla imprisoned without trial since 1972 and recently placed in a cell with

Luís Molina, a homosexual sentenced in July 1974 for the "corruption of minors." The plot unfolds on two basic levels. The relationship between the two men develops from antagonism to friendship to love as they share conversations, food, and Molina's narrative recreation of B-grade movies he remembers seeing. At the same time, Molina has a deal with the warden of the prison: he may be granted an early pardon if he is able to obtain information about Arregui's guerrilla group. As it becomes clear that Molina is in love with Arregui, that he will not be providing any information, the warden releases him in the hope (unknown to Molina) that he will lead authorities to Arregui's group. And indeed he does, but (according to the official police report) as Molina is confronted by police agents, he is gunned down by rebels in a drive-by shooting, ostensibly to prevent his capture, and dies shortly thereafter. Valentín is interrogated and tortured and ends the novel in a hallucinatory dream induced by the morphine mercifully administered him by a nurse in the prison infirmary.

The characters of *El beso de la mujer araña* make leaps like Horacio Oliveira. In Puig's text, however, they land in the arms of the enemy, entangled in that from which the utopian leap was supposed to liberate them. Yet characters do not therefore abandon their faith in utopia, conceived of as an existence completely liberated from the alienation that permeates their daily lives. In this sense, the abstract concept of utopia is brought into crisis, to a crossroads. For it is simultaneously constructed and deconstructed in this text. The text also inscribes a historical crisis of utopia. The utopian project of the sixties, to generate entirely new spaces free from alienation, remains the only mode of liberation as the novel opens. Freedom involves the occupation of a position "outside," whereas repression means staying "inside." But by the novel's end this binary logic unravels. In passing through the formal and thematic demands of this particular text, the utopian dream of liberation has been seriously questioned. The firm boundaries between an oppressive existence inside and a liberated existence outside are eroded. The text, a kind of mill through which the exhilarating utopianism of the sixties is run, seems relentlessly to convert those aspirations into shattered illusions and ambiguous middle-class fantasies. Horacio's enthusiastic leap becomes a tired hobble.

For this reason, perhaps, critics have viewed Puig's work as escapist, alienating, or paralyzing. They argue that Puig bolts the hatch on revolution and leaves open no trap doors for genuine social change. Much of this political evaluation of Puig's work turns on his incorporation of the forms and codes of mass culture. Some critics feel Puig turns to these forms to

avoid political engagement.[2] Many of Puig's own autobiographical statements seem to support the "escapist" assessment. He said, for example,
answering a question about the significance of "living through movies,"
that "for me it was survival because I couldn't accept the reality that was
presented me."[3] He also observed, in a similar vein, of the autobiographical
protagonist of *Betrayed by Rita Hayworth:*

> The principal character which is the one that reflects my vision of things—he
> reflects it because the novel is totally autobiographical, it is the story of my
> youth—is a boy that doesn't accept the reality imposed on him because it is,
> above all, repressive. His unconscious and disarticulated rebellion takes him to
> what you quite rightly called "alienation." That reality can't be changed but
> simply avoided. What alternative did I have at that age besides simple evasion?[4]

However, Puig here puts his finger on the problem with left-oriented critical evaluations of his politics. Evasion—and for that matter, entanglement
with a commodified mass culture—is neither good nor bad in itself, but can
only be evaluated in terms of historical necessity. In this sense, Puig's
honest engagement with the mass cultural forms that were his life happens
to reflect that broader challenge to high modernism's "great divide" that is
often attributed to postmodernism. Moreover, the novel's seemingly ambiguous politics acutely register a more general crisis of politics at the time
of Puig's coming to political consciousness in the early seventies. Ambiguity and conflict within the text express the contradictions of a nightmarish,
failed attempt at liberation. This text does not turn its back on social repression and the agency required to resist and overcome it. On the contrary, it confronts the complex nature of that repression. In this sense, it
anticipated texts such as Luisa Valenzuela's "Los censores," in which the
most insidious and perhaps dangerous, if not immediately frightening,
censors are those who reside within us. In fact, we might, on account of
Puig's attention to the interior spaces of repression, wish to situate him as a
precursor to some postmodern women's writing in the Southern Cone:
Diamela Eltit's *Lumpérica,* Marta Traba's *Conversación al Sur* and *En cualquier lugar,* Cristina Peri Rossi's *La tarde del dinosauro* and *La rebelión de los
niños.* For that matter, it may be worth noting that Puig himself conceived
Beso as an attempt to understand Latin American, and particularly Argentine, patriarchy from the angle of women's internalization of its oppressive
structures.[5] Puig believed that patriarchy, like other forms of authoritarian oppression in Argentine society, was most dangerous in its internal

form. The real enemy, perversely, was the perceived advantages oppression brought its victims. Rather than focusing only on external institutions and discourses, Puig believed that in the absence of internalization, such exterior trappings of power could not persist. Only by understanding the perceived advantages of being oppressed could one hope to dismantle oppression. In the process, Puig's work comes to demand that the nature of liberating praxis be rethought.[6] The novels that followed Puig's in the 1980s began to think liberation and resistance from a point beyond the crisis of utopia represented in, but certainly not initiated by, Puig's text.

The first scene of *El beso de la mujer araña* is marked by the presence of two textual features that structure the entire text: first, metafiction, and second, a complex representation of the dynamics of imprisonment. The beginning of *El beso de la mujer araña* coincides with the beginning of the narration of the panther woman film. This formal ambiguity forces the implicit acceptance (through an initial disorientation), if not an explicit recognition of a certain relationship between the reality of the cell and that of the film. They literally are inseparable. We as readers are left in the dark as to the status of the narrative. What is the object of the narrative? Is the woman being described a character within the world of the novel? Or in some other fictional world? Who is speaking? Will the narrator of the scene at the zoo also be the narrator of the novel? Of course, as the novel progresses and we become acquainted with the characters, we rely on conventions of reading to draw such distinctions. But we have nonetheless been forced to recognize that the films have a very close relationship to the events in the cell. This receives emphasis by their identity in the first lines of the novel.

These first lines also highlight this relationship through their content. The film/novel begins with Irena, a young Romanian woman, seated in front of and sketching a caged panther at the zoo. This creates a model of the situation within the prison cell. Molina, like Irena, is representing imprisonment—not only that of the panther, but also of Irena, who, we shall see below, is in a prison of her own. The boundaries between cell and film are blurred. But a perhaps still more significant implication of this blurring now becomes visible as well. For if the image of Irena sketching the panther echoes Molina's narration of the film, then it also models our own activity as readers, and Puig's as author.[7] Though we are not aware of it yet, we too are engaged in the representation of imprisonment, and certainly Puig is engaged in precisely such a representation. This metafictional layering, in which the text contains miniature replicas of itself within itself, blurs boundaries between film and cell within the text, as well as between text and world.

Two major theoretical works on metafiction—*Narcissistic Narrative* and *The Mirror in the Text*—imply, by their very titles, the self-obsessive character of such fiction.[8] We may be tempted to agree that metafiction refuses narrative's outward gaze. If the metafictional text gazes at itself (as in a mirror) and is about itself (meta-) as fiction, then it would appear that the "real world" referent that novels once represented has receded over the horizon of novelistic concerns. Thus, Robert Alter writes that metafiction intends "to draw our attention to fictional form as a consciously articulated entity rather than a transparent container of 'real' contents."[9] Transposing the discussion to the field of Latin American literature, Alter's view allures. Though there, this apparent flight from reality through formal technique is criticized as an escapist and overeager embracing of "foreign" techniques.[10]

This view presupposes a distinction between a "realist" novel, which represents "reality," and a "metafictional" (or formally innovative) novel, which represents the "text" itself. But this binary opposition between text/metafiction and reality/mimetic fiction is finally untenable. All literary texts, as Paul de Man has shown, are about themselves, and all literary texts, as Fredric Jameson has shown, are about the social conditions in which they were produced.[11] What seems to be at stake in the debate on metafiction is which of these referential functions a given text will foreground. But this cannot be resolved because these are not two isolable components of a text: to speak of one of these dimensions is automatically to speak of the other. The uniqueness of a metafictional device is not that it withdraws into itself, but rather that it simultaneously draws attention to both these textual dimensions. Patricia Waugh writes that metafiction "systematically draws attention to its status as an artifact."[20] This definition of metafiction encompasses precisely its double dimension, to which we may wish to add that it is artifact that is *socially* constructed. "Metafiction is about the social construction of a literary text" or "metafiction is about a literary text that is socially constructed": the difference lies only in the emphasis. Metafiction sets itself apart from "regular" fiction (that is, it constitutes itself as a critical category) by dramatizing the inseparable coexistence of and tension between these two dimensions of the literary text.

Linda Hutcheon approaches this view in her discussion of the metafictional paradox. However, she displaces the social conditions of production of the text to the generative activity of the reader:

> Its [metafiction's] central paradox for readers is that, while being made aware of the linguistic and fictive nature of what is being read, thereby distanced from any unself-conscious identification on the level of character or plot, readers of metafiction are at the same time made mindful of their active role in reading, in participating in making the text mean. They are the distanced, yet involved, co-producers of the novel.[13]

She is interested in metafiction as the representation of literature as "process" (rather than ossified, eternal product).[14] But Hutcheon reduces this "process" to the interactive dynamic—the "metafictional paradox"—between text and reader. Her blindness to the social implications of her insight becomes more visible to us when she explains her decision not to take up the question of "postmodernism" with which metafiction has (as in her own later work) been associated: "The focus of a debate on the causes of [the trend toward metafiction] must necessarily be on the perpetrator of the change—the author. The interest here is rather on the text, on the literary manifestation of this change, and on the resulting implications for the *reader*."[15] This view of literary history as focused on the author (even in conjunction with text and reader) at the apparent expense of its social conditions of possibility excludes the understanding of metafiction I argued for above. The metafictional text does not represent merely the inseparable dimensions of text and reader. Rather, it represents those of text and its real social conditions of production. These may include, but should not be limited to, the activity of the reader. An evaluation of a metafictional representation should not be separated from the context in which it appears because the text partly refers to its conditions of production and these are always ultimately concrete, social and historical.

In *El beso de la mujer araña*, the metafictional blurring of boundaries between text and world contrasts with the utopian function attributed to the films by their narrator, Molina. Molina feels that his film narrations are prompted by their *distance* from the reality of the cell: "I'd forgotten about this filthy cell, and all the rest, just telling you about the film" (23/17). But these films evoke, by escapist negation, the repression of their lives in the cell. And they actually reflect it in their form and content. Molina's escape hatch becomes problematic. He retreats to the film as to a utopian space of freedom. But that space represents repression (Irena and the panther are both caged). Furthermore, it is generated only because of the repression of the jail cell (Molina narrates to "escape"). The space, therefore, already contains the trace of the original state of repression it was created to transcend.

Molina himself expresses this contradiction in his description of Irena: "No, she's not thinking about the cold, it's as if she's in some other world, all wrapped up in herself drawing the panther" (10/4). Though Valentín points out the contradiction—being "inside oneself" means that one is within *this* world, and not some "other world"—Molina resolves it by suggesting that Irena carries the "other world" within her. But this explanation only displaces the contradiction. Her problem (from a curse or some sort of psychosexual neurosis she is afraid to consummate her marriage) is completely tied to her self. Irena's escape to an other world within is as contradictory and illusory as Molina's escape to a cinematic world which is a replica of the repressive one he inhabits. Indeed, from a psychoanalytic perspective this contradiction would be far from coincidental. Molina's film narrations, like Irena's panther drawings, would be ways of narrating, from a distance, their own much more painful and immediate situation. Such psychoanalytic speculation, however, must be complemented with attention to the social determinants on that situation.

Now, if the autonomy of aesthetic representation in the form of Molina's narrations and its escapist (or utopian) function have been eroded, this carries implications for the reader of *El beso de la mujer araña* as well. The reader of the novel may no longer approach the text as autonomous. Instead of looking to fiction as pure escape, totally divorced from the "real" world, the reader must wonder if that fiction somehow contains traces of that real world. How, the reader may ask, is the world of the novel similar or related to my own world? But, if that utopian escape is an illusion because it carries within it the seeds of the repressive state, then that the mechanism of repression is more complicated than the simple erection of a barrier separating an undesirable inside from a utopian, desired outside.

This scene, and the novel as a whole, problematizes an older model of the dynamic of repression or imprisonment:

—. . . the black panther at the zoo, which was quiet at first, stretched out in its cage. But when the girl made a noise with her easel and chair, the panther spotted her and began pacing back and forth in its cage and to growl at the girl, who up until then was still having trouble with shading in the drawing.

—Couldn't the animal smell her before that?

—No, because there's a big slab of meat in the cage, that's all it can smell. The keeper drops the meat near the bars, and it blocks out any smell from outside, *that's the point, so the panther won't get excited.* (9/2; emphasis added)

To the effective, but clumsy, repressive machinery of the cage, this passage couples a second, more subtle form of control. The panther's desire or, more properly speaking, instinct cages the animal as effectively as the bars. Because of the palliative effect of the meat, the panther is prevented from confronting the restrictions under which he lives. The panther will not become "excited" by the prospect of something outside the cage because there is something inside the cage that appears as a substitute, not only for the outside object but also for the very freedom the attainment of that object would presuppose. The meat displaces freedom as the desired object. In other words, the "utopian" impulse to leave the cage is contained by the immediate gratification represented by the meat.

But we may also trace the meat's capacity to fulfill its function to something in the subject—the panther. We must recognize that the meat's ability to distract the panther depends on a relationship between the meat (object) and the panther (subject), and not on some overwhelming enchanting spell the meat casts on the panther. In fact, it is the panther's instinctual desire for the meat that allows the latter to function as a repressive substitute for real gratification. Only because the meat serves some genuine need in the panther can it activate the instinct which finally constrains the panther's behavior.[16] Thus, something within the panther himself (his instinct) fuels the repressive illusion of freedom in which the panther lives—pacified by the slab of meat—and in which genuine freedom is effaced from the horizon of desired objects. In this sense, we are once again before a problem of alienation. The panther's capacity to regulate and satisfy his own desires is predicated on his freedom in the wild. By contrast, in the zoo, these desires are, in a sense, alienated or removed from him and presented to him in the external and objectified form of a routine of feeding and the slab of meat. This "new" mechanism of repression goes beyond the external repression of imprisonment. Instead, it manipulates the desires and internal, psychological processes of repression already existing within the subject, redirecting these processes toward its own ends.

Perhaps to refer to a panther's utopian impulses, desires or internal repressions strikes as slightly anomalous. If so, then let us move to the more plausible level of the human in this cat woman film. Irena fears that she has inherited a curse in which she will be transformed into a deadly panther if she has a sexual relationship. This curse affected the women of her mountain village in Romania and knowledge of it was passed on through legends. Therefore she has fled that village and arrived in New York. Gradually, through her relationship with the architect, she begins to lose her fear. Or he encourages her to believe that she has nothing to fear. In any case, she marries him and assures him that it is only a matter of time before she overcomes what is understood by both to be an irrational superstition. But that which she fled, the curse that she perceived as an external agent of terror to be left behind, lies within her. Indeed, this fact is represented rather dramatically when a woman from her village recognizes her in a restaurant. The zombie film narrated later in the novel also provides a helpful image for this: the young bride, fleeing the huge black zombie male in the old abandoned house, breathlessly escapes into a bedroom and locks the door behind her only to realize, as she becomes accustomed to the dark, that there is a zombie in this room as well (179/174). The zombie movie as a whole also represents this dynamic: the young and carefree newlyweds approach the utopian, bountiful island only to have their worst nightmares realized there as a result of the groom's repressed past. It matters little here whether one accepts Valentín's crude Freudo-Marxist reading of Irena's behavior or whether one takes the story of the curse at face value. In either case, the message seems simple enough: there can be no escape if one carries, like the panther and Irena, the mechanism of repression within.

But then where will liberation come from? This first scene certainly does not offer the possibility of a space in which one would be free of this burden of internalized repression. And at the same time, it offers no liberation without such a space. It simultaneously desires and denies Cortazar's utopia of a radically new space. It both posits and seals off such a totally pure, utopian space as the only space of freedom. For her part, Irena seemingly realizes that this utopia is unattainable, and yet is unable to conceive of liberation in any other terms. Finally, she lets herself be killed by the panther. This is the crisis of utopia as inscribed in the first scene of the text: a nightmarish image of utopia that is simultaneously dystopia. But this is not just Irena's problem. This first scene, with its dense metafictional layering, prohibits the reader from constructing the text as a utopian space apart from his or her real world. He or she must recognize in *El beso de la mujer araña* the traces of his or her own world. He or she must, like Irena, realize that the escape route is already closed off. Therefore, the reader must either put the book down or begin to conceive of the liberating function of the book in a different way.

I evoked above the brutal nature of the Argentine world of the seventies. This is the nightmare of the world of *El beso de la mujer araña,* and it makes not only a coded appearance, but is in fact the explicitly named object of the narrative. The terror of the seventies is thus telescoped into the space of the novel. If so, the implications of the crisis of utopia within the novel must therefore resonate out into the "real world." There, the utopian imaginaries of the sixties gave way, one by one, to the counterrevolutionary, monstrous realities of the seventies. In Argentina, left-wing Peronism found itself savagely undermined by the emblem of its utopian imaginary: Perón himself. These histories remain to be examined more closely as a way of historicizing the particular form and content of *El beso de la mujer araña* and as a particular moment in a shift in Latin American societies from the 1960s to the 1980s. First, though, we should probe the crisis within the text more deeply.

If *El beso de la mujer araña* rethinks repression and liberation, then we might focus, to begin with, on the most evident form of repression and alienation in the novel: the prison cell itself. But the cell as such appears only negatively. That is, there are no descriptions of the cell and the characters mention it only in projecting their desire to transcend it. It is as though its image were cut out from a piece of fabric and the novel represents not the cell, but the hole in the fabric. It is a strangely absent presence in the novel. Valentín and Molina appear as diametrical opposites at the beginning of the novel. Molina is perceived by both characters as "female"; as sensitive, emotional, sensual, and uninterested in politics. Valentín, on the other hand, is a hard-boiled Marxist revolutionary, highly rational and very macho. Molina absorbs himself in the seemingly frivolous images of the romantic Hollywood films of the 1940s; Valentín spends his time studying political theory. And yet, even in these two contrasting practices we may perceive a similarity that refers back to the cell. For both characters perceive these practices as means of transcending the reality of the cell.

Molina responds angrily to Valentín's intrusive political commentary on the panther woman film: "It makes me angry the way you brought all this up, because until you brought it up I was feeling fabulous, I'd forgotten all about this filthy cell, and all the rest, just telling you about the film" (23/17). And later, in defense of his Nazi propaganda film: "I'm locked up in this cell and I'm better off thinking about nice things, so I don't go nuts, see? . . . let me escape from reality once in a while, because why should I let myself get more depressed than I am" (85/75). For his part, and against this open escapism, Valentín posits the realism of his studies. But they actually serve the identical function. As he tells Molina in the following dialogue:

> —I put up with all of it . . . because there's a purpose behind it. Social revolution, that's what's important, and gratifying the senses is only secondary. While the struggle goes on, and it'll probably go on for the rest of my life, it's not right for me to cultivate any kind of sensual gratification, do you get my point? because, really, that takes second place for me. The great pleasure's something else, it's knowing I've put myself in the service of what's truly noble, I mean . . . well . . . all my ideas [*mis ideas*] . . . My ideals, . . . marxism, if you want me to spell it out in only one word. And I can get that pleasure anywhere, right here in this cell, and even in torture. (33–34/28; translation modified)

He insists that his unswerving commitment to the cause, manifested in ascetic discipline and study, link him, beyond the bars of the cell, to his friends: "I'm not alone! I'm with her and with everybody who thinks like her and me . . . I'm not far from any of my comrades, I'm with them! Now, at this very moment! . . . It doesn't matter if I can't see them" (48/42). Finally, in the same argument over Molina's Nazi film, Valentín cautions that Molina's "escapist" films are "like a drug. Because listen to me, reality, I mean *your reality* isn't restricted by this cell we live in. If you read something, if you study something, you transcend any cell you're inside of do you understand what I'm saying? That's why I read and why I study every day" (85/78). Thus Valentín seeks in his studies precisely the same metaphysical, utopian escape from the reality of the cell that Molina sought through his movies. To assert the transcendent value of his studies, Valentín relies on the autonomy of the written artifact. He believes that the written text constitutes a world apart from the material reality of the cell. He celebrates his studies at the expense of the material reality of the cell. He may feel solidarity and support from his comrades, but he is not, materially speaking, with them.

Valentín is not alone in his fabrication, nor are the cell bars the only repressive force affecting him and Molina. Both characters fashion a stable sense of identity—a primary task of survival within a prison cell, when all of the social structures (friends, family, home, etc.) from which one draws meaning as a subject are stripped away[17]—through a series of pyschic and interpersonal repressions. Each represses certain forces within himself in order to assert more strongly his identity within the cell. But the qualities each represses in himself strikingly are the qualities asserted by the other and expressed in *his* practice. Thus, repressing unwanted qualities within oneself, for these characters, also requires the interpersonal repression of those qualities as they are expressed by the other. For example, Molina denies the political nature of his self; he denies analysis and reason, asceticism, and the violence associated with the figure of the macho. He also resents Valentín and tries to quiet him when he brings up these values. Conversely, Valentín denies his private self, emotional and sensual pleasure, and the gentility associated with the figure of the female, and he punishes Molina for "giving in" to these qualities. The stability of these denials (we may call them repressions) and of the oppositions they produce forms the basis for the utopian practices of each character at the beginning of the novel.

We may spot, even at the beginning of the novel in these initial assertions of self-identity and of metaphysical transcendence, the traces of both psychological and physical repression. We detect the repressed contents "leaking" into and manifesting themselves in the two men's respective discourses.[18] This leak relates to the historical implications of Puig's representation of the crisis of utopia. It implies the possibility of identifying, in the early moments of some utopian project, the seeds that will lead to its downfall. In narrating several of the films, Molina draws our attention to a detail that is interpreted as an omen. For example, as the new bride arrives on the zombie island, an orchid falls unnoticed on the beach. In one sense, this is nothing more than the focus on the marginal or that repressed from one's field of vision. But it was put explicitly to political use by Puig himself who wrote of the eagerly awaited but disillusioning return of Perón in 1973: "When he was ousted from government in 1965 he chose Franco's Spain for his residence, and he was on the best of terms with the Spanish dictator. That was one of the many indications of his true political tendencies. And the moment he came back to power he eliminated the leftist members of his cabinet."[19] Perón certainly was never "utopian" in the sense that *Rayuela* or Valentín give to the term. But the point is that the Argentine Left attached its own utopian project to Perón without properly confronting those early leaks that indicated the potentially fatal contradictions inherent in that attachment.

We can attribute this "return of the repressed" in the novel to the pressure exerted on each character by the visible, tangible, and unavoidable embodiment (in the form of their cellmate) of the repressed contents of their unconscious. The cell guarantees, by forcing their interaction, the build-up of this pressure. This pressure gradually erodes the stability of their identities and of the utopian, escapist practices founded on those identities.[20] For example, Valentín betrays—in his sermon on discipline, solidarity, and Marxism—the role of pleasure in determining his self-constituting beliefs. He tells Molina that the "great pleasure" is "knowing." In Valentín's discourse, if not in his invented hierarchy of values, pleasure literally appears prior to knowledge. Strictly speaking, the two terms are identical: pleasure *is* knowing (and in Spanish, of course, the verb *saber*, "to know," is also "to taste," making knowledge indistinguishable from a certain sensuality). Thus, even as Valentín expresses his freedom from them, such "hedonistic" impulses lurk within him like the cell within the reader's textual space, an absent presence exerting an invisible force.

At another point in the same conversation, Valentín calls Molina "over-sensitive" and equates this quality with women, finally saying that "this excess [*ese exceso*] can get in a man's way" (35/29; translation modified). Valentín can accommodate neither women nor sensitivity in his own constitution or in the movement. Because of these exclusions, he represses Molina, who represents these characteristics to Valentín. He praises only women who, in effect, have subordinated what he sees as their "female-ness" and have become more "male." And yet, this repressed constellation (female/sensitivity) surfaces at the center of his definition of what makes a man: "It's not humiliating someone else with an order, or a tip. Even more, it's . . . not letting the person next to you feel degraded, feel bad" (70/63; translation modified). Now it appears that the essence of being male requires one to be sensitive; a previously disparaged female characteristic. Valentín must, according to the logic of his own definitions, be like a woman to be a man; but being like a woman can get in a man's way.[21] Valentín betrays his inability to overcome this false contradiction (false because evidently being sensitive, as Molina points out, has nothing whatever to do with being a man or a woman, male or female) through his striking and repeated violations of his own standard of "manliness." More than once, he gives Molina orders, humiliates him, degrades him, and makes him feel bad. He does this, however, precisely because Molina represents femininity and thus threatens Valentín's identity, grounded on the repression of the feminine within him. However, Valentín's discourse reveals a glimmer of consciousness in the ellipsis marks just before he refers to the person "next to" him. He recognizes, perhaps, that something is amiss, though he is not yet sure what. We can see, then, in some of Valentín's most strident assertions of identity and of the utopian function of this identity, the return of the repressed. These are the traces of the absent, but determining, terms on whose repression Valentín's very "freedom" seems to depend. And yet Valentín will continue, in spite of the contortions it forces him into, to operate on the basis of those repressions for some time.

Molina constitutes his self-identity through an equally fundamental repression, but in his case it is of the political. Molina sees "politics" (understood not as an everpresent struggle for power and social resources, but as a narrow field of professional specialization) as an uninteresting nuisance, to be kept separate from his personal affairs. He avoids, for example, the political implications of the Nazi propaganda film, of which he tells Valentín: "If I had the chance to choose one film to see all over again, it would have to be this one" (63/56). When Valentín answers in disbelief that it is a piece of "Nazi junk, or don't you realize," Molina at first remains silent. This silence, like Valentín's ellipses, represents, among other things, Molina's expression on politics. His expression must be rendered only as silence because to confront Valentín's criticism verbally would require Molina to use a discourse, that of politics, on whose repression his identity depends. After regaining his composure, Molina responds by sobbing that "it's well made, and besides it's a work of art, you don't under— . . . understand because you never even saw it" (63/56). He successfully, though not without trauma, reinstalls the barrier separating his movies from politics. Such a separation is crucial if the films' reflection of the uncomfortable repressions lived by both Valentín and Molina is to remain invisible to them. Valentín's relentless political commentary forces the emergence of symptomatic "returns," like this tearful rejoinder, of Molina's repressed political consciousness.

The most striking return of the political in Molina's early, apolitical activities results from his secret deal with the warden. Molina, recall, has made a pact with the prison warden (who receives orders directly from the military president) to obtain information on Valentín's comrades in exchange for his own (Molina's) release. Molina's desire for freedom is motivated by his wish to help his ailing mother, whose condition has declined since his conviction. He expresses, by this arrangement, a belief that politics are a neutral tool to be implemented toward the achievement of one's personal affairs and then left aside again. He is not conscious of the political as a perpetually conditioning factor, even though it is an indispensable part of his own emancipatory project. This repressed fact, of the irrepressibility of the political, returns dramatically when Molina must eat the poisoned prison food meant to debilitate Valentín. Molina fails to recognize this "mistake" as symptomatic of politics' determining influence on him.

This misrecognition will permit Molina to intensify his relationship with Valentín, and to continue to repress the less-savory aspects of politics and power, to the point when he will promise to relay, on his release, a message to Valentín's cadre.

In the first half of the novel the characters appear to be opposites. Each presents an identity to the other and to himself upon which he founds his transcendent, utopian practice. But each is also the mirror image of the other's repressed. Physical restriction forces each to daily, continually confront those repressed contents, and gradually fractures the facade of self-identity and coherence. The first cracks are, as we have seen, detectable immediately. But not until early in the second half of the novel will each come to accept in himself those previously repressed qualities projected onto the other.[22] Only then do they transform themselves and, at the same time, transform their conceptions of liberating practice.

Let me approach these transformations by way of an apparent detour through the footnotes that appear periodically between pages 66/59 and 211/214. The footnotes (with the exception of one, which is an excerpt from the imaginary press release on the invented Nazi film *Her Greater Glory*) provide summaries of the development of social scientific discourse on homosexuality. Most of the theories described come from the field of psychoanalysis. This fact, together with the content of some of the theories, foregrounds the theme of repression. And repression (psychically of "politics" or "sensuality," or intersubjectively of each other), we have seen, forms the flawed foundation of the characters' self-constituting, transcendent, and utopian practices.

This is not, however, the footnotes' only relationship to the reality of the cell, nor to the practice of repression. The footnotes constitute a scientific, theoretical representation of homosexuality. Meanwhile, the representation of the cell, to which they are formally juxtaposed, includes a homosexual. We therefore must address another level of the relationship. One important critic has found support for a psychoanalytic reading of the novel in the presence of the footnotes.[23] Although I would not thereby negate the validity of a psychoanalytic reading, it must be said that these notes do anything but praise the relevance of psychoanalytic theory, which is found wanting in its understanding of homosexuality. Especially interesting in this regard is that the most acceptable of the sources, Taube's work, is invented by Puig. Indeed the footnotes fall woefully short of "explaining" or "accounting for"—or even predicting for that matter—the complex behavior of Molina.[24] The various theories of homosexuality, like any discourse, operate on the basis of an exclusion. Although claiming empirical validity, they actually are grounded on the repression of that portion of reality that does not buttress their theoretical claims to truth. Without these claims to truth, the very identity of scientific discourse is undermined and it loses its privileged status.[25] In this sense, the footnotes are engaged in the same process as the characters: they constitute themselves on the basis of a repression of a threatening Other. In the case of the footnotes, the "portion of reality" that they marginalize, repress, or exclude—their "threatening Other"—is the character of Molina himself. They form in this way another appendage to the repressive machinery of the state that has physically imprisoned Molina.

Theodor Adorno understood this relationship between conceptualization and repression: "The name of dialectics says no more, to begin with, than that objects do not go into their concepts without leaving a remainder, that they come to contradict the traditional norm of adequacy. Contradiction . . . indicates the untruth of identity, the fact that the concept does not exhaust the thing conceived."[26] To the extent that the footnotes constitute "conceptual" activity, we might recall Adorno's emphasis on the repressive dimension of "conceptual" thought. For Adorno, the German word for "concept" [*begriff*] permitted the connection to "seizing" or "capturing" (for which the German word is *begriffen*). Thus, Adorno's reflections make more explicit the connection I am arguing for here between imprisoning with bars and with concepts. For that matter, Adorno—who fled Nazi Germany and whose writing is strongly marked by that period—gives us a reason to address the one footnote that appears not to fit *my* theory here. But even the Nazi press release footnote supports this interpretation. For the Nazi press release paints a very different picture of the Nazi film than does Molina. This disjuncture between the two representations of the film foregrounds the essential inability of representation to fully "capture" the "thing itself."

The footnotes are guilty of separating their discourse from the reality of the cell. But, at the same time, they are formally inscribed within that reality for they are marked by an asterisk in the text. This formal inscription demonstrates their dependence on that reality, their inseparability from it. Yet the footnotes sometimes draw our attention away from the cell for pages at a time, creating an illusion of self-sufficiency and of autonomy from its reality. In this way, they echo the discourse of the aestheticist reader (and that of Molina and Valentín) who separates the text from the reality of repression—political and otherwise—in Argentina and other parts of Latin America and the world. The metafictional nature of the filmic narratives blurs those comforting boundaries. So also the footnotes come to an abrupt conclusion and the reader is jolted back into the reality of the cell that, as becomes apparent, these footnotes are unable to explain. The confrontation of footnote with textual reality challenges the practice of separating these discourses. We may not comfortably occupy the seemingly self-contained discourse of science and truth. And it is not just the distance of science that is questioned. It is the repression involved in any kind of unselfconscious, exclusionary self-fashioning—whether on the part of the characters, the film protagonists, the reader of *El beso de la mujer araña,* or the producers of the utopian imaginaries of the 1960s.

Until now, we have been considering the footnotes as a homogeneous unit. But in fact they represent a diversity of theoretical opinion arranged polemically, leading up to what appears as the most plausible scientific discourse on homosexuality—plausible, that is, in terms of what we witness in the cell. They range from D. J. West's rejection of physiological theories (66–68/59–65) to the refutation of West's own reliance on biblical interpretations of homosexuality (102/97); and from Freud's diagnostic interpretation (103/100) to the celebration of "polymorphous perversity" in Marcuse (155/153). The footnotes thus foster the impression of a theoretical development that progressively accounts for more and more of the reality of the cell. This development mirrors the development of the characters who appear to expand their self-images to include characteristics they previously rejected. Ultimately, in the last footnote, from a source invented by Puig, "Dr. Anneli Taube" establishes the link between homosexuality and revolutionary political practice (211/214). This apparently prefigures Molina's (the homosexual's) own political intervention (on behalf of a revolutionary cause) at the end of the novel. But when we focus on the apparent growth and development of both footnotes and characters, we may tend to forget the repressions these self-constituting conceptual practices are founded on. This teleological image of development toward a utopian (pure and uncontradicted) truth is an illusion. In fact, this development carries its own negation: for if a given theory may be subject to criticism and replaced by another, so we must consider that the second, more "truthful," theory may in time be subject to criticism and replaced, and so forth and so on. Unless this internal self-negating function and the repressive foundation of the truth claims of such teleological narratives of theoretical development are recognized, the illusion of knowledge that they foster will surely be rudely shattered by the intrusion of some unaccommodating reality.

With these insights in mind, reconsider the cell and to the transformative process in which the characters are engaged. This process, initiated by the confrontation of each character with his own repressions in the form of the other, is accelerated by Valentín's illness (on account of *his* eating poisoned prison food). This illness makes visible a vulnerability and dependency that Valentín would not wish to have acknowledged earlier in the text. He can barely do anything for himself. He does not wish to go to the prison infirmary fearing that they will drug him to get him to talk, a significant fear in view of the novel's ending. He therefore must rely on Molina to take care of him, a role Molina welcomes. But this physical dependence on Molina only manifests tangibly the psychological dependence that has existed from the beginning. Valentín's psychological coherence, as we have seen, ultimately derived from the repression of the "Molinian" characteristics within himself. In this sense, his identity was dependent on Molina. This dependence was reflected in his growing attachment to the films. His illness forces that repressed dependence into the realm not only of consciousness, but of the physical. Not only his psychological identity but also his very physical existence, his machista image of self-reliance, depend entirely on the good will of Molina. He physically could not afford to engage in the self-denying practice of avoiding the infirmary without the support of Molina. This support expresses those very characteristics—tenderness and sensitivity—Valentín previously saw as "feminine" impediments to his self-constituting practices. Valentín thus comes face to face with all that he has lived to repress and the confrontation causes him to unravel. He by no means welcomes this seeming change in their relationship. He expresses his resistance as a desire not to be "beholden" to Molina. This eventually erupts into a full-blown crisis when a fully recuperated Valentín violently rejects Molina's offers of assistance (196–99/192–94).

Another interesting inscription of this dependency, and its larger ramifications, is that part of Molina's apparent manipulation of the warden involves getting bags of groceries that he then feeds to Valentín to help him recover. From a different angle, this implies that Valentín's resistance to the system (that is, his recovery) is accounted for by that system itself. On the other hand, this is problematic only from the modern perspective, which requires pure unrecuperability or uncooptability as a standard for its political strategies. By contrast, the postmodern viewpoint, for which Puig's text begins to clear a space, does not require such purity but rather views it as a myth. Moreover, the attempt to realize this myth historically must involve some kind of violent cleansing. Perhaps Valentín begins to realize this as well as a result of this experience.

At any rate, out of this crisis will be born their new relationship. Molina gets more groceries out of the warden and refrains from pushing them on Valentín. The latter apologizes for his outburst. Valentín explains that if "I got all uptight because you were being . . . generous with me . . . it's because I didn't want to see myself as obligated to treat you the same way" (205/201). In a similarly conciliatory gesture, Molina claims to understand that "when you're involved in a struggle the way you are, you're not supposed to . . . well, become attached . . . to anyone. Oh, maybe attached is saying too much, but why not, yes to become attached . . . like a friend" (205/201). Both characters here make very uncharacteristic statements of apology and reconciliation. And both statements are essentially articulated from what has up to this point been the other's point of view. Valentín recognizes the importance of sensitivity in interpersonal relations, and Molina admits the validity of Valentín's need to avoid such relations because of his politics. The ellipsis marks within their statements mark the unfamiliarity of this territory for each of them.

This transformation quickly takes the form of a project of liberating praxis proposed by Valentín:

> —in this case, the two of us are locked up here, so there is no struggle, no fight to win, you follow me?
> —Mmm, go ahead.
> —Then are we so pressured . . . by the outside world, that we can't act civilized? Is it possible . . . that the enemy, out there has so much power?
> —I don't follow you . . .
> —Well, that everything that's wrong with the world . . . and everything that I want to change . . . is it possible all that won't allow me to . . . behave . . . even for a single minute, like a decent human being?
>
> . . . .
>
> —I don't know if you understand me . . . but here we are, all alone, and when it comes to our relationship, how should I put it? We could make any damn thing out of it we want; our relationship isn't pressured by anyone.
> —Yes, I'm listening.
> —In a sense we're perfectly free to behave however we choose with respect to one another, am I making myself clear? It's as if we were on some desert

island. An island on which we may have to remain alone together for years. Because, well, outside of this cell we may have our oppressors, yes, but not inside. Here no one oppresses the other. (205–6/202)

This passage is extremely relevant to the process we have been tracing in *El beso de la mujer araña*. In it the terms of freedom have been reversed. We suggested above that utopia had previously been grounded on a logic of freedom = outside/oppression = inside. But here Valentín speaks of an oppressive world on the outside and grounds their possibilities for freedom on their being inside. This reversal, however, does *not* negate the utopian logic whose essence is the *stability of boundaries* separating bad old from good new. It only presents this logic's inverted image. Valentín still depends on boundaries—now the impermeability of the cell walls themselves—for the construction of a utopian space. Valentín rhetorically converts the cell into a utopian, repression- and alienation-free island in the tradition begun by Thomas More in 1516 and culminating four and a half centuries later in Fidel Castro's Cuba. But the contradictions inscribed in More's very title— "utopia"—are doubled in Valentín's contemporary expression of it.

Valentín posits a prison wall as a precondition for freedom. This astoundingly contradictory statement echoes Molina's treatment of politics as a neutral and passive tool for manipulation in one's personal interest. Valentín explicitly suggests not only that freedom can be achieved within their nine-by-nine-foot prison cell but also that it actually depends on the limitations of that space. He ignores the external connections of those prison walls to a larger apparatus of repression that preserves the capacity to control the contents of those interior spaces. Valentín ignores the cell in the same way the reader might feel entitled to do given the absence of any descriptions of it in the text; the same way that the recent Harold Prince Broadway production of *El beso de la mujer araña* ignores the cell, representing it only as a table and two chairs in a dimly lit corner of the stage, while the transcendent projections of each character's imaginations, in living color, hold center stage.

This leads to the second source of the instability of this utopian space. The forces of repression are much less visible, and therefore much more insidious, than Valentín acknowledges. In other words, the cell walls are more permeable to the bad "outside" forces than he recognizes. Recall the internalization of repression in the novel's first scene. In similar fashion, Valentín and Molina themselves transgress the boundaries of their utopian space by carrying *within* themselves unexamined pockets of repression.

They have smuggled in—even as they celebrate the walls that "protect" their utopia—the explosive elements that will shatter it. Valentín does manifest some doubt in the interrogative tenor of his comments. He perhaps feels unsure as to the viability of this utopian space. But he posits it nonetheless. And the gradual disappearance of those healthy doubts from the minds of both characters precipitates the tragedy of the novel.

But not all is doom and gloom in this cell turned utopian island. For, its contradictions notwithstanding, this utopian space generates genuine growth on the part of the characters. Valentín opens up and recognizes his desire to live and his love for the middle-class Marta. For the first time, he does not see sensuality as incommensurate with revolution. Eventually the two men develop a sexual relationship on the basis of the new values they instituted in their moment of crisis. This sexual relationship in turn initiates the final illusion of a utopia, represented by the dissolution of all alienating oppositions between the characters themselves. As Molina himself says: "It seemed like I wasn't here . . . as if now, somehow . . . I . . . were you" (222/219).

The last piece of this utopia is now in place. The characters first constructed the image of a space free from repression. Now they claim to have dissolved the repressions that existed within themselves, and that preserved an alienating barrier between them. When Molina claims to have become Valentín, we may believe that the characters have achieved a union beyond all their differences. This utopian space is further registered by the end of the footnotes. It is as though, confronted with this radically new behavior, the discourse of science had finally given up its attempt to contain the reality of the cell. Or alternatively, as though given this new relationship of absolute identity, the discourse of science, grounded in the alienation between thinking subject and material object, were obsolete.

If this space does generate real transformations on the part of these characters, then one might reasonably ask how important the contradictions signaled above really are. They might even appear as mere theoretically constructed objections needlessly impeding a project with obviously positive consequences in the realm of daily practice. However, the novel undermines such separations between theoretical discourse and "real" practice. Moreover, the text itself finally reveals the limitations of the utopian space—founded, as it is, on the psychological repression of psychological and state-sanctioned repression—constructed by Molina and Valentín. I may also advance my conclusion somewhat and suggest that the Latin American postmodern political and cultural discourse of impurity would acknowledge the importance of concrete gains. It would fault the characters only for hastily taking their utopian dream as fulfilled when in fact it necessarily remained only partially, albeit significantly, realized.

Molina, as we noted above, has an agreement with the warden of the prison. However, the warden, pressured by the government which is planning a major offensive against the insurgents, becomes anxious. He gives Molina just one more week to obtain information from Valentín. Molina, for his part, continues to believe that he can manipulate the arrangement for his own ends. Though his ends have changed from gaining freedom in order to take care of his mother to staying in prison with Valentín and preserving their new relationship. By the end of the week, the warden has changed his plan. He decides to release Molina in the hope that he will lead the secret police to the rebels. In his interview with Molina, the warden first pretends to move Molina to another cell in order to squeeze any information out of him. When it is apparent that Molina really knows nothing, the warden releases him anyway in accordance with his new plan.

Neither Molina nor Valentín seem ever to question the logic of this release. Instead, they apparently view it as an unambiguous stroke of good fortune. Molina feels saddened at the prospect of their separation, but he brightens at the possibility that he might help secure Valentín's release. They both separate the release entirely from the repressive state apparatus that issued it and they both believe themselves able to use it for their own purposes. With this attitude, they reinforce their repression of repression and further destabilize their utopia. Molina and Valentín seemingly believe, in effect, that they can generalize the limited space they created within the cell to the outside world. When Molina agrees to take the message to the revolutionaries, he may not be acting on a political conversion experience. He does display his expanded image of romantic love, which now encompasses, where it previously excluded, such political activity. Moreover, he expresses the hope that he and Valentín could be reunited on the outside. In this final attempt to extend their utopian space to the "outside," the two men intensify the logic that prompted the change in their relationship to begin with. They previously repressed the repression embodied in the cell walls and operant within their own psyches. Now they fall completely under the spell of their illusion. They repress the state's political repression (related to these first two forms) outside the cell as well.

As we expect, Molina, two weeks after his release, tries to contact the revolutionaries and is followed and gunned down in a confrontation with the police. We have no idea whether or not Molina knows he is being followed, but the cold, dry tenor of the police report reveals the power of the terrorist-state apparatus. Surveillance is total: Molina's every move and conversation is monitored. If ever we were lulled into believing in the general viability of Molina and Valentín's utopian space, that illusion is systematically dismantled by the terse police communiqués. We read the chapter simply waiting for Molina to walk into the trap, powerless to help him avoid it.

For his part, Valentín, as we might also have expected, is tortured and interrogated. He is injured so severely that a nurse takes pity on him and gives him a shot of morphine to help him sleep. The dream sequence that follows ends the novel. In it Valentín wanders through a hallucinatory landscape, led by his middle-class lover Marta. He imagines a desert island, much like the one in Molina's movies and the one Valentín earlier imagined their cell to be, on which he meets a native girl who asks him about the death of his cellmate:

> There's no point in being so sad because the only one who knows for sure is him, if he was happy or sad to die that way, sacrificing himself for a just cause, because he's the only one who will ever have known, and let's hope, Marta, how much I wish it with all my heart, let's hope that he may have died happily. "For a just cause? hmmm . . . I think he let himself be killed because that way he could die like some heroine in a movie, and none of that business about a just cause," that's something only he can know, and it's possible that even he never knew, . . . (284–85/279)

This passage apparently confirms that we cannot know Molina's state of mind at the time of his death. But if so, then perhaps it is the very ambiguity that is the point. This ambiguity foregrounds our interpretive activity as readers. We must, denied an authoritative conclusion within the text, confront our own role in the construction of this text. This again blurs the distance between ourselves and the text. But it also, as we shall see below, parallels the position of the two cellmates at the conclusion of Molina's last film narration.

Valentín's dream ends with his own movie narration of a woman on an island with maracas and drums. The woman that emerges

> can't move, there in the deepest part of the jungle she's trapped in a spider's web, or no, the spiderweb is growing out of her own body, the threads are coming out of her waist and her hips, they're part of her body . . . she's crying, or no, she isn't, she's smiling but a tear rolls out from beneath the mask, "A tear

that shines like a diamond?" yes, and I ask her why she's crying and in a close-up that covers the whole screen at the end of the film she answers me that that's just what can never be known, because the ending is enigmatic, and I answer her that it's good that way, that it's the very best part of the film because it signifies . . . and at that point she didn't let me go on, she said that I wanted to find an explanation for everything . . . (285–86/280)

This image, we must first observe, seemingly underscores the importance of acknowledging the ambiguity of Molina's death. But the image itself appears to be of Molina. This interpretation is strengthened when Valentín implies that he had sex with the spider woman because she was so sad, and that the spider woman fed him and showed him the way "through the forest." In this sense, Valentín's hallucinated movie is none other than *El beso de la mujer araña* itself. This reinforces the metafictional of the novel.

But this image signifies on a related, but even more crucial level. The web which traps the woman is spun from her own body. This rejects the utopian logic that distinguishes, through fixed and rigid boundaries, an inside from an outside, the pure from the impure, the just from the un-just, and the oppressed from the oppressor. The spider woman struggles against not something imposed externally, but rather something within herself—a web produced by her own body. Now, a whole series of figures—the panther trapped by his own instinctual desire for meat, the movie characters struggling with their own internal prisons, and the characters within the cell who face their own internal repressions, but fail to connect them to the external mechanisms of repression—align themselves beneath the sign of the spider woman, caught within her own web. This final image of the spider woman, a metaphor both for the novel as a whole and for the various characters within it, unravels the logic of utopia. But if the utopian projection, carried over from *Rayuela* and longed for by the characters in this novel, finally comes undone in this striking image, then what form of liberation remains? Again, this moment—when Puig appears finally to convert utopian energies into pathetic paralysis—must not be subject to dogmatic evaluation, but rather to historical contextualization. Only by tracing the condition of possibility of this image can we begin to conceive of the form, if any, that liberation might now take.

5

Beyond Valentín's Dream

From the Crisis of Latin American Modernity

> Today, at the hour of our awakening, we must be our own historians.
> —Justino Quispe Balboa

On 20 June 1973, General Juan Perón was scheduled to arrive at Ezeiza Airport in Buenos Aires, Argentina, after eighteen years in exile.[1] The Montoneros, a group of leftist Peronist guerrillas who had helped to secure Perón's return by destabilizing the military junta in power since 1966, organized a mass march to welcome their returning leader.[2] As they assumed a central place—amid a crowd of half a million—in front of the platform on which Perón was scheduled to speak just two hours later, they were met with machine-gun fire from the platform. Hundreds were killed, thousands arrested. Others were hunted down in the subsequent confusion, even as they sought first aid, and either beaten or taken to the nearby airport to be tortured.

What happened? How was this event, expected to mark the jubilant reunion of an aging leader with his young "soldiers" (some of whom born after Perón's exile in 1955), turned into a confusing and bitterly disappointing bloodbath? Press coverage at the time shed little light on the massacre. Even today, some authoritative historical sources remain undecided as to the cause of the violence.[3] Conservative groups at the time claimed only that an attempt on Perón's life, planned by the Montoneros, had been averted. However, neither the Montoneros' relationship with Perón nor the logistics of the event support this claim. The Montoneros, on the other hand, observed that the armed guards defending the platform were all members of various para-police outfits organized by and under the command of one Jorge Osinde, the undersecretary for sports within the Ministry of Social Welfare and the man in charge of security for the event. This answer, most plausible in view of subsequent events, is supported by contemporary historical sources.[4] For it turns out that the head of the Ministry of Social Welfare and the man who appointed Osinde to his post as undersecretary and who put him in charge of security for Perón's return was none other than José López Rega, Perón's right-hand man and close confidant of Perón's wife, Isabel. López Rega himself, a rosicrucian who earned the popular nickname *el brujo* (also the title of a novel), "the witch," was also a genuinely fanatical anticommunist. In the months and years that followed, López Rega supervised the para-military death squads of the Alianza Argentina Anticomunista (Argentine Anti-Communist Alliance, or Triple A) that conducted fierce and sweeping raids on "subversive infiltrators." In the fall of 1973, Perón instituted stiff penalties for acts of terrorism while turning a blind eye to the paramilitary activities of the Triple A. At a huge May Day gathering in 1974, Perón publicly condemned the Montoneros. After his death on 1 July 1974, with his wife Isabel installed as president, the situation only worsened such that, by early 1975, the Triple A was murdering fifty "leftists" a week.[5]

Thus, the very moment of the Peronist Left's supposed reunion with its leader was violently shattered by a bloody omen (an orchid fallen on the beach of a desert island?) of what was to come under Perón's administration. Puig may not have had this specific event in Argentine history in mind, or even the state of the Argentine left—though that is difficult to imagine given the setting of the novel and Puig's own comments on Peronism.[6] It seems safe to argue, however, that Puig's capacity to imagine unalienated, liberated utopian spaces was partly restricted by the fate befalling the concrete production of those spaces in his society. I take the bloody ambush at Ezeiza as emblematic of serious contradictions within the project of the Peronist Left, contradictions which are in turn embedded both in Peronism itself and in the Cuban revolution and the various attempts to extend it to continental Latin America in the 1960s.

Recall the Cuban revolutionary discourse of the leap as traced earlier. Throughout the revolution, Castro's 26 of July movement projected an explicitly vanguardist self-representation. After victory in 1959, the movement represented itself overtly and publicly as absolutely identical with the "Cuban people." At the same time, there persisted, on a more subtle level, an intolerant and socially, politically and culturally modernizing vanguardist discourse. These incompatible extremes—of transparent identity and of opaque vanguardism—governed the generalization of the Cuban model to the continent throughout the 1960s. But it is also important to recognize that they contradicted, as Castro was later to acknowledge, the reality of the Cuban revolution's own actual struggle for power.

In its early stages, the Cuban *foco's* survival depended on the political mobilizations of an urban resistance movement in Havana and Santiago that effectively commanded Batista's attention and resources. Consequently, Castro's rural guerrillas were left more or less alone to develop their survival skills, organize peasant support, and thus consolidate the revolution in large areas of the countryside. However, the rural *foco* grew in strength and reputation at the expense of a series of crippling defeats to the urban resistance. Ultimately, the weakened urban group came to be seen, by Castro himself, as a hindrance to what he came to consider the central force of the revolutionary movement, the rural *foco*. This rift, and the resulting mythologization of the vanguard *foco* educating and mobilizing peasant masses, persisted in the postvictory rhetoric of Castro's government, filled mostly with veterans of the guerrilla war. The point is that the government's retrospective tale homogenized what was a rather more-complex and heterogeneous revolutionary movement. This was recognized by Castro himself and by Debray by 1967. Before this rectification, however, Latin America would experience a series of failed attempts to launch Cuban-style *focos* in various parts of the region, punctuated by the death of Che Guevara at the hands of U.S.-trained Bolivian counterinsurgency forces on 8 October 1967. In other words, had the revolution written a different history of itself, its future history might have taken a different turn.

The so-called Latin American revolution, which the Cuban revolution initiated, was partly a response to the economic, political, military, and cultural expansion of the United States after World War II. Dependency theorists, as we saw above, presented the alternatives facing Latin America in stark terms: "underdevelopment or revolution." This social condition was certainly felt differently depending on the terms of each country's engagement with global capitalism as well as on the state of the struggle between each nation's own internal social forces. But it is nevertheless possible to speak in general of a crisis facing Latin American governments caught between the demands of, on the one hand, an increasingly pauperized peasantry and urban working class, articulated with a radicalized activist and intellectual left, and, on the other, a *comprador* bourgeoisie, a reactionary military corps, and United States' corporations and government. To this general crisis, Guevara's *Guerrilla Warfare* seemed to offer a clear blueprint to follow the course of Cuban revolution.

In Argentina, the Cuban blueprint was implemented according to the exigencies of both Argentina's particular historical relationship with global capitalism and the peculiar force exerted on the Argentine political imaginary by Peronism. Argentina was initially incorporated into the rising world capitalist economy toward the end of the nineteenth century. At that time, it exported processed beef to feed Europe's rapidly growing industrial working class.[7] A small class of wealthy landowners maintained political power, and a newly emergent professional and merchant class sought its share of the burgeoning export economy. At the same time, working-class immigrants from southern Spain and southern Italy, many with radical backgrounds, came to work in the meat-processing plants on the outskirts of Buenos Aires.[8] In 1911, threatened by the possibility of an alliance of the increasingly autonomous middle-class and a radical working class, the oligarchy of landowners established universal male suffrage for natives over eighteen. Because the majority of workers were non-natives, this "universal" male suffrage effectively excluded not only women but also radical immigrant workers. The newly enfranchised middle class, however, gained and held political power until 1928. It was, on the one hand, legitimized by the continuing growth of the Argentine economy on the basis of its agricultural exports. On the other hand, it did not shy away from the use of repression to whip the intransigent working class—stirred by events in Europe from Russia to Germany—into conformity, most dramatically during the *semana trágica* of January 1919 in which hundreds of workers were killed and thousands arrested.[9] Juan Perón, later to be real leader and symbolic hero of the Argentine revolutionary Left, was a young lieutenant in charge of one of the platoons that fired on the striking workers.[10]

The world depression of 1929 dramatically revealed, beneath the veil of an expanding economy, the reality of Argentina's dependent position within the world economy.[11] Agricultural markets crashed and, while affected less severely than other Latin American nations, the Argentina economy contracted sharply.[12] The military responded with a coup inaugurating what was to become a grim tradition in Argentine politics, and intended to return the agricultural export elites, or oligarchy, to power. Through electoral frauds which excluded not only the middle class but also the recently increasing numbers of Argentine nationals in the working class, the military successfully propped-up civilian governments throughout the 1930s. Economically, these regimes sought to shore up foreign, particularly British, markets for Argentine beef by granting generous concessions to British capital. But the regimes' policies, though designed to promote the interests of the agricultural elite, also had the effect of priming the process of import-substitution-industrialization whereby domestic industrial production was fostered as a substitute for increasingly expensive foreign imports. Though lured to the cities by this process, workers were not protected from the economic policies of the governments of the 1930s. As Charles Bergquist points out, other countries in the Western hemisphere were engaging in political and institutional reform as a way of defusing popular frustration with the crisis in global capitalism. But in Argentina, not only were these reforms not initiated, but popular discontent was once again actively and violently repressed.[13]

Faced with what he perceived to be the inevitability of global people's revolution after the Russian model, Juan Perón developed his strategy of defusing worker·discontent through preventive measures of economic, political, and social redistribution of power. For Perón, according to historian Donald Hodges, "communism is best resisted by a strategy of absorption."[14] Out of this would emerge his ideology of *justicialismo,* or social justice, as a means of ameliorating conditions that contributed to the attraction of communism among the working class. To that end, and in his capacity as vice-president and minister of labor from 1943 to 1945, Perón oversaw the organization and dramatic expansion of labor unions throughout Argentine industry. Moreover, he carefully screened union leaders, permitting communists to hold key posts only when they cooperated with his larger plans. His belief that Marxism and communism were acceptable provided they accommodated themselves to his nationalist scheme for social redistribution came to be legitimated in his official discourse by the principle of *verticalismo,* or direct hierarchical authority beginning with Perón. For that matter Perón's nationalism extended to a distancing of the U.S. and NATO allies whom he considered part of the cause of communism. Democratic liberalism in the United States and Western Europe was part and parcel of imperialism and a mask for capitalist generation of social inequalities. The threat of communism could only be "killed with an embrace" of its social values, though not its international institutions. Through Import Substitution Industrialization policies, industry had surpassed agriculture as the source of national income by 1945. The massive industrial working class was organized along nationalist, justicialist as opposed to internationalist, communist lines. And Perón himself was the leader of a mass movement.[15] Indeed, Perón was freed by these very workers in an apparently self-directed mass rally after he was arrested by liberal army officers on 17 October 1945.[16] In the elections that were held in February 1946, Perón put forth his "third position": domestically, between communism and capitalism and internationally, between the Soviet Union and the United States.

Perón's first administration, from 1946 to 1952, included reopening of diplomatic ties with the Soviet Union, the enfranchisement of women (of whom 2.5 million voted in 1951 elections) and the establishment by

Eva Duarte Perón of the feminine branch of the Peronist party. Constitutional changes included a charter enumerating the rights of the worker. Economically, Perón nationalized mass-communications industries as well as the British-owned railroads—long-standing symbols of Argentine dependence—and ports and U.S.-owned electrical companies, restricted the repatriation of capital by foreign companies, liquidated foreign debt, and subsidized and created new industries at the expense of agriculture. Between increases in wages and fringe benefits, workers' real wages were effectively nearly doubled between 1943 and 1948. Through these changes, Perón produced a relatively stable state bureaucracy, empowered at the expense of the traditional oligarchical leaders and middle-class party politicians, that helped consolidate his power base. He won reelection in 1951 by a landslide margin of almost two to one.[17]

Many mark Evita's death on 26 July 1952, just a month and a half after Perón's second inauguration (and coincidentally one year before Castro's mythic assault on the Moncada barracks in Cuba), as the beginning of the end for Perón.[18] Evita was a crucial link not only to women but also to workers. In a twentieth-century twist on Doris Sommer's nineteenth-century "foundational romances" in which Latin American nation-building projects are figured through romantic novels, Evita herself bound their marriage and Peronism in the same rhetoric of romance. Speaking in her autobiography, Evita wrote of how Perón won her hand: "He never promised me anything! Speaking of the future he spoke to me only of his people and I ended up convinced that his promise of love was there, in his people, in my people. In our people!"[19] Their marriage was inseparable from their politics: "To divorce himself from the people, the head of the government would have to begin by divorcing his own wife!"[20] If their romance was the symbolic and real cement holding together the Peronist movement, then the movement, in turn, sustained the marriage: "Now I love Perón differently, as I did not love him before: before I loved him for himself . . . now I love him because my people also love him!"[21] The romantic discourse also crept into Perón's own public discourse. On the fifth anniversary of the 17 October uprising, Perón explained to the nation that "the two arms of Peronism are social justice and social aid. With them we give to the people an embrace of justice and of love."[22] We have already noted the importance of a quasi-erotic rhetoric in Che Guevara's understanding of Castro's relationship to the people. Guevara also famously wrote, "At the risk of appearing ridiculous, that the true revolutionary is guided by great sentiments of love. . . . Our vanguard revolutionaries must idealize that love for the people, for the most sacred causes, and make it one, indivisible."[23] In the case of Perón, we should not fail to note that this romantic discourse is attenuated by the ambiguity Perón himself attributed to romantic "embraces" capable of killing an enemy.

Perhaps Perón's romantic rhetoric was less convincing without Evita at his side. At any rate, it is undeniable that Perón's second administration, coeval with his post-Evita government, fell into a stagnant, conservative maintenance of the status quo. Perón was also hit with economic crises. Droughts in Argentina hampered the government's capacity to agriculturally subsidize industrial expansion. And the postwar boom in the United States and Europe led to a contraction in global markets for Argentine agricultural exports and a decline in the terms of trade. The net effect was the restriction of domestic industrial growth and the loss, from Perón's coalition, of the crucial national bourgeoisie, who turned instead to the United States. Moreover, economic belt-tightening contributed to the straying of significant numbers of Perón's labor constituency. Perón's careless negligence or hostility to the Roman Catholic Church was epitomized by his legalization of divorce in 1954 and the banning of religious instruction from the schools in 1955. In the ensuing escalation of events, Perón was excommunicated by the Vatican. But these political losses may not have been crucial had they not been duplicated within the military that was Perón's most important bastion of support. His alienation of deeply religious nationalist army officers coupled with the disenchantment of liberal army officers who echoed the national bourgeoisie's dissatisfaction with Perón's economic and foreign policy led to a coup on 16 September 1955. Perón was sent into exile and the resistance was born.[24]

The development of the Argentine Left up until the publication of *El beso de la mujer araña* in 1976 is complex, but can for the present purposes be understood in terms of the relationship between these two major sources: the Cuban revolution and the Peronist national revolution. The relationship is complicated further by the complexity of and mythology surrounding both these movements as well. The Cuban revolution first provided symbolic hope not just to Argentines but to people all over Latin America. Hope that imperialism could be defeated, that social inequality and poverty could be eradicated, and that Latin Americans could live in human dignity. Beyond this symbolic hope, however, we also know that the concrete history of the rural *foco* as ultimately traced in Guevara's *Pasajes de la Guerra revolucionaria,* would first be transformed into a blueprint for guerrilla warfare in other parts of Latin America and the Third World.

Interestingly, although the Guevarist and Peronist Left would later go through multiple separations and realliances, one of the first rural *foco* actions patterned on the Cuban revolution in Argentina was headed by a Dr. John William Cooke. Perón wrote of Cooke on 2 November 1956 from Caracas, Venezuela, that the latter was "to assume his representation in all political acts or action. In this concept his decision will be my decision and his word my word. In him I recognize the only chief, who has the mandate to preside over the totality of peronist forces organized in the country and in foreign lands, and his decisions, have the same value as mine. In case of my death, I delegate to Doctor D. John William Cooke command over the movement."[25] Cooke's continuity with the Cuban revolutionary discourse of the leap is suggested by the letters he wrote to Perón, urging the latter to continue supporting the revolutionary potential of the resistance: "A movement like Peronism nourishes itself on absolutes. It is the glory . . . of national liberation movements. They must arrive uncorrupted, they must be above politicking."[26] Cooke launched the first rural *foco* patterned on the Guevarist model in December of 1959, and several other camps were established between then and 1962.[27] Though it failed, there was a renewed effort in 1963 to establish *focos* in both the countryside and the city. Both were wiped out by the armed forces in April of 1964. Then, in 1968, the Peronist Armed Forces (FAP) reestablished a rural guerrilla force. They were wiped out in September of that year and Cooke was killed.[28]

Parallel to the rise and defeat of the rural revolutionary armed groups, the revolutionary leader of the Peronist unions, Amado Olmos, was ousted in an internal struggle by the reformist Augusto Vandor.[29] Thus within the Peronist resistance already at this point, in 1962, Cooke identified two contrasting tendencies within Peronism: a revolutionary tendency and a negotiating tendency. Cooke identified the revolutionary tendency with the populism of Perón's heyday and the negotiating tendency with a small circle of powerful union bureaucrats.[30] In fact, the revolutionary tendency was itself fractured mainly between Guevarist, internationalist forces and Peronist, nationalist forces. Perón himself partly raised Cooke's expectations by identifying the Peronist "Third Position" with decolonization in the Third World.[31] According to Donald Hodges, Perón actually alternated his preference between the tendencies but ultimately leaned toward the negotiating wing "because revolutionary Peronism had acquired a Guevarist complexion at odds with the populist philosophy of Justicialism. Initially, Perón had sought to use Guevara and Guevarist tendencies to strengthen the Peronist resistance, but important sectors of the latter had ended by becoming 'Cubanized.' "[32] This rift was symbolically resolved when in 1965, Perón chose to move his exile to falangist Madrid rather than revolutionary Cuba. Puig noted this early portent of Perón "true tendencies," and Olmos wrote that "Perón's residence in Spain is the tomb of the National Revolution."[33] Perón's ambiguity was intolerable, if not fatal, to the purist, absolutist discourse of the leap that informed the revolutionary, Guevarist tendency within the Peronist resistance from 1956 until the late 1960s.

It was in the wake of the repeated failure to implement the Cuban model rural *foco* in Argentina that, in 1969, Fernando Abal Medina founded an urban guerrilla group called the Montoneros. The name was taken from the gaucho militias that fought in the Argentine wars of independence. These new Montoneros consisted of a small group of Catholic Peronist youths active in the late 1950s in the right-wing Acción católica but radicalized throughout the sixties. Their retrospective ideology suggested a departure from the Guevarist *foco* in two ways. First, they recognized that the clandestinity required by the *foco* was much better afforded by Buenos Aires' "urban jungle" than by the relatively inhospitable rural terrains of Argentina. Second, they sought to base the urban armed struggle in the ready-made, ready-mobilized mass force of Peronism. Of course, Cooke also implicitly stood for a certain synthesis of Peronism with the Cuban revolution. However, Cooke seemed not to recognize that since the Peronist movement was urban based, the armed struggle that would fight alongside it also must be urban based. Furthermore, the state of urban unrest in the late fifties and early sixties, when Cooke was formulating his strategies, was nowhere near the state it was by May of 1969, for example, when the city of Córdoba was seized by tens of thousands of students, automobile workers, and members of the general population sympathetic to their demands. The rebellion was eventually repressed (nearly ten thousand police and fully armed soldiers participated, sixteen people were killed). But the *Cordobazo*, as it came to be known, created conditions much more favorable to the operation of a clandestine urban guerrilla group like the Montoneros than any Cooke had encountered earlier.[34]

That the Montoneros' retrospective populist self-portraiture was not quite consonant with at least its early realities was made clear by the near catastrophe of their first public operations. On the first anniversary of the *Cordobazo*, two leaders of the Montoneros, disguised in military uniforms, kidnapped General Pedro Aramburu (a leader of the 1955 anti-Peronist coup). After a "revolutionary trial," Aramburu was executed. At the time, the Montoneros consisted of only twelve guerrillas, and nobody had ever heard of them. In fact, the kidnapping and execution was accompanied by five press releases establishing the group's identity and objectives.[35] This may be contrasted with Uruguay's *Tupamaru* urban guerrilla group that worked progressively to establish popular support prior to confronting government forces directly. By the time of their first kidnapping in August 1968, they had already spent five years establishing contacts with sympathetic supporters, expanding their ranks, and developing an elaborate organizational structure designed to permit maximum resiliency for the movement as a whole in the event of a failed action.[36] The Montoneros sought, on the other hand, to establish popular support through spectacular, newsmaking bankrobberies and kidnappings. At this early stage, the Montoneros preserved the vanguardist, *foquista* ideology that undergirded the Cuban revolution.[37] However, by August of 1970, the Montoneros were only saved from extinction through the support and protection supplied by the Fuerzas Armadas Peronistas (Peronist Armed Forces, or FAP), an older insurgent group.

Nevertheless, as their notoriety grew, the Montoneros' leaders came to dominate the Juventud Peronista (Peronist Youth or JP) movement out of which they emerged. The JP became the legal and mass front for the Montoneros. After their near annihilation in August and September of 1970, the Montoneros devoted time to public relations and the development of political support. This marked their second departure—the first being the urbanization of the armed struggle—from Che's Cuban blueprint. Among their discursive weapons was a history of Argentina as the history of a manichean conflict between, on the one hand, an elite, liberal oligarchy allied with foreign interests and, on the other, *el pueblo,* defending the national interest. The gaucho militias in 1810, immigrant labor organizers in the second half of the nineteenth century, Radical (meaning, in Argentina, middle-class) party president Hipólito Yrigoyen at the beginning of the twentieth century, and, of course, Perón himself were the major representatives of the people in this historical narrative. The defeat of Peronism in 1955 was caused by internal impurities, specifically its alliance with a bourgeoisie indifferent to nationalism except insofar as it guaranteed profits. When the economy turned sour and domestic markets dried up, these opportunists sold the country to foreign interests. The hard years underground and in exile, disenfranchised and repressed, had separated the wheat from the chaff. What remained of the Peronist movement were the true nationalist revolutionaries, headed by Perón.[38] Thus, when the Montoneros actually did leave behind Guevarist *foquismo* and openly established the mass character of their movement, it was in somewhat contradictory terms. On the one hand, theirs was a relatively undiscriminating discourse in terms of class or politics. The pantheon of the Montoneros' heroes included right-wing military officials as well as Cooke, Eva Perón, and labor leaders. On the other hand, all these heroes were grouped together and distinguished from the villains by the supposed purity of their nationalism. They thus paradoxically retained the purity of the Cubans *foquista* discourse of the leap, even as they sought to shed it in favor of the support of a broad-based popular movement.

The Montoneros failed to mark, as they hitched themselves to the Peronist mass movement, the differences within the movement between those who sought simply the abdication of the military regime and the legalization of Peronism and those who sought the socialist transformation of society. Nor did they accurately assess Perón's motivations in cultivating left-wing support throughout the 1960s. Alicia Partnoy, born the year of Perón's defeat and exile, adequately expresses this position in the introduction to her moving collection of short testimonial narratives: "I grew up loving my country and its people and hating injustice. . . . I knew that Peronism was a very broad movement and that under the umbrella of economic independence, political sovereignty, and social justice, there was room for all ideologies. However, like most of the younger generation, I thought that the movement bore the seeds of the change to socialism."[39]

The Montoneros preserved an apparently blind faith in Perón's conversion to their form of national socialism. Rather than believing themselves to be within the scope of Perón's manipulative politicking, they felt that it was the other, more conservative groups and individuals in the Peronist coalition that Perón was keeping around merely for strategic purposes. They believed themselves to be immune, uncontaminated, outside the realm of such strategic manipulations. Again, they reproduced the discourse of purity that marked the discourse of the leap found in the Cuban revolution and in *Rayuela*. Perón certainly did not criticize, and even encouraged, the Montoneros in this belief, at least in his direct statements. At the same time, however, Perón showed every indication of pursuing a more moderate electoral path to power, keeping the guerrillas on board as an ace in the hole to be played should the military balk at more moderate proposals. For example, even as the Montoneros celebrated Perón's appointment of the left-leaning Héctor Cámpora as his delegate in charge of the electoral initiative, they overlooked Perón's simultaneous appointment of Lieutenant-Colonel Jorge Osinde as his military and political advisor. And

Osinde, we know, takes us full circle to the Ezeiza massacre, where these contradictions seemed to explode tragically in the face of Perón's staunch Montonero supporters.[40]

Yet even after Ezeiza, where their ranks were thinned by machine-gun-toting thugs in the employ of Osinde and standing beneath thirty meter posters of Evita and Perón, the Montoneros continued to spin their myth of a Perón genuinely converted to the socialist cause but surrounded by right-wingers alienating the leader from the people and the movement. But López Rega's Triple A death squads operated with the tacit, and sometimes active, support of the federal police under Perón's administration. Perón enacted tougher penalties for acts of terrorism while ignoring the frequent right-wing massacres. The "University Law" passed in March of 1974 banned politics on campus, restricted student unions, and discriminated against leftist lecturers, but the leader of the University Peronist Youth claimed his organization was "convinced . . . it was not thought up to throw us out."[41] Even after Perón directly denounced the Montoneros and Peronist Youth as "callow and stupid" during a May Day celebration in 1974, the Montoneros refused to abandon Perón. Only after his death on 1 July 1974, the assumption of the presidency by his widow Isabel, and the rapid escalation of right-wing attacks organized by López Rega did the Montoneros, in September 1974, finally go back underground in an alliance with other disappointed Peronist and Guevarist guerrilla groups.

I argued that Puig's novel registers this transitional crisis in the revolutionary utopian politics of the Latin American Left. Many convincing theories of postmodernity, however, argue the importance of articulating such transitions to mutations in international capitalism. Jameson's thesis, we know, is that the period since the end of World War II witnessed the emergence of what Ernest Mandel called "late capitalism." The problem with this from the perspective of Latin American modernity and postmodernity is that it does not permit us to track the shifting fortunes of the revolutionary Left from triumph in Cuba—at the height of U.S.-dominated late capitalist expansion—to catastrophe in Chile, Uruguay, and Argentina in the 1970s. In part, this is a problem of scale. The scope of a historical concept like late capitalism, defined by Jameson in terms of its effacement of regional differentiation, hardly permits the kind of detailed focus on the specific trajectories of given countries like Argentina. Indeed, we have seen the contradictory image that emerges from Jameson's attempt to integrate the Third World into the theory of postmodernity. But does this then require us to lapse back into a nativist vision of Latin American cultural autocthony? Is the course of the revolutionary Peronist resistance to be understood independently of global economic conditions?

I believe not. Instead, we may need to adjust the conceptual framework through which we interpret the crisis of the Argentine Left. It is true, for example, that Mandel identifies the beginning of late capitalism with the end of World War II. He describes the conditions as follows: "The weakening (and partial atomization) of the working class determined by fascism and the Second World War permit a massive rise in the rate of profit, which promotes the accumulation of capital. This is first thrown into armaments production, then into the innovations of the third technological revolution, which significantly cheapens constant capital and thus promotes a long-term rise in the rate of profit."[42] Mandel's periodization here roughly coincides with Alain Lipietz's history of Fordism. For Lipietz, the reorganization of the industrial capitalist "regime of accumulation" and "mode of social regulation" that occurred in the wake of the great depression "came into its own in the post-1945 period."[43] So far so good. Jameson seems correctly to have identified late capitalism with the postwar period.

However, for Mandel, late capitalism is what is called a "long wave" of capitalist development. This means that it consists of "an initial phase, in which the technology actually undergoes a revolution, and when such things as the production sites for the new means of production have first to be created. This phase is distinguished by an increased rate of profit, *accelerated accumulation*, accelerated growth, accelerated self-expansion of previously idle capital."[44] But Mandel also observes that within a single long wave, "this first phase is followed by a second, in which the actual transformation in production technology has already taken place . . . The force that determined the sudden extension by leaps and bounds of capital accumulation thus falls away, and accordingly this phase becomes one of retreating profits, *gradually decelerating accumulation*, decelerating economic growth."[45] Mandel published *Late Capitalism* in 1972. Writing in the late sixties and early seventies, Mandel was trying to explain both the postwar boom of late capitalism *and*—and this is what Jameson omits in his borrowing of Mandel—its crisis in the early seventies. Lipietz and the "French regulationist" theorists also focus on the crisis of the early seventies. For them it is a "crisis of global fordism that went "from latent erosion to open crisis (1967–1974)."[46]

In Argentina, Perón's return partly filled an economic need. The pact between organized labor, national industrialists, and the state had secured Argentina's partial industrialization in the period immediately following

World War II. Perón was the symbolic, but effective, glue cementing that alliance. When the country was hit with economic crises, Perón was abandoned. His return was, in one sense, an admission on the part of other social sectors that only Perón could piece together the increasingly antagonistic fragments of that earlier moment and restore growth to the Argentine economy. But conditions had changed, particularly in the world economy. Thus:

> In 1974, the social pact among organized labor, the national bourgeoisie, and the state fell victim to the *coup de grâce* delivered by the Arab Israeli war of the previous year. Argentina's favorable terms of trade were suddenly reversed as OPEC oil prices (and the prices of exports from the industrial countries) sharply outdistanced the price of primary exports in international markets. Industrialists abandoned the price freeze, followed immediately by the General Confederation of Labor (CGT) and the unions, who demanded large wage increases. Inflation, which had declined greatly in 1973, rebounded sharply upward.[47]

Mandel located the oil crisis and the effects just described in Argentina within the general downturn of the long wave of late capitalism. This downturn is produced by capitalist overproduction and, as Mandel observed, "any capitalist over-production crisis strikes the weak more harshly than the strong, the poor more harshly than the rich."[48] Specifically, in the Argentine case for example, the balance of payments deficit reached $352 million in 1974.[49] The need to cover this deficit is, we shall see, part of what induced the borrowing binge of the military regime from 1976 to 1983.

Puig's spider woman was trapped by a web of her own production. The Montoneros also spun an ideological web of the purity of the Peronist resistance, of the integrity of Perón's declared commitment to socialism, and of their own position as vanguard spokesman for a mass movement of students and workers. Like the spider woman, the Montoneros were trapped within that web, attempting vainly to break free only in September of 1974, when it was already too late. Their utopian vision was shattered from within, by unrecognized contradictions within its very foundation. At the same time, the whole development of the Left in Argentina was constrained by a crisis in global capitalism. The periodization of geographers such as David Harvey, which draws on Mandel and especially Lipietz, permits us to see this moment—so crucial in terms of concrete Latin American history—as equally important within a global picture of capitalist mutations since World War II.[50] For as a result of this crisis, global capital had to restructure itself in what Harvey calls more "flexible" (Lipietz uses the term *post-Fordist*) directions. It is this moment, and not World War II, that for Harvey ushers in the postmodern. And the postmodern is thus linked, by affirmation or negation, to the restructuring of global capital in response to the crisis of 1973–75. Puig's novel does not yet mark the postmodern, but rather this space of crisis. The limitations on the social imaginary of the Argentine Left may well restrict Puig's capacity to continue to project Cortázar's utopian leap, but it also accounts for the particular, partially self-destructive character Puig attributes to that leap. And the crisis that Puig registers now shows itself to be the concentration of Argentine, Latin American, and global cultural, political, and economic forces. At the same time, it is at this moment that these various forces shatter the imaginary of Latin America as a unified conceptual and political whole and leave in its place a cluster of politically isolated, particular regions and subregions.

In the wake of Molina's death and Valentín's hallucination, amidst the bloody death-squad massacres and violent guerrilla actions, what kind of liberation remains possible there? The last movie that Molina recounts to Valentín also ends ambiguously. It tells the story of a pair of "star-crossed" lovers whose relationship ends when the man dies in his lover's arms, singing a song, in a hospital room. The film concludes with "a giant giant close-up of just her face, with her eyes flooded with tears, but with a smile on her lips" (263/259). The film apparently also mirrors the novel as a whole. And the ensuing conversation prefigures Valentín and Molina's own endings:

—Such an enigmatic ending, isn't it, Valentín?
—No, it's right, it's the best part of the film.
—Why is that?
—It means that even if she's left with nothing, she's content to have had at least one real relationship in her life, even if it's over and done with.
—But don't you suffer more, after having been so happy but then winding up with nothing?
—Molina, there's one thing to keep in mind. In a man's life, which may be short and may be long, everything is temporary. Nothing is forever.
—Yes, but let it last a little while, at least that much.
—It's a question of learning to accept things as they come, and to appreciate the good that happens to you, even if it doesn't last. Because nothing is forever.
—Yes, it's easy to say. But feeling it is something else.
—But you have to reason it out then, to convince yourself.

—Yes, but there are reasons of the heart that reason doesn't encompass. (263/259)

In this passage, we might first note the extent of the transformation of the two characters. For in an earlier argument about "living for the moment," each took the position opposite from that which they adopt here. But more importantly, each character here expresses the attitude that will determine his position at the end of the novel. Molina cannot accept anything less than utopia in the older sense. He cannot bear the possibility of losing what he thinks he has had. This leads to his attempt to preserve and extend his relationship with Valentín through his actions outside the cell. His death is the most tragic marker of the crisis of utopia in the novel. Valentín, on the other hand, expresses the sentiment that will permit him to accept the morphine and revel in the hallucinatory dream with Marta, all without forgetting that "my comrades are waiting for me to resume the age old fight" (286/281).

Marta's final statement, "Este sueño es corto pero es feliz" (this dream is short but this dream is happy) (287/281), further inscribes the inescapable contradiction that figures the crisis of utopia. The concept of utopia as a radically new space is decidedly unambiguous. It permits no traces of the old—it is freedom, the old is oppression and misery. But the problem with this concept is that it fails to account for transition. How does one move from a repressed space to a utopian space without bringing something "old"—namely, one's self—into the new space? Indeed, we might ask if in leaping from the asylum window and so constituting the utopian space of *Rayuela*, Horacio Oliveira could really have shed his old self entirely—whether he could have, in effect, leapt without himself. At any rate, in *El beso de la mujer araña* neither character recognized this contradiction when they declared the prison cell a repression-free zone, or when they unilaterally extended the scope of that declaration to the outside world by sending Molina on his fatal errand. Neither recognized that their space was limited, like a dream, by definition. And so, we see in retrospect, it must have been with all the utopian spaces posited in the novel. All were flawed from the beginning by their failure to take into account their connections with the system or reality to which they constituted a liberating response.

The Argentine resistance attempted to extend the utopian project of the Cuban revolution. However, it did not reflect on the contradictions within that project or those within its own. The bewilderment of a leftist movement that has witnessed its figure of hope—Perón—turn into the harbinger of catastrophe forms, at least partially, the social conditions of possibility for a novel like *El beso de la mujer araña*. For this reason, perhaps, the novel provides no alternative formulation of liberation. If the utopian purity characteristic of the Cuban revolutionary discourse of the leap was ever realized or realizable, objective conditions in Argentina—and in other parts of Latin America—had, by 1974, turned that dream into a grisly nightmare.

The Argentine case suggested that perhaps the heterogeneity of subjective identifications in the world of contemporary capitalism rendered inadequate not only the politics of purity, but also the purity of historical narratives such as those invoked by the Cuban revolution and the Montoneros as justification for such a politics. Puig himself occupied one of these alternative subjective positions. As a homosexual, sympathetic to the anti-authoritarian, emancipatory impulses of the movement, Puig was nonetheless painfully aware of the ways the movement could reproduce authoritarian exclusions. Puig criticized Castro's treatment of homosexuals and dissidents and felt marginalized by the Peronist Left's intolerance of criticism. Perhaps this marginalization, particularly over what dominant machista discourse takes to be a private issue, homosexuality, helps explain how Puig's writing seems to prefigure certain trends in women's writing. In both cases, the challenging of the boundaries between public and private that is the hallmark of feminism, becomes a fundamental means of pointing up the gaps in an ostensibly emancipatory project. Take this as a subjective accounting for Puig's representation of the crisis of the Latin American modernist discourse of the leap. He spoke from one of the repressed, absent spaces in the revolutionary picture.

However, Valentín's dreams—recognizing both the liberating function of the dream ("it is happy") and its necessarily limited nature ("it is short")—appears to originate from a point beyond the paralyzing crisis of utopia. Attending to this ambiguity, one critic nevertheless criticized Puig's ending: "It seems that Puig can promise his readers only a short but happy dream."[51] But this is, if one views the text historically, precisely the point. Historical conditions are such that a nostalgic return to heroic revolutionary practices of the past—an endless happy dream—are worse than useless. On the other hand, the most critical act consists in naming those conditions and contradictions as the first step in a rethinking of strategy. "The postmodernism debate in Latin America," John Beverley has written, "has to do above all with its connection to the ongoing process of democratization in the hemisphere and, contingently, to the need for a revision (or replacement) of the discourse of the Latin American Left in the wake of, on the one hand, the defeat of both the armed struggle strategy represented by guerrilla *foquismo* [and urban guerrilla warfare, we might add, in Argentina] and the 'peaceful road to socialism' represented by Allende's coalition-building electoral politics (and the problematization of Cuba as a model for an achieved socialist society), and, on the other, the general crisis of the socialist project on the world stage."[52] In the present context, we may tentatively conclude that simply recognizing and acknowledging the crisis of utopia so poignantly evoked—recognizing, that is, the repressions on which every utopian liberating project must be founded—is the indispensable basis for whatever new form liberation might take. Part of this project, in turn, is recognizing the crisis of the conceptual unity of Latin America. This means shedding the presupposition of a Latin America and attempting instead to work up such a concept through the articulation of various local realities throughout the region. We can now explore, to speak metaphorically, the extension of Valentín's dream. What are some of the cultural forms taken by an emancipatory political practice beyond the failed utopian projects of an earlier period? One of the literary forms that such a practice took in the 1980s in Argentina is what I will term the Latin American postmodernist *historia*.

Argentine Postmodernity

6

Resuscitating History in *Respiración artificial*

> A chronicler who recites events without distinguishing between
> major and minor ones acts in accordance with the following truth:
> nothing that has ever happened should be regarded as lost for history.
> To be sure, only a redeemed mankind receives the fullness of its past—
> which is to say, only for a redeemed mankind has the past become
> citable in all its moments.—Walter Benjamin

In the last chapter, I emphasized Manuel Puig's ultimately liberating representation of a totalizing utopia in crisis. But a representation of utopia in crisis presupposes the continued existence of utopia, even if in crisis. This presupposition was possible for Puig for two reasons. First, that although the Peronist Left's decline had clearly begun, forces of repression had not yet been consolidated to the point that the Left was annihilated. The Argentina represented in Puig's novel still resounds with voices of resistance and struggle, however beleaguered. This incomplete character of the emergent authoritarian structures of repression thus forms the first condition of possibility for the persistence of a utopian dream. The second condition of possibility is Puig's condition as a writer in exile. Though Puig's novel was censored in Argentina in 1976, as an exile Puig was free from the reprisals of the regime—he could not be tracked down and made to disappear, tortured, or killed for his representation. The very possibility of representing state repression the way Puig did in *El beso de la mujer araña* might be the final dimensions of that utopia whose crisis he represented. In other words, the possibility of confronting and representing the catastrophe of massive state terrorism and repression will itself be the final utopian space blotted out when repression becomes generalized after 24 March 1976.

During the period of Argentine history that begins on that day and continues through 1983, a military junta, self-baptized as the *Proceso de reorganización nacional* (Process of National Reorganization) or simply the *Proceso*, threatened, abducted, tortured, raped, disappeared, killed, and exiled thousands of Argentines. Some numbers offer a crude approximation. James Cockroft places the number of assassinations at "20,000 or more" and notes that within the first month of the coup "10,000 peo-

ple were arrested, mostly workers, leftists, and young people."[1] Donald
Hodges writes that in the first two years alone, the Military process was
responsible for "30,000 disappearances, at least four times as many cases
of torture, and another 10,000 assassinations."[2] These numbers, however
staggering, are inadequate precisely because they give the confident, if
painful, impression of accurately representing the military's brutality. After
the restoration of democracy, the president convened the National Com-
mission on the Disappeared (CONADEP), which issued an institutionalized
version of a representation of the military's violence: a book called *Nunca
más* containing testimony from survivors and lists of the disappeared. This
was intended, in a sense, to finally clear the air, to exorcise the demons
haunting the Argentine national spirit after the "excesses" of the *Proceso*.
But it was precisely its problematization of such representations—as we
shall see—that was perhaps the *Proceso's* most powerful weapon. In the case
of *Nunca más,* one of the major responses was dismay at the inadequacy
of the representation. *Nunca más* was able to document only about nine
thousand disappearances, just one-third the number that many human
rights organizations estimated to be accurate. Imagine how much more
difficult a representation of military violence would be at the height of
military rule.

Unlike Manuel Puig, Ricardo Piglia wrote *Respiración artificial* inside
Argentina during those savage first few years of the *Proceso*.[3] For this reason, because he remained in Argentina, Piglia remained subject to certain
constraints on expression that Puig eluded in exile. Piglia could not confront the *Proceso* head on. To him fell the task of representing a regime most
of whose repressive practices aimed, in one way or another, at the elimina-
tion of all such representations. Indeed, the concrete feeling of the military's omnipresence is internalized—but also, perhaps, partially disabled—
by the novel itself through the character of the censor, Arocena. This is the
case not only because the regime disposed of the bodies of its victims in the
River Plate estuary, or secretly detained journalists and other would be
witnesses to its violence, but also because the military appropriated the
discourse of *historical* representation. If then, one wanted, like Piglia, not
only to narrate what the regime was doing but also how it came into existence—what its conditions of possibility were—one had to negotiate the
various means by which that regime imposed a reign of silence and absence, foreclosing the production of any historical discourse other than its
own. For Piglia, then, writing in this context, neither the utopia of partial
openings in the military's repressive structure nor that of representation

existed any longer. In this sense, *Respiración artificial* registers a resistant cultural politics out of the dissolution of that utopian trajectory marked by *Rayuela*, with its euphoric, transformative leaps, and *El beso de la mujer araña*, with its dystopian, self-destructive dead ends.

Because of the fundamental and ineluctable pressure exerted by the military regime on cultural production, I want to begin this chapter a little differently than my previous ones. There I moved from close studies of textual surfaces to an account of their more general sociocultural conditions of possibility. Here, however, I believe that an adequate understanding of the novel must be preceded by an evocation of its sociocultural conditions of possibility. Of course, a certain reading of the novel might be produced without such an evocation. But *Respiración artificial* might, in such a reading, wind up among the ranks of *Cien años de soledad* in the catalogues of "historiographic metafiction" or "postmodern fantastic historiography." It is, of course, precisely such a reading and such facile assimilations into Euro–North American postmodernism theory that I wish to combat by my own reading. In this case, an understanding of the peculiarities of the local sociocultural historical moment out of which the text emerges will recast all those devices and technical features that might make it a candidate for Euro–North American postmodernity in the light of a politically oppositional Argentine postmodernity.

Beyond the initial phases of widespread physical repression, and its residual persistence, the military in Argentina recognized the need to open up a cultural front. In one sense, physical repression had operated under the umbrella of a total war on subversive ideologies. That is, the military saw what it called "terrorist" acts as the material symptom of a properly spiritual malady: the infiltration of foreign, specifically non-Western and communist, ideas into Argentina. But its evacuation of leftist discourses from traditional official and non-official arenas for public expression compelled the military to produce some cultural image—to complement its more brutal political, military, and economic practices—on which it could rely for justification of its own existence. Thus, even among the earliest statements of the *Proceso's* objectives, we find a recognition of the need "to impose the restitution of those fundamental values that contribute to social integrity: order, work, hierarchy, responsibility, national identity, and honesty in the context of Christian morality" and to "promote in youths social models that underscore these values to replace and eradicate the present values."[4] The primary ideological terrain in the military's struggle was a single vision of national and world history.

The military produced silence and absence in Argentine society, silences and absences it then filled with its own discourse. First, the military regime intervened directly in the production of historical representation. Partly, this occurred through the takeover of the autonomous university system and the removal of faculty and students unfavorable to the regime. The official institution for the production of knowledge about the society thus came under the *Proceso's* control.[5] The regime also widely, if somewhat erratically, censored books, publications, films, multimedia installations, and theatres.[6] The regime's production of historical discourse also consisted in minimizing (and even flat-out denying, in some cases) the extent and nature of the military's repressive campaign, as in its "documento final" (among other prior statements), issued at the time of its abdication in April of 1983.[7] But its production of historical discourse was not limited to its retrospective self-portraiture nor to the crude denial of the existence of repression during its tenure. On a discursive level, the military operated, much more diffusely, by mobilizing the historical language of Argentine nationalism to generalize what was in fact its limited class and institutionally based interests.

A week before Christmas, in 1977, General Videla, the first president of the junta, stated:

> Argentina is a Western and Christian nation, not because this is written at Ezeiza Airport; Argentina is Western and Christian because it comes from its history. It was born Christian through the direction of Spain, it inherited from Spain Western culture and it never renounced that condition, but rather justly defended it. It is to defend this Western and Christian condition as a lifestyle that this struggle against those who did not accept this system of life and wished to impose a different one was launched . . . For merely thinking something different within our lifestyle no one is deprived of their liberty, but we consider that it is a grave crime to attempt against the Western and Christian lifestyle, wishing to change it for one that is foreign to us, and in this kind of struggle, not only he who assaults with the bomb, the gunshot, or the kidnapping is considered an aggressor, but also he who on the level of ideas wants to change our system of life through ideas that are precisely subversive; which is to say that subvert values, change, invert values . . . The terrorist is not only one because he kills with arms or places a bomb, but also for activating others through ideas contrary to those of our Western and Christian civilization.[8]

According to this and various other pronouncements, the junta's war was a defensive one, charged with saving the cornerstones of the Argentine "lifestyle": the family and Christian morality and the national identity as the offspring of Western civilization.

Western and Christian are inseparable within the junta's discourse. Brigadier General Agosti noted that Argentina was

> a bastion of Christian and Western civilization. This definition, which rests on the affirmation of its own values, is not conditioned by the open and erratic attitudes of other Western nations. That West is for us a historical becoming more than a geographical location. A becoming that is born in Greece and projected through Rome, and fertilized by the Catholic religion. The West is found where the ideas of liberty and faith in Christ govern the activity of man.[9]

But Western and Christian values are not only essential to a spiritual war. They are, rather, to be seen as the spiritual fundament undergirding the material interests of America. Thus, in a series of statements, Brigadier General Graffigna insisted that "the West is for us a spiritual location. We occupy a place of honor and responsibility in the Southern Cone that is vital for the security of America," that the "Southern's Cone's defense is vital to the security of America, and thereby, of the West" and that "we Argentines have an inheritance that comes from the depths of history: liberty, order, justice, property, family, lifestyle, faith in God. We are the custodians and the protectors of the inheritance." All of this received an important seconding from U.S. General Gordon Sumner, former head of one of the United States' inter-American defense-training facilities: "Your country and in fact all of the Southern Cone, have a geographical position and strategic resources that will require the development of a role in the future . . . This region of the world is terribly important to the whole free world."[10]

This articulation of Christian values with the material and ideological interests of capitalism via the invocation of "Western civilization" was crucial for the junta's consolidation of support from two major sources: the Argentine (and international) Catholic Church and the United States and international banks—and we will return to examine their role in the *Proceso*. But this particular discourse was also important because of its meaning within Argentine history.[11] Within that context, the major enemy of the church and of unbridled capitalism was Peronism. Thus David Rock argues that the *Proceso* was a "revolution in government whose aim was the total dismantling of the Peronist state."[12] Peronism, if not Perón, had to be depicted as the source of the civil and economic chaos into which Argentina had slipped steadily since the 1930s. The version of national history underlying this was basically a mirror image of that of the Montoneros.[13] Argentine history had, from the early nineteenth century, been propelled by the struggle between two great forces—popular nationalism and elitist liberalism—incarnated in famous individuals and groups and played out on well-known battlefields. How these forces were evaluated within a historical narrative depended entirely on who was telling the story. We have seen that for the Montoneros, the struggle for national sovereignty extended from their namesakes in the wars of Independence, through Rosas, Yrigoyen, and Perón. Theirs was a 150-year struggle against a minority, conservative oligarchy whose survival depended on tight links with international capitalism. The military, by contrast, based Argentina's national identity first in its Spanish colonial heritage and then in the prosperous years of the agro-export economy of the late nineteenth and early twentieth centuries. The golden years extended from 1880 to 1916, with brief resurgences in 1930 and 1955.[14] Otherwise, the military, as the guardian of Western and Christian values, had been on the defensive, a resistant force against the invasion of the godless, immoral, foreign, and anti-individual values of communism.

In this way, the same abstract appeal to Western and Christian values spoke to three distinct but equally indispensable audiences: the Argentine upper classes, the Catholic Church, and the United States. Perón, because he had been a common enemy of the three groups, came to function as the concrete embodiment of the erosion of those values. This, we will see, is one reason why Tomás Eloy Martínez's book *La Novela de Perón* functions so effectively as a resistant, Latin American postmodernist *historia*. By representing itself as the only viable endpoint of a homogenized, manichean national history, the junta papered over its own conditions of possibility, establishing itself as the only possible present and thus the only source of all possible futures. *Respiración artificial* and *La novela de Perón*, I will show, break open this closed vision of history. But they do not engage the military on its ground, denying the military version of its own history (which in any case would be impossible given conditions within Argentina at the time) and resubstituting the left version. Such strategies, according to José Pablo Feinmann, would only preserve an essentially antidemocratic philosophy of history whereby "the truths of political adversaries are confronted in terms of war" and in which the realization of one's own truth requires the destruction of the truth of the adversary.[15] Instead, these novels work on the material of other historical moments showing them to be, not the seamless products of the famous presupposed by the military's historical discourse, but rather shaped by the multiple repressed and for-gotten—the subaltern—histories of the everyday.

In the case of Piglia's novel, it is important to note two other dimensions of the military's occupation of history. The *Proceso* foreclosed the pos-sibility of an oppositional historical representation by fragmenting the so-cial, by so suffusing social spaces with its terrifying authoritarian logic that all such spaces became radically privatized. The decentralized nature of the regime's apparatus conferred on the violence an aspect of terrifying randomness whose ultimate effect was the shattering of whatever sense of collectivity might have survived the first round-up of intellectuals, labor leaders, and guerrillas. If not only these people but also their neighbors, or people with the same surname, could be victimized, then why not you too? If not just a soldier in uniform but the person next to you at the market could be an informer or a torturer, then how could you risk establishing the sorts of relationships from which a collective resistance might emerge? This generalized state repression produces the effects attributed by Fou-cault to Bentham's panopticon: "To induce in the inmate a state of con-scious and permanent visibility that assures the automatic functioning of power. So to arrange things that the surveillance is permanent in its effects, even if it is discontinuous in its action."[16] It is in this way that after a pe-riod of widespread violence, the same effect of terrorizing and atomizing the population can be generated by the *absence* of violence.[17] This diffuse structure of repression does not lend itself to ready representation: neither artistically, nor legally in the form of a chronicling of its crimes. A by-product, already hinted at in the above description, of this diffuse repres-sive structure is the radical atomization of society. Terror produces an everyday life experience in which the obsessive desire for privacy, the fear of social contact, registers the complete saturation of the private by the public. The experiential reality of living one's daily life without forging any social bonds presupposes the diffuse public apparatus of repression that renders such bonds potentially fatal. However, the unrepresentability of this repressive structure masks the causes of social privatization, such that one's life experience appears only as sheer fragmentation. In this way, the regime severs the link between private experience and public events and practices. Once again, *Respiración artificial* attacks this separation, at-tempting to reestablish the connection between the private and the public, indicating—again on the site of past histories, but also now on the site of the present—the ways in which private and public mutually construct each other and together shape the movement of history.

Finally, disappearance occupies perhaps a central position in the *Proceso's* repertoire of repressive strategies, one fundamentally, though perhaps obliquely, linked to the foreclosure of historical representation.[18] It may appear obvious that disappearance produces absence and silence. After all, the space once occupied by a certain individual suddenly becomes vacant and their voice suddenly suppressed. But the paralyzing effects of disappearance on the production of historical discourse are even more insidious. Ariel Dorfman has argued that the tragic history of Latin America is such that even death takes on the aspect of creative act by which myth and memory and therefore resistant histories are activated.[19] Certainly birth and death are the (once) ineradicable markers testifying to our place in history. Disappearance, by robbing us of death, by consigning us to a limbo outside of life and death, stalls our agency in history. It immobilizes or silences us (in obvious ways) and paralyzes those who would invoke our name and memory, because there is no proof of our death, let alone of the regime's responsibility for it. In this way, the concrete repressive practice of disappearance suspends the representation of history, leaving vacant the public sphere in which it is conventionally (and however distortedly) produced. And it is therefore against this practice that *Respiración artificial*—dedicated to *desaparecidos* who showed Piglia "the meaning of history"—makes perhaps its most concrete intervention. For the novel, on a most basic level, is about a man—a professor of history, no less—who is disappeared.

The notion that the novel can be read as a coded or allegorical condemnation of disappearance must not be dismissed as a simple minded or crude political valorization. Under conditions of severe repression and restriction on cultural production such coded narratives become a fundamental component of cultural resistance. Moreover, support for this kind of an allegorical reading appears in the answer to the novel's opening question: "¿Hay una historia?" The narrator tells us that the *historia* begins in April of 1976, the first full month, of course, after the installation of the *Proceso*. Thus, in one sense at least, if there is an *historia* in *Respiración artificial*, it is exactly the *historia* of the *Proceso*.[20] But my reading of the novel will not focus directly on these allegorical questions, though they are also inevitably addressed by it. Rather, although the allegorical reading seeks to raise up the novel's secret "message" as its politically resistant "content," I want to focus on its "medium"—its "form"—as providing at least as telling an indictment of the crimes of the *Proceso*. Instead of suggesting that the novel answers its initial question with an embedded history of the regime, I want to suggest that its initial question can only be asked under the conditions created by that regime. The question ¿Hay una historia?—with its multiple ambiguities (story/history, a/one)—presupposes that the terrain of history has been radically destabilized. The novel provides then, in my view, an extended elaboration of this initial question insofar as it evokes the conditions under which its own distorted and tentative *historia* can emerge. Finally, I will argue, it does not only represent the violence done to history by the *Proceso* but also proposes and realizes means by which that violence can be resisted. The novel, to put it most simply, produces solutions (ways of narrating *la historia*) to the problems that its own existence marks (is there an *historia?* How can one narrate it?).

That it is difficult, at best, to write history under these conditions has already been demonstrated, and is further betrayed by Piglia's need to code the more directly political messages of his novel. But this difficulty is also manifested formally and thematically. History as the *Proceso* narrates it is told straight on as it were, through the subjectivity of a single individual in command of the facts and the voices of those who constitute history: its models are the *pronunciamento,* the political *discurso* or speech, and the various physical practices of repression. Here history, or perhaps—for reasons that will become clear—I should retain the Spanish term *historia* (signifying both "history" and "story"), can only be accessed obliquely; now not only because of censorship but because of the myriad problems the junta has presented to representations of its own coming into being.[21]

One figure for this kind of oblique representation of history is the genealogy. Think of the patriarchal lineage as the model of the military's discourse of history. And recall as well the centrality of the "traditional Christian family" in the military discursive arsenal. In this novel, we find a constant displacement of that model. This displacement is itself present from the beginning of the novel. The initial scene finds the narrator, an Argentine writer from Buenos Aires in his early thirties named Emilio Renzi, recalling the beginning of the *historia*. It all started when he received, three years ago (in April of 1976, remember) a letter and a photograph from a long lost uncle. Renzi had published, also three years ago (and this is what prompts the letter), a novel based on this uncle's scandalous personal past. Now the photograph that Renzi receives shows him, three months old, in his uncle's arms. Renzi's father is not in the picture and "in the background, blurred and almost out of focus, is my mother" (13/11). Thus, the conventional linear model of the genealogy is replaced by one that proceeds obliquely, from uncle to nephew.

But this oblique figure repeats itself backward through succeeding generations that circumvent the father-son relationship. Renzi's uncle, Marcelo Maggi, for example, descends from his father-in-law (the father of his divorced and now dead wife), with whom he shares a passion for history and, in particular, for the history of the father-in-law's family. The father-in-law Luciano Ossorio never knew his own father, who died in a duel protecting the honor of *his* father, Luciano's grandfather Enrique Ossorio. But Luciano's father never knew his own father, Enrique (for whom he died), because the latter himself died before the son (born illegitimately of Enrique's cousin) was born. Thus at every point in the *historia,* the clear and continuous lineage from father to son is disrupted, either by premature deaths or for other reasons (all of which, we will come to see, bear their own relationship to the broader movement of social history). We can approach the significance of this oblique genealogy by imagining a subject attempting to reconstruct the *historia* by looking for the line between fathers and sons. For this subject, the *historia* would present itself as riddled with gaps and inexplicable absences. What such a genealogy requires instead is a subject in the present who looks askance, off-center as it were, at the deviations and disruptions in the conventional lineage. In fact, this genealogy requires Nietzsche's "genealogy," which seeks events, Michel Foucault tells us, "in the most unpromising places."[22]

On the one hand, this conclusion can be understood as reinforcing the call for a savvy detective—and Piglia, incidentally, has also written on the detective genre—who can disinter the secret significance of what Newman calls Piglia's "*novela política/policial.*" Nietzsche's genealogist, like the reader of *Respiración artificial,* must know where to look, or at least must know to look in unusual places. But the invocation of a genealogist, like the presence of coded political allusions, necessarily also refers to the conditions that necessitate his or her existence and strategies. Thus, the shadowy image of the *Proceso,* restricting communication and producing a generation of decoders, surfaces again. And finally, the call for a genealogist registers the conditions under which *historia* itself undergoes such distortions and deviations. To reformulate these three levels as questions the first asks, What is the real *historia?* The second asks, Why can't we tell the *historia* straightforwardly, as a linear narrative? And the third asks, Why is the *historia* itself so convoluted? In fact, the three levels, though not identical, operate dialectically. The representation of the regime cannot be separated from the damage it has done both to the subject that would represent it and the object of its representation. Ultimately, it is precisely this damage to representation that becomes in turn the object of a damaged representation.

We can approach this problem formally in *Respiración artificial* as well. The novel consists entirely of letters, conversations, what Newman calls "embedded conversations," diary entries, and interior monologues. Thus, the novel gives a first impression of extreme fragmentation. Once again, this fragmentation, as a formal object of study, permits several interpretations. On one level, it may simply register the atomizing power of the *Proceso*, which leaves no aspect of the social, including literary production, untouched. But interpretation at this level reduces the novel's form to a passive instrument through which social catastrophe can be gauged. It certainly must be this, but it must be something else also. Thus, on a second level, we can understand this formal fragmentation as an evasive response to the totalizing, if diffuse, operational logic of the authoritarian regime. The novel fragments formally in that case as a means of survival. This leads us back to the question of censorship and the means by which a text eludes it. In this case, it is not a matter of masking one content with another, but of masking that content with a form that doesn't correspond to it. A collection of letters and diary entries, some from a century ago, to say nothing of complexly interwoven private conversations, appears an unlikely venue for a denunciation of a military regime, to say nothing of a historical representation of that regime. Not only is this formal fragmentation less accessible than other conventional forms of protest, but it also seems precisely to deny any access to that historical representation that would be anathema to the regime. But, in fact, this formal fragmentation relates back to the model of history and historical thought established in the context of the family tree. For we took from that discussion the lesson that history must be sought in "unpromising places"—such as, for example, texts whose form seems precisely to deny history. But we needn't leave a characterization of the text's form at the generality of "fragmentation." The novel fragments in specific ways whose specificity is itself significant.

I want to argue that the novel's various formal fragments can be best grasped through the Spanish term *cita*. Why I choose this term in particular—and choose to render it in Spanish—will become clear shortly; for now, let me emphasize the term as signifying a quotation. In this sense, the various letters, diary entries, and conversations (and of course, "embedded conversations") are all *citas*. That is, they are all discourses which are quoted within the discourse of a character in the text. Thus, for example, all of Maggi's letters to Emilio are quoted within Emilio's own narrative discourse. Similarly, within his letters, Maggi quotes from the diary entries of Enrique Ossorio and from his conversations with his friend Tardewski. Later, in a letter to Maggi, Emilio will quote from his conversation with Luciano (who, during the conversation, quoted Maggi among others). The final section of the book consists of a long conversation between Tardewski and Emilio, divided into two parts, one narrated by the former and one by the latter. During the conversation, Emilio (quoted by Tardewski in his first-person narrative) quotes from Borges and Arlt. And Tardewski, who was earlier quoted (by Maggi) as wanting to write a book made entirely of *citas*, comments that he is "a man made entirely of *citas*" (273–213). In fact, he (quoted by Emilio in his first-person narrative) quotes often and at length from a special notebook he has full of quotations, especially from Kafka and Hitler. And both characters, throughout the conversation, quote their own separate conversations or (in the case of Emilio) correspondence with Maggi. What does this proliferation of *citas*, often interconnected via complicated networks, signify?

I should perhaps first recall the importance of the *cita* in the Latin American literary tradition. I argued earlier that Argentine literature, from Sarmiento to Borges, has critically appropriated European aesthetic models and that the *cita* may be the emblem of this activity.[23] However, although Borges may be the most conspicuous "citer" in Latin American letters, and although Piglia certainly writes, in one sense at least, out of a certain Borgesian tradition (also shared by Cortázar), we should not fail to note the difference between Piglia and Borges. For Borges, the critical appropriation of Western culture took place within the hermetically sealed, ahistorical or timeless, vacuum of the "universal library"—totally protected from the unsavory aspects of social inequality and violence. As Marta Morello-Frosch has pointed out of Piglia: "Unlike Borges, he places literary practice in the social realm, in the collective spaces of discourse and action, even at a time—the seventies—when historic events had pushed cultural practice to the most private places."[24] We can see this in the various functions of the *cita* in *Respiración artificial.*

On one level, the specific form of the *cita* reinforces the effect of the text's more general formal fragmentation. Often, a series of *citas* are chained together in the text. Thus, Emilio, within a letter, writes, "You, he told me, I write Maggi, look like Marcelo" (23/18). No quotation marks serve to mark off the various levels of the *cita*. In this example, the outer frame of the discourse consists of Emilio's narrative to us, the readers.

Within this he quotes from his own letter to Maggi, and within that letter he quotes a statement made by Luciano. Later, Emilio writes: " 'I study and think and exercise, he informed me' said the Senator that Marcelo had had them tell him" (53/42). Though Renzi employs quotation marks here, the Senator's (that is, Luciano's) quotation of Maggi within his own discourse, plus the succession of cuing phrases naming the origin of the various discursive fragments, both serve to destabilize the origin of the discourse. Are we hearing Maggi, or Luciano, or Emilio's words? Perhaps such chains of *citas* serve to reveal the uselessness of such a question. The words "belong" to whomever utters them at a given moment, but they no more originate with Emilio than they do with Maggi, to whom we intuitively would attribute them. Again, this dislocation of the coherent subject as an author of his or her own discourse can be read both as symptom and strategy. As symptom, one views all such fragmented, de-subjectivizing discourse as conditioned by the absent presence of the *Proceso*, and beyond it, I would argue, of some form of history as the social. But this symptom can function as a strategy when the regime's own discourse presupposes precisely the coherence and stability of the Cartesian subject incarnated in itself. If the regime believes and propagates the myth that it moves and writes history (and to some extent it is clearly justified in this belief), nothing can be more dangerous to it than to have it revealed that it is itself moved—like the Wizard of Oz, or Benjamin's chess playing automaton[25]— by an agent it must keep out of sight.

On a related level, the *cita* can only function in this way—continually displacing the origin of discourse—by presupposing an absence, namely, that of the quoted speaker. Then, given the local historical conditions of the *Proceso*, we should promptly rewrite absence as disappearance. In that case, the *cita* becomes the formal clue to the secret or allegorical content of the novel, which, as I observed above, is about a *desaparecido*. Everyone can only cite Maggi's words because Maggi himself is unable to cite them himself. But it is not only into Maggi's disappearance that the *cita* clues us. Or rather, in so far as Maggi's is the concrete embodiment of a widespread practice of disappearing individuals, it intersects with the *Proceso's* other major *desaparecido*: that is, the historical past itself. Now the absence marked by the *cita* is that of the past which, by definition, is not present. Thus when Maggi quotes Eliot to Renzi (or when Renzi quotes Maggi quoting Eliot to us as in the text's epigraph) the *cita* presupposes Eliot's pastness, his nonpresence. The *cita* presupposes not only the spatial distance of the disappeared person whose words must be repeated by others, but the temporal distance of the disappeared past whose messages must be resuscitated by us in the present.

This notion of the *cita* as a marker of temporal distance, of the absence of the past brings me to why I elected to retain the Spanish term. I could, after all, have easily substituted for it certain theoretical concepts—"intertextuality" (Kristeva), "reported speech" (Volosinov), or *citation* (Compagnon)—which the dynamics of quoting within the text might have appeared to call for.[26] But these concepts do not mark as explicitly the second, related, function of *cita,* namely, that of "(re) present-ing" the absent.[27] Thus, while theories of intertextuality or reported speech acknowledge and even play on this presence of the absent, the term *cita*—which also means appointment, encounter, or engagement (as well as court summons)—actually inscribes the double action within itself, in a way that even the French *citation* fails to do. *Citas* then also bring the disappeared past or individual back, (re)presenting them and sending their silenced messages back into circulation. (It seems worth pointing out that the etymology of our own English word *cite* sends us back to the Latin *citare,* frequently *ciere* or *cire,* "to set in motion" and "to call"; and that *resuscitate*—as in the title of this chapter—derives from this same root, with the additional dimension of "raising up" or "reviving" as from the dead.)[28]

I now want to demonstrate that simply clipping *citas* is not sufficient. Rather, one must, to "cite" Benjamin, "brush *citas* against the grain": look for not-famous or infamous *citas;* or (what amounts to the same thing) take famous ones and work on revealing their repressed. *Respiración artificial* represents various subjects engaged in precisely this practice. These subjects in the present go into the past, searching in its "unpromising places" and receiving its textual fragments—its *citas*—as so many messages left for the present. The significance and aim of this practice will only finally be apparent at the conclusion of my reading. However, I may give a more helpful preliminary notion of it by referring to the text's own first *cita,* its epigraph from T. S. Eliot: "We had the experience but missed the meaning, and approach to the meaning restores the experience." In one sense, the *cita* is precisely that "meaning" the various subjects of the novel "approach" in order to "restore the experience." This is *cita* as both leftover quote (the fragmentary residual meaning of a past experience) and encounter (the approach that will restore the experience). The *cita* is thus also an appointment. In other words, these subjects approach their respective and usually marginalized, repressed, or private *citas* as keys through which to reconstruct the secret, broad social forces underlying the more famous, well-known history of a period.

For example, Luciano tells Renzi the *historia* of his own father's death in 1879; an *historia* whose point of departure is the note his father left for his family on the morning of his death (59/47). Thus, a *cita* begins the *historia*. The note, however (quoted by Luciano, quoted by Renzi in his letter to Maggi, quoted by Renzi in his first person narration), not only permits Luciano to reconstruct the story of his father's death. It also opens up a vista on that conjuncture of Argentine history. How? Luciano's father died in a duel defending the honor of his own father, Enrique Ossorio. The duel, Luciano tells Renzi, represented a Hegelian operation between Argentine gentlemen by which they produced themselves as masters to their defeated opponent's slave. In the case of his father's duel and death, however, an Argentine court, for the first time, convicted the victor of murder. This court decision brings to a halt, then, the practice of dueling as a means of establishing honor and mastery. But the real historical significance, Luciano says, lies in that the liberal elites—the Argentine gentlemen—had discovered that they could establish themselves more effectively by banding together against those who challenged their mastery as a class, namely, "immigrants, gauchos, and Indians" (63/50). Rather than decimate their own numbers through duels, they now, in the face of emergent middle and working class demands, consolidated their power. In this way, Renzi tells us that Luciano concluded " 'the death of my father in a duel and the subsequent trial is an *event* that in a sense is linked, or rather, I should say' said the Senator, 'that accompanies and helps explain the conditions and the changes that brought to power General Julio Argentino Roca' " (63–64/50–51). Thus a *cita*—the note from his father—represents the means (Eliot's "meaning") through which the experience of the consolidation of oligarchic power in the late nineteenth century can be approached.

Tardewski, Maggi's friend, provides a similar example, also in conversation with Emilio. Tardewski was a student of Wittgenstein's at Cambridge in 1939. He wants to explain to Emilio how he came to be "surprised" by the war in Poland (instead of being in Cambridge) in the summer of 1939 and thus how he wound up in Argentina, talking to Renzi. His story therefore recounts the conditions of possibility of his own personal present. But, as will soon be clear, this recounting cannot be separated from the emergence of a different event, namely, the Second World War and Hitler's army, which he left Poland to escape. This is so not only because World War Two was the immediate social condition to which his flight to Argentina was a response, but because, as I will show, his discovery of (one of) the conditions of possibility of World War Two itself caused him to be in Poland at the time of the invasion.

Like Luciano, Tardewski's *historia* begins with a *cita,* or rather with two. In this case, the first *cita* is a footnote to an annotated edition of Hitler's *Mein Kampf* (which edition was given to Tardewski by mistake at the British Museum in London when he asked for a volume of writings by the Greek sophist Hippias for research on his thesis on Heidegger and the presocratics). Tardewski was interested, he tells Renzi in the "least historical" or "least public" (251/197) period of Hitler's life. Specifically, he focuses on an absence. Hitler's disappearance from Vienna between October 1909 and August 1910 (255). "His official biographers," Tardewski tells Renzi, "alter the chronology and Hitler himself modifies the dates in *Mein Kampf* to erase that void" (255/200). Hitler, Tardewski learns by looking away from the center of *Mein Kampf* and toward its own margins, footnotes, and appendixes, spent that period in Prague dodging the Prussian draft. And in Prague, Hitler especially frequented the Arcos café, a meeting place for German-speaking Czech artists, writers, and bohemians. All of this would be no more than an interesting irony were it not for the second *cita* Tardewski ran across that weekend in the British Museum. This came from a double review in the *Times Literary Supplement* of volume 6 of Kafka's complete works and Max Brod's biography of Kafka. Emilio tells us that Tardewski writes that "among the quotations [*citas*] and texts of Kafka or of Brod transcribed in that review" there was the following: "Max Brod encouraged the always indecisive Kafka to connect with the intellectual circles of the Arcos café, Tardewski read, and he prevented Kafka until at least 1911 from isolating himself from the world that surrounded him" (258/202). It was, then, the desire to discover the relationship between these two *citas,* and between Hitler and Kafka, that moved Tardewski to return to Varsovia, Poland in the summer of 1939. What was this relationship?

To put it most simply, Hitler talked and Kafka listened. But already this presents an oddity because Hitler, we are told, was a painter and according to Kafka, painters are mute. Kafka, the writer, should be the one telling stories. Tardewski reads Renzi a *cita* from Kafka's diary dated 12 May 1910:

His seriousness kills me. With his head stuck in the neck of his shirt, his rigid hair combed onto his skull, the muscles of his jaw tense, in his place . . . , ellipsis, read Tardewski. Right after that, on the next line, Kafka writes this:

Discussion A. I didn't mean that, he tells me, Tardewski reads. You know me by now Doctor. I am a completely harmless man. I had to relieve my feelings. What I said were just words. I interrupt him. This is precisely what is so dangerous. The words prepare the way; they are the precursors of acts to come, the sparks of future fires. I had no intention of saying that, A. replies to me. That's what you say, I answer, trying to smile. But, do you know what aspect things really have? It could be that we are sitting on a barrel of gunpowder that turns your desire into reality. (260–61/204)

Later Kafka would write that he told A. "Tell me everything from beginning to end, read Tardewski. I won't listen to anything less, I'm warning you. But I am burning to hear the whole thing from you. Because what you are planning is so atrocious that only when I hear it can I conceal my terror" (262/205). This relationship between Hitler the dictator and Kafka the listener, initiated in obscurity in Prague in 1910, is underscored in 1924 when Kafka lies dying, literally muted by tuberculosis, in the Kierling Sanatorium while Hitler dictates the text of *Mein Kampf* to his assistants in a castle in the Black Forest. What is the importance of the relationship that Tardewski claims to have discovered between Kafka and Hitler?

It has significance both for Tardewski and for our discussion of *Respiración artificial*. For Tardewski, Kafka knew how to listen. He knew, like Marx, that humans only produce imaginary solutions to real problems when the conditions for the realization of those solutions already exist. He knew that if the deeds described by Hitler could be imagined, then they could be completed. Kafka, therefore, in his novels, responded to Hitler with anticipatory representations of the horrors of the world Hitler would produce in reality. How, Tardewski asks himself, could nobody have realized this? In other words, Kafka read Hitler better than anybody read Kafka. For if someone had read Kafka with the same attentiveness and sense of history with which Kafka read Hitler, then perhaps the lessons learned after the holocaust could have been anticipated, as they were by Kafka. But this clearly has implications for our own reading. These implications are themselves here underscored by another allegorical allusion. In referring to Kafka's *Trial*, Tardewski sees in it the representation of the terrifying randomness and anonymity of all totalitarian regimes (265/207–208). But *The Trial* in Spanish is *El Proceso* (*Der Prozess* in the original German), and Kafka therefore literally can be said to describe the regime in power in Argentina. There are thus clear resonances to our own historical present. In that present, we are again called upon to listen to the "sickly murmurs of history" (266/208)—to research the marginal *citas* in which we can discern the movement by which history will bring the future. And, we are called, like Kafka, to amplify those murmurs, to make the future visible and therefore, perhaps, rewritable. But we are not only left to draw these implicit connections between Kafka and Hitler and our reading process during the *Proceso*. For Maggi's own *citas*, his engagement with the fragmentary messages bequeathed (literally) by Enrique Ossorio operates in precisely the same way as Luciano and Tardewski's readings of the *citas* of their own pasts, but on the site of Argentine history—and ultimately, as I will show, on the history of the *Proceso*.

Maggi received from Luciano a chest of documents that had been handed down from Enrique Ossorio to his son, from his son to Enrique's wife, and from his wife to Luciano. Just before his death, discussed above, in 1879, Luciano's father (Enrique's son) compels the family to swear that the chest of documents would not be opened for one hundred years. That interdiction brings us to the present, where Maggi takes it upon himself to reconstruct Enrique Ossorio's life. The documents consist of letters, diary fragments, and plans for (and portions of) a utopian novel consisting of letters written by Argentines in 1979. From these documents (*citas*), Maggi pieces together the following *historia* of Enrique Ossorio, a brief recapitulation of which will be helpful in understanding its implications within our reading of the novel.

He was a brilliant philosophy student whose Argentine professor wants to send him to Paris to study with Jules Michelet. For "unknown reasons" (32/25) he does not go and instead, in 1837, becomes a private secretary and confidant of Juan Manuel de Rosas, a federalist dictator of Argentina during the first decades of its independence. Rosas's dictatorship actually spanned a period of violent civil war following independence. Rosas himself headed the *Federales,* mostly *estancieros* and gauchos from the outlying provinces who sought to federalize the national government, granting broader power to provincial governments, and resisting the Europeanization of Argentina. Resistance forces, or *Unitarios,* consisting of liberal elites from Buenos Aires, sought to centralize power in the port of Buenos Aires. This opposition, of course, was recast in terms of *civilización y barbarie* by Domingo F. Sarmiento, who was among a group of intellectuals—Mármol, Alberdi, and Echeverría, some exiled in Montevideo and some in Chile—seeking to undermine the Rosas regime. Enrique Ossorio, then, begins in Rosas's camp. But he quickly establishes ties with various clandestine *Unitario* subgroups and even furnishes them with confidential information and documents that are used in an unsuccessful plot to overthrow Rosas. After the foiling of the plot, though he is not suspected of any wrongdoing by Rosas, Ossorio flees, first to Montevideo, where the exiles reject him as a double agent, to Chile, to California (in 1848, where he strikes gold and becomes rich), to Boston, and, finally, to New York. Eventually, he apparently loses his mind, is implicated in the death of a woman in Harlem, and is deported to Chile, where, two weeks before the overthrow of Rosas in 1852, he kills himself with a shot to the head. After his death, his *historia* divides, one branch following his documents, the other following his gold. The son keeps the gold, invests it in land, and becomes a member of the elite agricultural oligarchy of Argentina (whose legacy the *Proceso* invoked repeatedly) until he dies at the moment when that oligarchy circled its wagons against liberal democracy and working class insurrection. His widow keeps the documents which will eventually come into the hands of Maggi.

The task Maggi puts to himself, confronted with the fragmentary textualized remains of Enrique Ossorio, is to "show the movement of history that is enclosed in an essentially *eccentric* life" (36/28). Maggi therefore wants to reconstruct the founding of what would become the Argentine national cultural identity (by Sarmiento and others) not by looking in a "promising place"—Sarmiento's *Facundo*, for example—but by looking away from it, at its margin, "its reverse," in the writings of the disgraced Ossorio. The history that must be told, he tells Renzi in a different context, is the history of defeats (18/15). But he also wants to explore these writings in the mode of the genealogist; he believes that the historical significance of Ossorio's misfortunes can only be discerned by reversing the chronology of his life. Therefore, Maggi's point of departure, the first lines of his book, will be the letter (quoted by Maggi in a letter quoted by Renzi), written to Alberdi, to which letter Ossorio—in the suicide note that forms the last lines of *Respiración artificial*—directed the finder of his corpse. Once again, a *cita*, wholly marginal to, indeed, repressed by the historical record, acts as the means by which one can approach the meaning of a lost experience and thus restore that experience.

But Ossorio's case is not only of interest because of what it can tell us of a foundational moment of Argentine history. Ossorio has an instructive consciousness of his relationship to his own moment of history, and it is this consciousness that ultimately represents the paradigmatic genealogical mode of the novel and leads us to understand its relevance for the present moment in history. Specifically, Ossorio understands himself to have been marginalized from the historical events of his day and therefore considers himself to be in a better position to evaluate the present's relationship to the future—or, in other words, to evaluate the future as a present whose history is Ossorio's own time. How does this work?

Exile, for Ossorio, is utopia. This is not because it is a perfect place. Rather, because it is a no-place; a site defined negatively in relation to homeland (94/76). Moreover, exile is utopian in that temporally it represents a kind of limbo between the memory of one's past presence in the homeland and the dream of one's future presence. The exile, as Maggi paraphrases Ossorio, has "a nostalgia for the future." Ossorio also considers himself utopian in that as traitor he lives "between two sets of loyalties" (96): "He must pretend, remain in the wasteland of perfidy, sustained by impossible dreams of a future where his evil deeds will at last be rewarded" (96/77). A subject in Ossorio's position then, marginalized from the dominant discourses of the present, lives with an eye on the relationship between that present and its possible future.

Already in this respect, Ossorio is paradigmatic for the other figures in the novel. Maggi, Tardewski, Luciano, the various figures in Concordia, and Kafka can all be seen as, in Tardewski's words, *fracasados,* "failures." History has exerted a particularly displacing force on these characters, who have all lived periods of intense social crisis. It has swept them aside and deposited them in their various marginal locations. They become the best witnesses to the movement of history, but also those with the least access to the discourses through which history is narrated.

This utopian (marginal) subjectivity dictates a certain, by now familiar, mode of representing history. And in this too Ossorio provides the model for the other figures of the novel. Ossorio, imagining the future, focuses on the everyday, looking for the future in "unpromising places." The *cita* Ossorio decides to leave for the future is a utopian novel. But "the utopia of the modern dreamer [*soñador moderno*]," Ossorio writes in July of 1850,

> departs from the classic laws of the genre in one essential respect: one must refuse to reconstruct a nonexistent space. Thus—*a key distinction*—one must not situate the utopia in an imaginary or unknown place (most commonly on an island). One must instead make a date [*cita*] with one's own country, on a date (1979) that is itself fabulously distant. There is no such place: in time. There is *as yet* no such place. As I see it, this is the equivalent of the utopian point of view. To imagine Argentina as it will be in a hundred and thirty years. (97/78, translation modified)

Ossorio thus sets out to write this utopian novel, entitled *1979*. The protagonist will be a historian who finds himself confronted with a set of "trivial and everyday" documents from the future (101/83); and the model for the novel will be the *cofre*, or "coffer," containing his own—that is, Enrique's—documents. Thus the protagonist, whose own real time would be March 1837 to June 1838 (the beginning of Rosas's regime, a French blockade of Buenos Aires, and the *terror* in which Rosas's secret police detained and murdered thousands of *Unitarios*), will receive, or rather will intercept, letters from the future. Why letters?

On one level, we may interpret a letter as a kind of marginalized discourse of history. They are the privatized underside to the official acts, statements, decrees that seem to govern the course of history. Renzi implies as much when he writes of his desire to write an autobiography composed of letters (40–41/32). The changes in style, in handwriting, in thematics would then refer obliquely back to the experience of the life. An "approach" to the "meaning" of the letters would "restore" the "missed experience" of the life. On another level, though, Ossorio gives two reasons for writing letters. First, given that the epistolary genre seems anachronistic in the age of realism, Ossorio explains that letters themselves are an inherently anachronistic mode of communication. "To write a letter," he says, "is to send a message to the future; to speak from the present with an addressee who is not there, of which knowing nothing about how that person is (in what spirits, with whom) *while* we write him and, above all, *later* when he reads us. Correspondence is the utopian form of conversation because it annihilates the present and turns the future the only possible site for dialogue" (103/83). Letters, moreover, are conditioned by exile. Exile is a social condition that requires "us to substitute words for the relation among close friends, now far away, absent, scattered in different places and cities" (103/83). Exile, in other words, by calling for correspondence, implicitly defers dialogue to the future. This seems reasonable because the exile is, after all, the one with the "nostalgia for the future."

Letters then, are the paradigm for the *cita* that speaks to the future. But in this sense, they simply formally embody a characteristic shared by all forms of writing; especially those informed by a sense of history, by the knowledge that all writing will one day, like the documents in Enrique's *cofre*, be in the hands of the future. The subjects of that future will then, like Maggi (or like the reverse of Enrique's utopian protagonist), try to reconstruct the movement of history, its own past, via these *citas* (fragmentary citations and engagements). But if this is the case, then all writing is necessarily historical writing, all writing constitutes the history of the future because all writing is directed to an addressee (reader) in the future. The question then is raised: How can we write that history of the future in such a way that, in narrating it, we shape it?

The paradigmatic answer, once again, lies in Ossorio's utopian novel. Thinking about the future, as he and his protagonist both do, consists in asking oneself, "How can it be that I wasn't able to see *then* what seems so obvious now? And what can I do to see in the present the signs that announce the course of the future?" (84–85/68). These are the special questions of the subject marginalized in the present. These are the questions that inform a writing directed toward the construction of history. Now we can see that this was the gift of Kafka, who could see in Hitler's words what would become Hitler's reality, and for that matter of Tardewski, who asks himself precisely, "How could no one have understood" that Kafka was writing about Hitler in his diary?—a fact evident to him now (261/204). But it is, moreover, precisely that attitude that Maggi calls *la mirada histó-rica,* "the historical gaze." "We are but leaves floating on a river and must know [*saber*] how to look at what comes as if it had already passed/past [*pasado*]" (20/16, translation modified).

The *cita* as the mode of apprehending and representing history now acquires an additional dimension. It is not only a quotation and an engagement with the past, but also now, as Enrique wrote, a *cita*—a "date"— with the future. For this reason, perhaps, Tardewski (as quoted by Maggi quoted by Renzi) wants to "write a book entirely made up of quotations [*citas*]" (20/16). Quotations? Or dates? How about summons? And Emilio, whose first novel Maggi tells him was precisely such a book, wants to write a novel/autobiography full of letters. Maggi, for his part, wants to produce the history of the Rosas period via the *citas* bequeathed by Ossorio. But all of these representations of the past, all these *citas,* now appear as so many modes of historicizing the present; by which I mean, as so many modes of thinking the present as a moment in time, linked dialectically to a past, as its future, and to a future, as its past—as in the double epigraph to my own book.

The final textual horizon for this operation is *Respiración artificial* itself. The novel, like all these hypothetical texts posited within it, consists of *citas.* It engages a variety of pasts on the basis of its resuscitation of various *citas.* But, extending the implications of the other texts within the novel, it also presents the letters and conversations, occurring in 1976 in Argentina, one month after the beginning of the *Proceso,* as so many *citas* from that present. Although these letters are, in one sense, the letters from the future to Ossorio's utopian protagonist in the past, they are also, in another sense, letters from the present to the future. They are, perhaps, letters from that present to us, the reader, inhabiting a different present that at once is that prior present's future. If *Respiración artificial* consists of so many letters to the future, then, as we have seen, it constitutes that future's past. It constitutes history. But a history of what? Namely, a history of the *Proceso* as it might be narrated by an imaginary subject from an imagined point in the future, say, a reader in 1994. *Respiración artificial*, in other words, brings together documents, textualized fragments, *citas* and sends them to us in the future. We are charged with reconstructing the shape of an epoch out of them.

Respiración artificial provides a model for historical thought. It displays that model in action on a series of historical sites. And then it includes itself as a *cofre de citas* within an operation in which we are called to think historically in accordance with that model. The model challenges us to look for history in the absences in the historical record. Of course, absences also means disappearances, and there surely is a key to the nightmare of the *Proceso*. But the *Proceso* not only disappeared people, it disappeared history itself. This fact reappears secretly as the novel's obsession with history and with the gaps and margins of the historical record. What do the various *historias* in the novel make us do? Do we rush to our History of Argentina to verify the court decision narrated by Luciano? Do we check through editions of *Mein Kampf*, or through Kafka's diaries? If we do, and we do not find these events where they should be, then are we led to dismiss these *historias* as so many "stories" or "fictions"—made-up histories? Perhaps, but in that case we may also want to check the "official history" of the *Proceso* to verify the supposed disappearance of thirty thousand individuals. Is the *historia* of their disappearance also then a made-up history? We presume not. But then, it is precisely the point of these *historias* to question the gaps in the historical record, to resuscitate the marginal, subaltern, or repressed stories that actually reveal the movement of history, the forces that condition the emergence of those more famous punctuation marks— events, "great men," dates—that delineate the official history. In the case of the *Proceso*, doing so represents a double challenge: one, a challenge to the content of the *Proceso's* pseudo-history, and two, a formal challenge to the discursive presuppositions of that history. Clearly this vision of the historical and oppositional function of the novel seems to place it at odds, stylistic similarities notwithstanding, with both of the models of postmodern historical fiction advanced earlier. Does this novel not represent an instance of Latin American postmodernism after all? To adequately address this question, we have to take up a sketch of the historical conditions of possibility of the junta.

Neil Larsen observes: "The recourse to 'authoritarian' forms of state power in the Southern Cone of Latin America must primarily be understood as a structural response to a 'crisis of hegemony' internal to the social formations in question."[29] Larsen here points out an essential coordinate of the military's assumption of power. In the previous two chapters I briefly traced the rise (and crisis) of the Peronist resistance in Argentina in the late sixties and early seventies. Together with the mobilization of workers, students, and intellectuals, these armed movements had toppled the existing military junta and forced the return of Perón. Faced with the growing polarization of Argentine society and the increasing violence of the confrontations between left and right, a new junta stepped into the de facto vaccuum of power to "order" what it saw as the chaos brought on by administrative incompetence in dealing with the virulent threat of immoral and "foreign" communist subversives. But this account begs further questions, such as, What was there in Argentine society that enabled the military to step in? What accounted for the specific tools it implemented in responding to the crisis in hegemony?

Since the end of the nineteenth century, facing a perceived threat from Chile, the Argentine armed forces were built up through the importation of German armaments, and trained, professionalized, and autonomized under the guidance of Prussian military advisers. The military espoused the ideology of the "nation in arms," which confers on the armed forces the role of guarantor of the public honor.[30] Beginning in 1930, the military interpreted this role as requiring its intervention during unstable periods of constitutional rule.[31] Of course, these military interventions had in fact, though rarely in rhetoric or in appearance, a class orientation. The armed forces traditionally stepped in to combat the perceived erosion of the privilege of agri-export oligarchical elites. Certainly, the *Proceso*—dismantling the changes initiated during Perón's first presidency in the 1940s—engaged a redistribution of national income from labor to capital, from industry to agriculture, from domestic to foreign capital, and of course, to the military itself.

Along with this historic role, the military counted on support, within Argentina, of two key social sectors that had also shared a historical antagonism with Perón: the church and the liberal agricultural oligarchy and national bourgeoisie. The Argentine Catholic Church was historically linked to the state through the principles of the *patronato*, which grants to the state certain powers with respect to the appointment of members of the church hierarchy.[32] However, as my discussion of the military's historical narrative indicated, this official linkage eventually gave way to a separation of church and state. Nevertheless, an unofficial alliance between the church hierarchy, the oligarchic elites, and the military remained. Leonardo Boff writes that "the church then allied itself with the dominant classes that controlled the state."[33] Perón alienated the church in part through his personal behavior but especially by legalizing divorce. The *Proceso* turned back the clock and drew institutional and rhetorical support from its renewed relationship with the church. The Argentine church, during a period when "liberation theology" was an integral component of the Sandinista revolution in Nicaragua, turned a blind eye not only to the socioeconomic injustices instigated by the *Proceso* but also to its brutal violation of human rights as recognized by even conservative world governments and organizations. The national bourgeoisie, in one sense, owed its very existence to the protective hand of Perón's industrialization programs. However, already by the end of Perón's second term in office, liberal sectors of the national bourgeoisie were frustrated by the combination of a saturated domestic market and Peronism's essential antagonism toward foreign capital. Both these groups, as represented within the armed forces, were instrumental in the 1955 coup that threw Perón into exile, and both were important supporters of the military "reorganization" of national life after 1976.

But these conditions and the *Proceso's* own assumption of power were also inextricably linked to developments in the world outside Argentina. Most obvious here is the cold war and the persistence of revolutionary movements in the wake of the Cuban revolution and the decolonization struggles in Africa. It was easy, especially after Richard Nixon's *Real War* marked the Third World as the site of an ongoing third world *war,* to link Argentina's own battle with "subversion" to a broader campaign in which the "free world" needed to secure every beachhead against the onslaught of communism.

And again, as with the case of Puig's transitional moment, all these developments can be articulated within the framework of changes in the structure and practices of international capitalism. We left postwar capitalism in the crisis of the early seventies and noted that for David Harvey and others, postmodernity as a concept should properly mark the ensemble of economic, social, political, and cultural changes that formed the response to the economic, social, political, and cultural crises ("crises" from the vantage point of Western culture, international capitalism, and bourgeois liberalism) of the sixties and early seventies. Thus Larsen adds to the internal conditions enumerated above "the longer term global crisis of overaccumulation of capital."[34] But how did the Argentine *Proceso* fit into the international response to these crises? What were its economic policies and how were they articulated to its political and ideological repression?

The regime saw itself, in the tradition of the *generación del 80,* as carrying forth the interrupted project of Argentine modernization within the orbit of world capitalism. This involved the dismantling of Peronist social and economic policies which were seen as an obstacle on the development of the agricultural sector (thought to be Argentina's "natural" source of prosperity) and the inflow of foreign capital. Thus, the regime's economic minister, José Martínez de Hoz, fully embraced the free-market economic theories of the so-called Chicago boys—economists trained at the University of Chicago whose economic policies were being implemented in nearby Chile under the dictatorship of Augusto Pinochet. A key feature of Chicago school neoconservative economics is, as Annie L. Cot has put it, "the way it extends economic discourse well beyond its traditional boundaries; thus it has produced an economics of marriage, crime, the family, cheating in school, drugs, pop culture, electoral behavior, philanthropy, painting, religion, altruism, fertility, morals, polygamy, law, suicide, adultery, conjugal roles and so on."[35] Clearly, the potential scope of such a discourse provided unique opportunities for a regime so concerned with extending its battle from military to ideological fronts.

Beyond this ideological versatility, the Chicago school economic prescription served the *Proceso* by granting up-to-date "scientific" grounding for the implementation of economic policies reminiscent of the agro-export, free-market days of the 1880s. This, above all else, according to William C. Smith, meant "a far-reaching 'opening' and reinsertion of Argentina's domestic economy into the world-economy according to strict criteria of efficiency and the law of comparative advantages."[36] Smith goes on to note seven points of this economic program:

[1] reduction of real wages to an "equilibrium" level about 40 percent below the average of the previous five years. . . . [2] export taxes on agricultural and livestock products would be eliminated. . . . [3] the domestic market would be

opened up by a progressive reduction in import tariffs (from an average of over 80 percent to about 40 percent). . . . [4] many of the subsidies that previous governments had instituted to promote non-traditional manufactured export goods would be abolished. . . . [5] foreign exchange markets would be liberalized and the financial sector reformed, and this would be coupled with policies designed to finance public-sector deficits and investments by selling government bonds in the local capital market. [6] public sector prices would be raised. . . . and [7] state activities would be cut back, especially by reducing public expenditure for social welfare (i.e., health, education, housing, etc.), rationalizing public-sector employment practices, raising taxes to cut the public deficit, and promoting the privatization of some public enterprises.[37]

These policies had the concrete effect of "deindustrializing" Argentina and thrusting millions of working-class Argentines into destitution. Military repression had, aside from their role in the "war against subversion," the additional value of securing acquiescence to these violent economic policies.

Of course, these were not the stated goals of the economic program. Nor were these domestic effects the only ones of importance to the junta. For this "streamlining" of the Argentine economy made it more attractive to international investors.[38] Argentina's total debt in U.S. dollars went from eight billion in the year prior to the military takeover to close to fifty billion by 1983. Thirty-seven percent of the debt incurred during the *Proceso* resulted from the service of the foreign debt itself. But another quarter went to arms and military equipment. By comparison, the figure of eight billion in 1975 represents an increase of only five billion since 1962.[39] The influx of foreign capital, beside obviously financing military extravagance, was intended as the fuel that would accelerate the stalled Argentine economy.[40] Moreover, the easing of consumer credit restrictions delighted middle-class Argentines who binged on deficit spending of this *plata dulce*, or "sweet money." Combined with their double fear of subversion and repression, this guaranteed middle-class silence during the *Proceso*.

The *Proceso* had thus linked its fortunes, culturally and economically, to the industrialized Western world. With its "war against subversion," the junta had successfully made its own internal interests consonant with the interests of the cold war United States. Now, economically as well, the military's desire for foreign capital corresponded to foreign capital's need for release into new financial markets. David Harvey shows how loans relieved the pressure of the overaccumulation of capital in the industrialized nations. The debt serves as a kind of valve for periodic crisis in flexible capitalism because, as Harvey writes, "It may, in short, prove possible to 're-schedule the crisis' by re-scheduling (for example) third world and other repayments until the twenty-first century."[41]

There is little question that *Respiración artificial* appears as a response to military rule in Argentina. The *Proceso*, in turn, can now be seen as appearing at the intersection of a complexly interrelated series of cultural, political, social, and economic developments occurring simultaneously in Argentina and Latin America and abroad. Writing a history of recent Argentine culture means taking all these factors into account. Ultimately, writing such a history requires us to use periodizing terms. And, in so complex a case, the flexibility of a term—able to accommodate and signal the tensions of the various forces combining to produce an event—is of paramount importance. George Yúdice has argued that "postmodernism" is a term that should refer to "the 'aesthetico-ideological responses/proposals' before, in front of, and within the capitalist transnationalization now not only in the United States of Europe but in the entire world."[42] This basically restates Jameson's understanding of postmodernism as the cultural logic of late capitalism. But Yúdice, crucially, understands the spatial dimension of the logic of late capitalism. It unfolds throughout the world producing not uniformity, but provoking rather a heterogeneous series of responses—both complicitous and antagonistic—and interlocking with a variety of existing social, political, and cultural problems. In that case, Piglia's text as a response to a political and cultural situation clearly imbricated with the economic logic of late capitalism can usefully be viewed, at least for the purposes of historical understanding, as "postmodern." But to insure that this historical term remains flexible enough to note the specificity of *Respiración artificial*'s local conditions of possibility, we should add the modifier "Argentine." This then is the cultural matrix of Argentine postmodernity within and against which *Respiración artificial* operates. It challenges the cultural and political forms produced by flexible capitalism in Argentina. And it does so, interestingly, by using the techniques and literary discourses—fictional incorporation and treatment of history, self-reflexivity—thought to be complicit with flexible capitalism by critics in the United States. History, however, became a fundamental site of military aggression in the early 1980s in Argentina. In such a context, the problematization and rethinking of historical discourse, although surely generated from within the cultural matrix of late capitalism, just as surely functions to destabilize the authority of the local structures through which it operates.

7

The Importance of Writing History; or,

On Louis Bonaparte and Juan Perón

> Just because he was nothing, he could signify everything save himself.
>
> —Karl Marx

Marx wrote these words, in *The Class Struggles in France, 1848–1850*, in reference to Louis Bonaparte, when he still believed that the appearance of working-class defeat during the revolutions of 1848 actually presaged a greater revolution to come.[1] But these hopes were dashed by Bonaparte's coup d'etat on 2 December 1851. Marx was left bewildered, and then *disenchanted.*[2] I emphasize "disenchantment" to draw attention to a meaningful irony surrounding Marx's account. *The Eighteenth Brumaire of Louis Bonaparte,* written between December 1851 and March 1852, is the work in which Marx attempted to account historically for a turn of events that had surprised him. Beginning in 1845, Marx produced a series of works—his most resolutely historical materialist—in which the empirically observable movement of history as class struggle was asserting itself in spite of the ideological *enchantments* of bourgeois society. *The German Ideology* (1845), *The Holy Family* (1845), and *The Poverty of Philosophy* (1847) were the philosophical expressions of this movement, *The Communist Manifesto* (1848) its political expression, and *The Class Struggles in France, 1848–1850* was the historical description of its taking place. But when Louis Bonaparte grabbed absolute power with the support of various, and otherwise *antagonistic* classes, Marx saw the mantle of enchantment resettling over the reality of class struggle. What appeared as Bonaparte's merely clownish character in *Class Struggles* became his crucially, effectively, almost strategically clownish character in *Eighteenth Brumaire.* The irony is, then, that Marx's disenchantment in *The Eighteenth Brumaire of Louis Bonaparte* derives from the *re*-enchantment of the world. This irony makes for a three-way tension in the text between Marx's begrudged recognition of the effective weight of "ideological" forces, his conviction that he remains immune to their effect and is thus capable of penetrating them, and his own rhetorical recourse to figures from the "ideological" realms of aesthetic and historical representation.

We have encountered disenchantment, or disillusionment, earlier in our own history of Latin American modernity. I argued, in my chapters on *El beso de la mujer araña,* that the 20 June 1973 massacre at Buenos Aires' Ezeiza Airport emblematized the Argentine experience of the coming to crisis of Latin America's utopian projects of the 1960s. On that day, millions of Argentines, including hundreds of Montoneros, awaited the return of General Juan D. Perón from Madrid after eighteen years in exile. This was to be the day of triumph for the leftist Peronist resistant movement that had only three months earlier won a convincing victory at the polls. Instead, just prior to Perón's arrival, right-wing Peronists allied with Perón's private secretary José López Rega, opened fire on the Montoneros lined up before the speaker's platform. This event set off a cycle of uneasy relations between the Argentine Left and Perón until the time of his death in July 1974 and was the source of the disenchantment of the Peronist Left in this period.

The epigraph above, and indeed many other portions of Marx's bitterly lucid account of Louis Bonaparte's coup, could serve as a basis for a Marxist account of Peron's "betrayal" of the Left and for the increasingly violent polarization of social conflicts in the country that finally led to the installation of the *Proceso* in 1976. But here I want to depart in particular from Marx's renewed, if begrudged, attention to the effective weight of ideology, and in particular, of history, of history *as* representation, of historical representation.

Marx begins *The Eighteenth Brumaire of Louis Bonaparte* by citing Hegel, who, he informs us with a rather uncharacteristic lack of precision, "remarks somewhere that all facts and personages of great importance in world history occur, as it were, twice."[3] This establishes what is already apparent in the title of the work (with its reference to Louis Bonaparte's uncle's own assumption of absolute power): that this is a work about repetition and so, about the force of the past, of history.

But in his famous amendment to Hegel's remark, Marx decisively shifts into a metaphorical register that is at least as important as this theme of the effectiveness of history. Marx continues, still referring to Hegel's remark: "He forgot to add: the first time as tragedy, the second as farce."[4] Marx has again appropriated the somber language of Hegel's world history. But where in his first appropriation, Marx "inverted" it to show that "idealist" world history was actually, or *really*, the history of class struggle, Marx here recasts that image into the language of theatre.

We continue reading. Marx famously reasserts the force of history: "Men make their own history, but they do not make it just as they please;

they do not make it under circumstances chosen by themselves, but under circumstances directly encountered, given and transmitted from the past. The tradition of all the dead generations weighs like a nightmare on the brain of the living."[5]

But once again, Marx follows this with a shift into a dryly comic metaphorical register of the theater. For this history appears, in all of Marx's examples, as the donning of a theatrical mask or costume. In the exception, it appears in response to the "anxious conjuring up of spirits of the past" by revolutionaries. Finally, the need of the present to recur to the past, is metaphorized in terms of language acquisition. One can *speak* a new language by means of translating in one's head back to the mother tongue, but one "has assimilated the spirit of the new language and can freely express himself in it only when he finds his way in it without recalling the old and forgets his native tongue in the use of the new."[6]

The importance of these metaphorical shifts appears on two levels. First, Marx's reliance on these particular metaphors (the theater, necromancy, language)—all drawn from the sphere of what he has already called "ideology"—presage his shift in emphasis from analyzing the unveiling of class struggle in the revolutionary period around 1848 as the triumph of the material over the ideological to accounting for its (merely) apparent disappearance under a cloud of illusion and ideology after Bonaparte's assumption of power. But on a second level, Marx's liberal and able use of metaphorical language (not only here, but throughout his work) itself suggests his awareness of the effectivity of ideological practice. It is not that Marx abandons a belief in a material substratum to ideology, nor even that he ceases to believe that his historical method offers privileged access to it. Rather, it is that he reveals the indispensability of ideology *to* his method. Thus, even his insistence on the coming of a future revolution whose "content goes beyond words," is rhetorically—through Marx's characteristically devastating use of *chiasmus*—inseparable from the recognition that in this revolution "words went beyond the content" (106).[7]

I begin with Marx for three reasons: first, because the particular content of his interpretation of Louis Napoleon lends itself to the period of Argentine history surrounding Perón; second, because his particular historical method of taking real appearances as costumes and showing both what they conceal and why they are effective offers itself as a model for the attitude toward history of Argentine postmodernity; and third, because the emphasis on historical representation that frames his interpretation helps to explain the importance of writing history for the novelists of Argentine postmodernity. Tomás Eloy Martínez's *La novela de Perón* illustrates this rationale and concretizes it in a fictional treatment of that figure—Juan Perón—who looms largest in the Argentine shift from modernity to post-modernity.[8]

In the novel, which is centered on the day of Perón's return to Argentina, Perón himself, with the aid of López Rega, is writing and revising his own memoirs. There are several occasions on which the two give us access to their thoughts on the representation of history. Early in the novel Perón remembers that Evita "had already intuited that when she published *La razón de mi vida*. The people [*el pueblo*] need fable and emotion, not the colorless pap of the doctrines with which, much to his regret, he has had to nourish them" (58/42; translation modified). Here, memory takes the form of fable and emotion (romance) counterposed to the dryness not of history, but of political doctrine; a doctrine, however, which in the case of Perón is not unrelated to his mode of representing history. Perón's political doctrine of *verticalismo* insists on the suppression of difference. All individual impulses must be subordinated to the will of the social embodied in the figure of the *caudillo*, Perón. Thus, in reviewing the first chapter in which a number of "embarrassing" family members and events are omitted, Perón applauds López Rega's editing: "All was in order, then. López had been able to clean up the smudge of cousins and aunts that was blurring the Memoirs" (72/53).

Later on, López Rega assures the General that intimacy ("fable," "emotion," "history in the flesh," "romance") has no place in memoirs such as his:

> Be more historic, General. See what I mean? Try to make the image look a little more like marble. Don't reveal yourself, don't let yourself be known. Greatness is made of silences. When have you heard that a great man leaves the bathroom, pulls the chain, going around in his underwear in front of people? Family? What is that? Turn it into forgetting [*olvido*]. You were never like that. (127/103; translation modified)

Indeed, López Rega's desire to erase from Perón's history the romantic style we might associate with Evita and the earlier period is also expressed in his bizarre attempts to invoke Evita's powerful spirit into the more manageable body of Isabelita, Perón's current wife. In both cases, López Rega's desires are mirrored by the desires of his arch-enemy—the Peronist Left—to keep Evita alive (in spirit and body) as the force of radical Peronism. All seem, as Marx wrote of the revolutionaries of 1848, "anxious to conjure up the spirits of the past."

As for Perón, his fear of the private, romantic side of history comes through even as he wills the repression of his fears in general:

> The only feeling he has experienced unblurred to any extent is fear, which he would like to efface from his memory: to assert that fear does not exist now and therefore it might (must) never have existed. It wasn't the trivial fear of death, but rather of that which is worse: fear of history. He has suffered thinking that history will tell in its own way that which he silenced. That others will come to invent for him a life. He has feared that history will lie when it speaks of Perón, that it will discover: the life of Perón has lied to history. So many times he has said it: a man is only what he remembers. He should say, rather: a man is only that of him which is remembered. (122/98; translation modified)

This suggests that Perón's greatest fear is the return of the repressed.

Perón, like Alberdi whose remarks on the desert Perón quotes (123/ 99), believes that the best way to deal with something unpleasant is to deny its existence. And in fact, Perón's celebrated ambiguity is not to be confused with an integrated and genuine respect for the impossibility of truth as the sole possession of an individual will, nor should it be attributed only to the violence of class contradictions in Argentina at the time of his political formation and therefore seen as merely a political strategy. We should also see it precisely as the enactment of his doctrine of making memory disappear.

Going over the General's role in the military coup against President Yrigoyen, of which so many versions circulate in the novel, López Rega is concerned that the General choose one version. Upon hearing this, the General scoffs:

> Look. If I've again and again become the protagonist of history [la historia], it has been because I've contradicted myself. You've already heard Schlieffen's strategy. You have to change plans several times a day and pull them out one at a time as needed. The socialist fatherland? I invented it. The conservative fatherland? I keep it alive. I have to blow in all directions, like the windvane. And never retract anything [retractarme], but rather keep adding phrases. (218/182; translation modified)

Perón doesn't want López Rega to confuse a strategic proliferation of contradictory signs with the unseemly return of repressed bits of living past.

The image of Perón as an empty, but omni-signifying, sign (like Marx's Louis Bonaparte) will reappear later in the novel when one companion remembers of Perón that

> he didn't seem human. Perón was an automaton, a golem, what the Japanese call a bunraku. Several times, I saw him distracted. That hasn't happened to many people: seeing Perón distracted. He was left unmasked. He was a hollow figure, without a soul. Later, returning to himself, he filled up with the feelings and desires of others, with the needs. . . . Distracted, one could not see hatred nor sadness nor joy nor fatigue nor enthusiasm. One could notice only the hollowness. Attentive, then yes: the feelings of others were reflected in him, as if instead of a body he had a mirror. (265/316; translation modified)

Thus, when Perón scoffs at López Rega's contradiction-anxiety, he is completing the equation between Perón as historical protagonist, Perón as empty historical sign, and Perón as historical narrator. Taken together with the general aim of his and López Rega's memoires—to show the General in command of everything, including contradictions—we can begin to form a negative snapshot of what a resistant or oppositional historical representation would look like. It would knock, so to speak, the General off his rocker. It would condemn him to face up to *his* construction, *his* shaping, by those very forces thought to be under his command (remember Benjamin's automaton and the Wizard of Oz!). This is realized much more explicitly toward the end of *La novela de Perón.*

In *The Class Struggles in France,* Marx described the entourage of *claqueurs* that accompanied Louis Bonaparte on his trips throughout France: "They put speeches into the mouth of their marionette, which according to the reception in the different towns, proclaimed republican resignation or perennial tenacity as the keynote of the President's policy."[9] Meanwhile, *La novela de Perón* ends with the journalist, Zamora, observing Perón's first, televised, speech after the Ezeiza massacre. Perón is accompanied by López Rega:

> Something in the image was unnatural, as if it were raining upside down. The peasants and the horses were getting nervous. Zamora paid closer attention. The General said:
> "I will soon make a trip throughout the Republic . . ."
> One of the men realized that López lips were moving ahead of the speech.
> —Pay close attention—he mused—. They're prompting the General.
> It happened again. In the secretary's [López Rega's] mouth one could read:

"and I would like to see the Jujeños in Jujuy" a fraction of a second before the phrase left the President's throat.

" . . . and the Salteños in Salta," dictated the lips.

"Salta," Perón repeated. (415)

The crowd watching the television breaks up in what the narrator describes as *desencanto,* "disenchantment." But it may be a politically enabling disenchantment. In Martínez's hands, Perón, like Bonaparte, has become an empty signifier: a dictator who is literally dictated to.

In fact, Martínez's historical tactic, which is implicitly modeled by Marx, was explicitly advocated by Nietzsche. In Nietzsche's own reflections on history—so important both to Benjamin and to recent theories of history—the nineteenth-century philosopher identified several types of destructive history.[10] Among them were "monumental" and "antiquarian." In the first, history appears a series of great men, deeds, and events that serve as models for the present. In the second, history appears as the continuity of the similar across time. Of course, these different histories can also appear as dimensions of the same vision of history. This is the case with the Peronist (certainly leftist Peronist) and the *Proceso's* versions of Argentine history. The antidote Nietzsche prescribed for these histories was parody and interruption. That is, to a monumental history one must respond by pulling the mask away from the great figures (did he have Marx's *Eighteenth Brumaire* in mind?) and to an antiquarian history one must respond by showing the gaps and breaks in what pretends to be a single, uniform and coherent historical line.[11] Martínez (and Piglia, for that matter) echoes these prescriptions with his representation of the underside of official history.

This task is taken up within the novel by the journalist Zamora whose editor expresses the challenge of representing Perón in the following terms:

> The official Perón is pumped dry. Another one has got to be found. Tell about the character's early years, Zamora. Nobody's really done it. Sure, there's been no end of glorifications, myths, collected papers, but the truth never appears anywhere. Who was the General, Zamora? Decipher him once and for all: Reconstruct the words he never dared to say, describe the impulses he must have repressed, read between the lines . . . The truth is what is hidden, right? (45/30–31)

But Zamora is more cautious about truth than his editor. He believes truth to "be in all the lies" (46/31). He decides to interweave the narratives of seven childhood companions of the General into one large chronological tapestry. As promotion for the piece, the seven "witnesses" (as they are called) will be at Ezeiza to herald Perón's return and to exhibit history, "but in the flesh" (46/31).

Perón and López Rega want to drain, like vampires, the vivid and contradictory memories of the general into a monolithic, granite monument to the general's historic dimensions. If their project is to transform memory into history, then Zamora (like the characters in *Respiración artificial*) attempts to take history, now in the objective, disciplinary sense, and somehow transform it into memory. The process is tantamount to the breathing of life into the dead and immobile artifacts, or *citas*, of the past and present.

Martínez's treatment of a concrete historical subject—Peronism—is a departure from the dominant and antagonistic treatments of Peronism offered by the Peronist Left and the *Proceso*. His transcendence of their discursive battle accompanies the transcendence of their physical conflict. It exemplifies, I think, what José Pablo Feinmann calls "la verdad democrática."[12] And Feinmann writes, recall, not of actually existing democracy in Argentina, but of a more genuine participatory social, economic, cultural, *and* political democracy.

But Martínez does not merely "redo Perón." Or rather, by doing so, he also redoes historical representation in general, precisely along the lines seen in *Respiración artificial*. Erase what doesn't fit—"Gobernar a la historia. Cogerla por el culo" (218/182)—this is Perón's mode of representation; a mode whose formulation here reminds us of its links to a patriarchal discourse of violation. Moreover, this mode, it becomes clear, is the tragedy of Argentina at the end of the novel after Perón's death, when one of the General's "daughters" "realized that the instant the casket disappeared from the screen they would all be left orphans forever. . . . Doña Luisa believed that anything was possible, that it only had to be said for it to happen: "Resurrect, big man! What's to stop you?" (423/357). As the reader leaves her embracing the television screen we must be reminded of Zamora's comment, "The past is something unreal here, like a movie screen. Every instant a new (and worse) exploit of reality changes it. It can't even be oblivion [*olvido*]" (242/204). Zamora expresses the problem of historical representation in Argentina and cinema's depthless screen becomes the figure for the unreality of history under such conditions as were lived in the region in the seventies and eighties.

Martínez's novel, also like *Respiración artificial* and like Marx's works, attempts to renegotiate the course of history, of society. But it does so neither by creating an elitist, utopian space that will somehow uplift the degraded detritus around it—the avant-gardist project of the boom of Latin American modernism—nor by reducing it to a best-selling patina of pastiched styles from another moment in history—the problem of "historiographic metafiction" or "postmodern fantastic historiographies." Rather it does so by *respiración artificial*: resuscitating not the dead General but the petrified image that the General carefully left behind; by appropriating *citas* not as dogma and doctrine but as living and life-giving letters to the future.

Conclusion

8

Speculations Toward
Articulating Latin American
Postmodernities

Near the end of chapter 1, I cautioned that the transition from modernity to postmodernity that I would be tracking on the site of Argentine fiction might look rather different if it were tracked instead in Central American poetry, or in Brazilian television. I also expressed my belief that no single volume could possibly accommodate all the different lines along which this transition could or should be tracked. Consequently, I wrote this book in the tension between the ungeneralizably particular, Argentine fiction from 1960 to the present, and the incomprehensibly general, Latin American modernity to Argentine postmodernity. Let me now, perhaps too speculatively, figure that tension more concretely by articulating the Argentine postmodernity I have been describing with two other postmodernities in Latin America. The two lines I will follow from my point of departure in Argentine narrative—one along a geographical axis to Central American writing and politics and the other along a formal and gender axis to women's writing and political activity in Argentina during the same period— must be understood as only two of many intersecting lines that could be traced from innumerable points of departure to equally countless points of destination across the region and perhaps beyond.

Let me also first elaborate on what I have already emphasized at various points throughout this book. The possibility of "Latin America" as a conceptual or political signifier with a real referent was a hallmark of the revolutionary Left during the period I have characterized as Latin American modernity. The subsequent shattering of this Left in the seventies brought with it a crisis in the semantic validity of the term. Today, we are faced, on the one hand, with the bourgeois, free-marketeer attempt to retake the term as a signifier for a regionally unified market and, on the other hand, with the progressive intellectual concern for homogenizing important intraregional differences under the heading of "Latin America."

What follows in this concluding chapter may thus be taken as an attempt to dialectically respond to this bind. I wish neither to abandon the term to the apologists of free-market capitalism nor to wish my way back to the 1960s, when Latin America was a term that made sense on the Left. Instead, I want to try to demonstrate how the term can regain provisional meaning in relation to a heterogeneous group of political and cultural phenomena that share the features I have already highlighted in the Argentine case.

It would appear at first glance that little could be further from the sophisticated novels of Cortázar, Puig, Piglia, and Martínez—geographically, politically, and culturally speaking—than the *testimonios,* or testimonial narratives, of Central America.[1] Testimonial narratives are first-person narrations of a real individual's experiences during a significant event or period in his or her country's history. They are unusual because the protagonist/narrator is often illiterate. They thus orally narrate their life story—sometimes in response to questions—to an interlocutor, often a writer, journalist, anthropologist, or political activist. The interlocutor records, transcribes, and edits the oral narrative and, usually, takes charge of the procedures involved in publication.

Surely when we here in the United States think of Latin American resistance culture, it is these *testimonios* that spring immediately to mind. In an apparently straightforward first-person narrative these texts tell the grimly triumphant stories of individual and emergent collective subjects struggling on a daily basis to transform their conditions of existence. For the most part, their celebrated reception not only by Latin Americanist critics but by the public at large, derives from an appreciation for the difficulties involved in this incursion of the genuinely popular into the realm of high culture. Especially for early celebrants of the form, *testimonio* was different because it was a representation by, of, and for the people; in marked contrast to the well-intentioned but finally colonizing representations offered by better-known cultural elites.[2] At the same time, the entrance into the previously exclusive domain of written expression in Latin America is hailed for its invigorating and transformative effects on the institution of literature. For more contemporary critics then, the *testimonio* is remarkable less for the changes it signals within literature than for its explosion of the very institution. *Testimonio,* it is argued, is not a representation at all, but rather a practice: the practice of identity-formation.[3] If nothing else, this view seems supported by the Nobel Prize committee's decision to award one testimonial author—Guatemala's Rigoberta Menchú—their prestigious award, not for literature but for peace.[4]

All this may suggest that the *testimonio* conforms more to Jameson's notion of those resistant, but not postmodern, cultural forms emerging from the Third World.[5] But there may also be grounds and good reasons for viewing the *testimonio* as a form of Latin American postmodern cultural resistance.[6] The appearance of simplicity and authenticity are belied by both the complex system of mediations involved in the production of the *testimonio* and by sophisticated narrative techniques employed by the protagonist/narrator.[7] Indeed, the resistance value of the *testimonio* as cultural practice and artifact, far from resting on either its transparently realistic openness or its arepresentational identity-forming praxis, seems rather to derive from the tension between these practically unrealizable theoretical poles. That is, even the most apparently realistic representation involves an interpretive transformation of reality into the cultural medium. At the same time, the identity-forming dimension of the *testimonio* depends on its representational dimension. If the *testimonio* did not represent to the protagonist/narrator, to her people, and to a general public a plausible "truth" about their lives, its political efficacy would be extremely limited. Only by sustaining the tension between openness, or transparency and opacity can the *testimonio* function as resistance in the broad circles it has.

Thus, like the Argentine *historias* it is not the *testimonio's* uncontaminated positing of some pure, truthful, native history that makes them so powerful, but their subversion of such a project. This may or may not run counter to the *testimonialista's* own beliefs or intentions regarding their project. In the case of Rigoberta Menchú, her migration into ever-widening circles outside her native culture—first she learns Spanish, then she learns to read, then she travels to France, etc.—would suggest a recognition of the fact that it is only the mutability of the form given different contexts that ensures its continued viability as a form of cultural resistance. Indeed, confirmation of this notion comes, surprisingly and perhaps unfortunately, from the neoconservative cultural observer Dinesh D'Souza. For *Me llamo Rigoberta Menchú y así me nació la conciencia* (the title of Menchú's *testimonio*) figures prominently in his harangue on curriculum revision at Stanford University. What bothers him so much—and it is the intensity of his irritation that I take as an index of the efficacy of this *testimonio*—is not that she tells a different version of Guatemalan history. It is rather that she both presents the appearance of being a "genuine" Guatemalan Indian and frustrates our expectations with regard to the proper contents of such an identity. She tricks us by being a Euro–North American Marxist and feminist in Indian's clothing.[8] Not the stability of her identity nor the fixed truth of her discourse, but the protean character of these confounds D'Souza and lends her work such "dangerous" power.

The notion of representation behind this view of *testimonio* is, I believe, a uniquely postmodern one in that it sheds the utopian absolutism of

both realist (representation as transparency) and modernist (representation as opacity) stances on the function of representation. Ernest Laclau
has articulated this view in the context of political representation as part
of his understanding of the post-Marxist (and postmodernist) "radical
democracy":

> Representation cannot simply be the transmission belt of a will that has already
> been constituted, but must involve the construction of something new. There is
> thus a double process: on the one hand, to exist as such, a representation cannot
> operate completely behind the back of the person represented; and on the
> other, to be a representation at all requires the articulation of something new
> which is not just provided by the identity of what is being represented. . . .
> absolute representation, the total transparency between the representative and
> the represented, means the extinction of the relationship of representation. If
> the representative and represented constitute the same and single will, the "re-"
> of representation disappears since the same will is present in two different
> places. Representation can therefore only exist to the extent that the trans-
> parency entailed by the concept is never achieved; and that a permanent dis-
> location exists between the representative and the represented.[9]

For representation to exist, and the efficacy of the *testimonio* requires that it
does, Menchú cannot be identical to the oppressed of Guatemala and the
testimonio can be identical to neither her spoken testimony nor the experiences of identity-formation that it narrates. Thus it is not necessary that
representation be abandoned in order for the *testimonio* to function as a
resistant, community-forming practice. On the contrary, it is essential that
representation (in Laclau's "translucent" or "impure" postmodern sense)
be operant for the *testimonio* as practice to fulfill itself. And this view is
precisely the one behind the subversions of history we find in *Respiración
artificial*.

This theoretical justification for articulating the *testimonio* to the Latin
American postmodernity of Argentine narrative is complemented by a
more properly historical one. Consider the Sandinista revolution in Nicaragua. The link between *testimonio* and revolutionary struggle is not one
that needs to be reestablished. *Testimonio* emerged out of the cultural
developments following the Cuban revolution and it accompanied, as in
Mechú's case, both successful and less successful revolutionary struggles
in Central America. But the February 1990 electoral defeat of the Sandinistas in Nicaragua, together with both the wave of guerrilla groups turn-

ing in their arms for ballots throughout Latin America and the dismantling of communist regimes in Eastern Europe, have raised questions about the future of revolutionary struggles in Latin America and, thus, about the future of a cultural form that seemed to draw its urgent force from those struggles.

But on my reading, the *testimonio* involved either a departure from or a redefinition of (I tend toward the latter) revolutionary culture. Its ambiguity and power in such a variety of contexts far exceeds the limits imposed by official restrictions on culture production in revolutionary societies such as Cuba. But if the *testimonio* redefines revolutionary culture with, if we are to believe Laclau, a decidedly democratic—though not bourgeois—inflection, then perhaps we can reevaluate not only its future and its relationship to seemingly dormant revolutionary tendencies in Central America, but the very status of those tendencies themselves. In the case of the Sandinistas an evaluation of the electoral defeat must be made in the context of world events, particularly those unfolding since the defeat. Given the overwhelming tide of international sentiment, it's hard to see the Sandinistas' capitulation to even an unfair electoral process as anything other than a strategically foresightful move. Consider the consequence of rejecting electoral arrangements: the protraction and intensification of a civil war not likely to end, especially given the new U.S. president Bill Clinton's continuation of Reagan-Bush policies toward Cuba and the rest of the region. Instead, the Sandinistas submitted to an election whose results, whatever their distortions by U.S. involvement, did reflect, as Beverley points out, the partial breakdown of the "identification between a radicalized intelligentsia . . . and the popular sectors."[10] But beyond this, the election signified a strategic retreat from an unwinnable position in favor of one that would secure first the continued existence and effectiveness of the Sandinista front, and second, and more importantly, its favorable public image as a flexible social force most interested in leaving a democratic legacy, even at the expense of its own power. Events in Nicaragua since the election suggest that the possibility of a return of Sandinista power, this time through internationally sanctioned elections, is not so far-fetched.[11] In the event of such a development, the United States may not be in the same position internationally to offer the kind of gruesome response with which it greeted Salvador Allende's UP government in Chile two decades ago. Thus, as I suggested in chapter 1, the recent trajectory of the Sandinistas in Nicaragua bespeaks a particular kind of postmodern, radical democratic practice in Latin America, one visible also in social movements throughout the region, and one whose cultural expression we may see in certain versions of the *testimonio* as well in the Argentine *historias*.

Having traced this line—of cultural impurity and radical democracy—from the Southern Cone to Central America, I want now to return, specifically, to the group of women known as the Madres de la Plaza de Mayo who hastened the abdication of the *Proceso*.[12] The Madres were initially a group of fourteen middle-aged women, mothers (and grandmothers) of course, whose paths had crossed too often in their search for loved ones disappeared by the *Proceso*. They gathered together, for the first time in April of 1977 and each Thursday thereafter, before the government house demanding "aparición con vida" (appearance with life) and "juicio y castigo a todos los culpables" (justice and punishment for all the guilty). Their numbers quickly grew, and by 1982 one of their marches drew five thousand demonstrators. May I note, before signaling what I believe to be the most important features of the movement—at least in the present context—the stunning courage of the participants. The mothers, powerless in Argentine society according to traditional political codes—silent, gathered to confront a power that, at the time, seemed to most to be total in its power and savagery.

The first point I want to make about the group relates to the question of history under the *Proceso*. For the Madres might be seen as restoring body and voice to the absences and silences produced by the military's occupation of the field of historical discourse. Marching in the face of the regime, carrying photos and names of their disappeared children, the Madres literally challenged and rewrote *la historia official*.[13] If the military had engaged in what seemed like the perfect repressive act—repressing not only the opposition but also the act of repression itself—and suspended history in the process, the Madres set history back in motion again by bringing to light the signs of the military's repression (the photos of their missing children), by resuscitating the memory of their loved ones. Their strategy and its effectiveness were made possible, I think, by the coincidence of two factors. First, the military's unprecedented suffusion of private lives with its ostensibly public policies, and second, the Madres traditional role as the guardians of this private sphere. Their resistance was, in a sense, sanctioned by the patriarchal bourgeois distinction that, in Latin America perhaps more than elsewhere, divides a public sphere from a private and assigns men custody of the former and women custody of the latter. Thus, when the military encroached on the former in so dramatic a way—through its disappearances—the mothers had a "legitimate" stake in reclaiming this territory.

For some Latin American feminists, these were ultimately crippling bases on which to form a women's social movement.[14] Grounding themselves on their claim to the private sphere and thus reinforcing the distinction, the mothers set themselves up to be hastily redispatched to that sphere once the military had "withdrawn from it." Indeed, the extent to which the mothers' demands went, and continue to go, unmet indicates the degree to which other groups and official political parties, who had attached themselves to the mothers' initial struggle, dominated the post-abdication public sphere and relegated the mothers to a marginal, even apparently extremist, position. It is difficult to counter these arguments if one measures the success of a social movement by its ability to enter existing public structures for the expression of needs.

Before addressing this objection directly, it can be usefully studied by examining the representation of the problem in some Argentine women's writing from the period. Take, for example, the case of the late Marta Traba. Traba is not so well known in U.S. literary circles as, for example, Luisa Valenzuela. George Yúdice had convincingly argued that this is in part due to the fact that Valenzuela's writing more reassuringly fills a need on the part of U.S. progressives to see Third-World women writers as dissidents that explicitly address the horrors of political expression, particularly as they affect women.[15] This may be the case. Traba's writing certainly seems more oblique and internally directed. It is not that her characters live only private lives, or that they are somehow insulated from public violence. Rather, it is that she represents them not at the height of their enmeshment with the public but afterward, when they must struggle to integrate their difficult encounters with the public with a now unrecognizably deformed private life. Let's look for a moment at her posthumously published *En cualquier lugar.*[16]

The characters in *En cualquier lugar* have suffered a catastrophic, violent defeat in their own country. This has left individuals terrified of living their routine daily lives, let alone a more explicitly political form of life. They find themselves dispersed in different areas of a large city in a foreign country whose language they do not speak. They are exiles. Exile, the title of the novel suggests, is fundamentally a spatial problem, specifically a problem of spatial dislocation. From one's native land, where one might have felt centered, one is propelled to a foreign land in which one becomes marginal with respect not just to the natives of that foreign land but also to those remaining behind in the exile's homeland. Enrique Ossorio, in *Respiración artificial,* you may recall, added to this spatial dislocation a temporal dimension: the exile has a nostalgia for a future—that is, for a future in which the spatial dislocation is repaired. This spatial and temporal marginality, then, becomes a central motif in the novel, expressed even on the first page when Mariana notes her own acute sense of detail. Even the exiled torturer, Torres, becomes marginal as he wanders the avenues of the new city, glued to the walls, longing for the narrow streets of the native country in which his presence was more dominating.

For both Torres and the more positive characters in the novel, this marginality also expresses itself as a loss of control. In the spatial sense, they find great relief in knowing where they are, this knowledge being an indicator of well-being, or at least of survival. Everyday, or private, life ultimately becomes the sphere in which this sense of control can be best nurtured. There, one can converse simply and freely, or children can play without fear. These private activities become events to be celebrated in this novel. Of course, the heightened self-consciousness of private activities also indicates the abnormality of their situations. How does one live in a situation and in a place where the everyday becomes extraordinary? The darker implications of this reveals itself most grimly when the elder of Alicia's two sons, Emiliano, threatens his younger brother with being returned to the station (through which they first arrived and will presumably return to the homeland).

Understanding the full force of this threat requires us to view this situation as not only an individual tragedy, but one of a collective, struggling to maintain its coherence as it passes through a hurricane of historical forces pulling it in various directions. These *directions*—which are both political in the sense of strategies and temporal in the sense of futures—are, appropriately enough, figured as material locales, spaces, in the novel: there is *la estación,* where they arrived and where a large group of exiles continue to plan for their return, there is *la tipografía* of Ana Cruz, *la pieza* of Mariana. Alongside these, there are the spaces more eccentric to the exiles' new lives: the new city's bustling center and the homeland. *La estación* becomes concretely and symbolically the exiles' public sphere and it is primarily occupied by men. By contrast, both *la tipografía* and *la pieza* are the places to redevelop a private sphere and they are occupied by women and their children. Emiliano's threat to send his little brother back to the station then, is a threat to exile him from the private to the public.

But this needn't be a bad thing. Indeed, according to the critics of the

Madres de la Plaza de Mayo, it is precisely the trajectory that a resistance movement must take. This view is shared by the men in the novel. For them, setting up shop as Ana Cruz literally does, or making oneself at home, as Mariana attempts to do, implies acceptance of the new situation, a renunciation of the struggle. Consequently, the men insist on remaining at the station where they plan strategies for clandestine resistance and their eventually triumphant return to the homeland. In a sense, they seem right. Certainly, Emiliano's little brother's fear largely comes, I think, from the instability associated with the station, sharply contrasted with the permanence, stability, and "normality" of his daily, private life at home.

This gender and politically inflected opposition between these spaces also takes on, in the present context, a certain historical dimension. At least, the men and their strategies are clearly marked as antiquated. Or perhaps, if antiquated is too strong a term, as not keeping pace with the exigencies of their concrete conditions of existence in the present. There is the sense that the men, in response to the defeat of the strategies associated with the leftist movements of the Latin American sixties and early seventies, simply replot those same strategies from exile. And the problem is not merely that they won't work from exile, but that they won't work because of the conditions that have forced the exile: the emergence of an unprecedented terrorist state in their homeland. Only through a massive denial—or repression—of the depth of this state's violence, can the men bracket their private lives and attempt to retake the public sphere in unmodified terms.

The women by contrast are painfully aware of the private damage—figured as physical violation in the case of Flora, who ultimately takes her own life—done by the regime. Their response seems to suggest not only that a *certain,* modernist, kind of public resistance is outdated, but perhaps more broadly that public resistance in general must, under these conditions, pass through and be inseparable from private healing. The concrete challenges the private women's spaces in the novel direct against the more conventionally political figures—Vázquez, Luis, and the other—recast the terms of a debate over what constitutes a collective, resistance, freedom, place, and survival. Thus the opposition between public and private—which both Piglia and Martínez challenged by publicizing private figure and events and privatizing public ones—becomes a prime locus for understanding the novelty of both cultural resistance and the new social movements and the importance of women in them. The assertion that women's writing or political practice in Latin American postmodernity turns on a recasting of the debate over public and private need not rest on any kind of essentialism. Rather, what seems to be involved is a kind of historical sub-version. Women in Latin America have been traditionally assigned—both in life and in literature, as characters and authors—private roles. Thus, rather than rejecting that role entirely and aiming at an occupation of the public sphere, writers such as Marta Traba and Cristina Peri Rossi, and activists such as the Madres, seem to be redefining the public sphere in terms of the private sphere, and consequently redefining the private sphere in terms of the public.[17] Perhaps a figure such as Rigoberta Menchú goes even further. While making the same kind of subversion of public and private (she renarrates her private life as a public one, and the nation's public events as private), she may also emblematize the kind of practice that also ultimately subverts, as I would argue the *historias* of Argentina do, the distinction between writing or culture and political practice.[18]

But let us also attempt to address the objections raised with respect to the Madres more directly. What if part of the significance of new social movements involves their redefinition of success? Perhaps they overcome, in concrete practice, the dichotomies that have long vexed Latin American politics: between a revolutionary fervor that brooks no compromise with an existing society and a bland and acquiescent reformism that all too often leaves fundamental structures unchanged.[19] Perhaps the fact that move-ments like the mothers' failed to integrate itself and its demands into a traditional public sphere and its dominant political organs is not, or at least not exclusively, a symptom of failure. Perhaps instead, or also, it can signify a strategic decision to remain in what Arditi called the "social"—the more fluid, less easily monitored regions adjacent to society's institutions. From this position, the mothers may have felt themselves—for the moment, I stress—to have a greater purchase on the political system and to better preserve the coherence of their demands. At any rate, rather than clearly remaining in the private sphere and so dooming themselves to fail to enter the public sphere, the mothers seem to me to challenge the dichotomy between public and private sphere, but without dissolving one into the other.[20]

This second point about the Madres and new social movements brings us back to questions raised by Latin American theorists of postmodernity in chapter 1 regarding the preconditions for progressive political action. For the mothers lacked any kind of formal program or theoretical basis—a fact probably not unrelated to their striking "audacity." They were unaffili-ated with any political party or social class. Rather, they coalesced—with-out any hand-wringing over lack of identity or unity, or any of the other prerequisites for political action so favored by many of us in the United States—in the face of a crisis with a simple desire: to have their missing children brought back to them alive. Of course, although they never abandoned this demand, they were able to accommodate new demands in the face of new crises. For example, they were among the first to publicly denounce, via the rhetoric of motherhood, the junta's militarism in the Malvinas (Falkland Islands) War with Britain. Moreover, their flexibility extended to forming coalitions with different prodemocracy and human-rights groups. Though at the same time they maintained the integrity of their position never yielding on certain issues, especially with regard to amnesty for the military and justice for the victims, issues the larger coalition eventually conceded to the abdicating junta. They were thus a diverse group, socioeconomically and ideologically, they were situational in both origin and demands, and—a coalition themselves—they eventually joined in larger coalitions, though often with crucial differences, demanding a halt to state terrorism and the return of democracy.

Judith Butler has written:

> The insistence in advance on coalitional "unity" as a goal assumes that solidarity, whatever its price, is a prerequisite for political action. But what sort of politics demands that kind of advance purchase on unity? Perhaps a coalition needs to acknowledge its contradictions and take action with those contradictions intact. Perhaps also part of what dialogic understanding entails is the acceptance of divergence, breakage, splinter, and fragmentation as part of the often torturous process of democratization. . . . Without the presupposition or goal of "unity," which is . . . always instituted at a conceptual level, provisional unities might emerge in the context of concrete actions that have purposes other than the articulation of identity.[21]

The project Butler theorizes seems to be already in progress in those realms of cultural politics I have just quickly sketched. The notion of a concrete and radical social politics of fragmentation—irreducible, contrary to its detractors' claims, to an exclusively textual variety of poststructuralism— might finally be the more abstract, theoretical image superimposed over these various locales and practices of resistances. Ernesto Laclau has written that "the radicality of a politics will not result from the emergence of a subject that can embody the universal, but from the expansion and multiplication of the fragmentary, partial and limited subjects who enter the collective decision-making process."[22] Such assertions have come under heavy attack from certain quarters of the Left today. But perhaps in Latin

America, at least in Argentina, such a politics may have resonance and reach unimaginable to us in the First World today. Jean Franco has written that "movements such as those of the mothers cannot be reproduced or essentialized. If we can learn anything from them, it is that they raise questions which may not have a single correct answer."[23] Following Franco's speculations, we might conclude that the oppositional politics of Latin American postmodernism renounce "the discourse of the universal and its implicit assumption of a privileged point of access to 'the truth,' which can be reached only by a limited number of subjects."[24]

I believe this intensely and concretely oppositional postmodern critique of identity politics finds expression in the *historias* of Argentina, which retain the oppositional impulses of an earlier generation without reproducing their absolutist presuppositions. The *historias,* like Piglia's, were not resistant because they stridently asserted an alternative history drawn gleaming with truth from the mire of repressive pseudo-histories. They resisted, rather, because they recognized and narrated—from their own painful experience of catastrophe—the project of remaking history, of reconstructing the future, as an ongoing and impure process; a process involving the recognition of limits, gaps, and compromises. But they also resisted because the history they embodied was not a history to be learned and slavishly followed, but one generated as the process of a group of subjects' confronting the present as the future of the past and as the past of the future.

Notes

Preface and Acknowledgments

1 George Yúdice, "¿Puede hablarse de postmodernidad en américa latina?" *Revista de crítica literaria latinoamericana* 29 (1er semestre de 1989): 109.

2 Nancy Fraser, "Rethinking the Public Sphere: A Contribution to the Critique of Actually Existing Democracy," *Social Text* 25/26 (1990): 56.

3 C. L. R. James, *Notes on Dialectics: Hegel-Marx-Lenin*, 1948 (Westport, Conn.: Lawrence Hill, 1980), 15.

4 For thorough catalogues of such gestures by critics as well known as Gerald Graff, Charles Russell, James Mellard, Christopher Butler, Ihab Hassan, and John Barth, see Carlos Rincón, "Modernidad periférica y el desafío de lo postmoderno: perspectivas del arte narrativo latinoamericano," *Revista de crítica literaria latinoamericana* 29 (1er semestre de 1989): 61–104 and Jorge Ruffinelli, "Los 80: ¿Ingreso a la posmodernidad?," *Nuevo Texto Crítico* 6 (año 3, segundo semestre de 1990): 31–42. And for a similar catalogue, but focusing on cultural studies, see George Yúdice, "Marginality and the Ethics of Survival," in *Universal Abandon? The Politics of Postmodernism,* ed. Andrew Ross (Minneapolis: University of Minnesota Press, 1988), 214–36 and *"Testimonio* and Postmodernism," *Latin American Perspectives* 70 (Summer 1991): 15–31.

1 Resisting Postmodernity

1 A bibliography of Hutcheon's work, excluding the numerous and well-attended conference lectures she has given, as well as widely circulated and programmatic journal essays, includes *Narcissistic Narrative: The Metafictional Paradox* (1980; reprint, New York: Methuen, 1984); *A Theory of Parody: The Teachings of Twentieth-Century Art Forms* (New York: Methuen, 1985); *The Poetics of Postmodernism: History, Theory, Fiction* (New York: Routledge, 1988); *Canadian Postmodernism* (New York: Oxford University Press, 1988); *The Politics of Postmodernism* (New York: Routledge, 1989); and *Splitting Images: Contemporary Canadian Ironies* (New York: Oxford University Press, 1991). All quotations from *A Poetics of Postmodernism* will be hereafter cited parenthetically in the text.

2 For a useful essay outlining the various strains of literary postmodernism in Europe and the United States, see Hans Bertens, "The Postmodern *Weltan-*

schauung and Its Relations with Modernism: An Introductory Survey," in *Approach Postmodernism*, ed. Douwe Fokkema and Hans Bertens (Amsterdam: John Benjamins, 1986), 9–52.

3 Michael Speaks has also traced Hutcheon's exclusions to the architectural model of postmodernism on which she depends in a manuscript he generously shared with me. It was later published as "Modernizing Postmodern Literature: Historiographic Metafiction and the 'Downtown Writing,'" *Dagens Nyuter* (Stockholm, Sweden) 27 April 1991, Lorsdag (Saturday): "Kultur & Nöjen," 23.

4 Fredric Jameson, *Postmodernism, or, The Cultural Logic of Late Capitalism* (Durham, N.C.: Duke University Press, 1990), 3 and 45–47. References to this work will hereafter be included parenthetically in the text. See also Jameson's comments to Anders Stephanson in the interview published under the title "Regarding Postmodernism—A Conversation with Fredric Jameson," *Social Text* 17 (Fall 1987): 29–54.

5 Fredric Jameson, "Periodizing the 60s," in *The 60s Without Apology*, ed. Sohnya Sayres et al. (Minneapolis: University of Minnesota Press and *Social Text*, 1984), 207.

6 Fredric Jameson, "Postmodernism and Utopia," in *Utopia Post-Utopia: Configurations of Nature and Culture in Recent Sculpture and Photography* (Boston: Institute of Contemporary Art, 1988), 14. See Jameson, *Postmodernism*, 307–11, for a similar discussion of historicity in modernism.

7 Fredric Jameson, *The Political Unconscious: Narrative as a Socially Symbolic Act* (Ithaca, N.Y.: Cornell University Press, 1981), 9.

8 I cannot resist including Jean Baudrillard's description for comparison with the previously cited passages from Jameson: "Our 'modern' civilisations have existed on a base of expansion and explosion at all levels, under the sign of universalised commerce, of economic and philosophical investments, under the sign of universal law and conquest. Undoubtedly even they have known how to survive, for a time at least, on a *controlled explosion*, on a liberation of subdued and progressive energy, and this was the golden age of their culture. But according to a process of boom and acceleration, this explosive process has become uncontrollable, it has acquired a fatal speed or amplitude, or rather it has reached the limits of the universal, it has saturated the field of possible expansion and, just as primitive societies were ravaged by explosion for not knowing how to curb the implosive process any longer, so our culture begins to be ravaged by implosion for not having known how to curb and equilibrate the explosive process." Jean Baudrillard, *In the Shadow of the Silent Majorities or, The End of the Social and Other Essays*, trans. Paul Foss, John Johnston, and Paul Patton (New York: Semiotext(e), 1983), 59–60.

9 Fredric Jameson, "Third World Literature in the Era of Multinational Capitalism," *Social Text* 15 (Fall 1986): 65–66; an essay that Jameson in a footnote (88) called a "pendant" to his general theory of postmodernism. This essay has generated far more detailed criticism than I can do justice to here. See, for central texts,

Aijaz Ahmad, "Jameson's Rhetoric of Otherness and the 'National Allegory,'"
Social Text 17 (Fall 1987): 3–25; Henry Schwarz, "Provocations Toward a Theory
of Third World Literature," *Mississippi Review* 49/50 (1989): 177–201, and most
recently and compellingly, Madhava Prasad, "On the Question of a Theory of
(Third World) Literature," *Social Text* 31/32 (1992): 57–83.

10 This sense is given if one substitutes "utopia" for "history" (and their respective variants, of course) in the following passage: "Historical representation is just
as surely in crisis . . . The most intelligent 'solution' to such a crisis does not consist
in abandoning historiography altogether, as an impossible aim and an ideological
category all at once, but rather . . . in reorganizing its traditional procedures on a
different level. Althusser's proposal seems the wisest in this situation: . . . the historian should reformulate her vocation—not any longer to produce some vivid representation of History 'as it really happened,' but rather to produce the *concept* of
history." Jameson, "Periodizing the 60s," 180.

11 See Pedro Henriquez Ureña's classic literary history of Latin America, *Literary
Currents in Hispanic America* (1945; reprint, New York: Russell and Russell, 1963).
Other classical texts in Latin Americanist cultural studies that usefully trace this
phenomenon include Irving A. Leonard, *Books of the Brave: Being an account of
books and men in the Spanish conquest and settlement of the 16th century new world*
(Cambridge, Mass.: Harvard University Press, 1949); Edmundo O'Gorman, *La
idea del descubrimiento de América: historia de esa interpretación y crítica de sus fundamentos* (México: Centro de estudios filosóficos, 1951) and *La invención de América:
El universalismo de la cultura de occidente* (México: Fondo de cultura económica,
1958).

12 For a history of radical geography, see Edward Soja's standard account, *Postmodern Geographies: The Reassertion of Space in Critical Social Theory* (London:
Verso, 1989).

13 Karl Marx and Frederick Engels, *Manifesto of the Communist Party* vol. 6 of
Karl Marx–Frederick Engels Collected Works (New York: International Publishers,
1976), 6:503.

14 V. I. Lenin, *Imperialism, The Highest Stage of Capitalism* (1916; reprint, Peking:
Foreign Languages Press, 1973), 76.

15 Samir Amin, *Unequal Development: An Essay on the Social Formations of Peripheral Capitalism,* trans. Brian Pearce (New York: Monthly Review, 1976), 9.

16 See Anthony Brewer, *Marxist Theories of Imperialism: An Critical Survey* (1980;
reprint, New York: Routledge and Kegan Paul, 1987), 158–59.

17 Neil Smith, *Uneven Development: Nature, Capital and the Production of Space*
(Oxford: Basil Blackwell, 1984), 152.

18 Arjun Appadurai, "Disjuncture and Difference in the Global Cultural Economy," *Public Culture* 2, no. 2 (Spring 1990): 6.

19 Ernest Mandel, *Late Capitalism,* trans. Joris DeBres (1975; reprint, London:
Verso, 1987), 102.

20 Norbert Lechner, "Some People Die of Fear: Fear as a Political Problem," in *Fear at the Edge: State Terror and Resistance in Latin America,* ed. Juan E. Corradi, Patricia Weiss Fagen, and Manuel Antonio Garretón (Berkeley and Los Angeles: University of California Press, 1992), 28. For an already standard analysis of the effects of modernization and modernity on Buenos Aires, see Beatriz Sarlo, *Una modernidad periférica: Buenos Aires 1920–1930* (Buenos Aires: Ediciones Nueva Visión, 1988).

21 Karl Marx, *Grundrisse* vol. 28 of *Karl Marx–Frederick Engels Collected Works* (New York: International Publishers, 1986), 28:201.

22 Ibid., 337, last emphasis added.

23 David Harvey, *The Limits to Capital* (Chicago: University of Chicago Press, 1982), 416, emphasis added. See also Harvey's *The Condition of Postmodernity* (Oxford: Basil Blackwell, 1989). For similar observations, but situated within a different disciplinary framework, see the "French regulationist school" work of Alain Lipietz, *Mirages and Miracles: The Crises of Global Fordism,* trans. David Macey (London: Verso, 1987) and Michel Aglietta, *A Theory of Capitalist Regulation: The U.S. Experience,* trans. David Fernbach (1979; reprint, London: Verso, 1987).

24 For accounts of contemporary capitalism stressing its disorganized nature, see Scott Lash and John Urry, *The End of Organized Capitalism* (Madison: University of Wisconsin Press, 1987) and Claus Offe, *Disorganized Capitalism: Contemporary Transformations of Work and Politics* (Cambridge, Mass.: MIT Press, 1985).

25 Michael Speaks, "Chaos, Simulation and Corporate Culture," *Mississippi Review* 49/50 (1989): 166.

26 Marx, *Grundrisse* 28:451–52.

27 Speaks, "Chaos," 166.

28 See, for example, Marx and Engels, *Manifesto,* 496.

29 Arturo Escobar, "Imagining a Post-Development Era? Critical Thought, Development and Social Movements," *Social Text* 31/32 (1992): 20.

30 Benjamín Arditi, "Una gramática postmoderna para pensar lo social," in *Cultura, política, y democratización,* ed. Norbert Lechner (Santiago de Chile: FLACSO/CLACSO/ICI, 1987), 170.

31 See Jürgen Habermas, "Modernity—An Incomplete Project," in *The Anti-Aesthetic: Essays in Postmodern Culture,* ed. Hal Foster and trans. Seyla Ben-Habib (Port Townsend, Wash.: Bay Press, 1983), 3–15.

32 It seems worth noting that in U.S. politics during the summer of 1992, a crisis of the two-party system and the shift from "voter apathy" to "voter anger"—both manifested in the groundswell of support for the candidacy of Ross Perot—opened, but left largely unrealized, possibilities for redefining democracy. See articles by Ralph Nader, Sandy Pope and Joel Rogers, and Lawrence Goodwyn in *Nation* 255, no. 3 (20–27 July 1992): 98–102, 102–5, and 114–17.

33 Even some of the most respected Latin Americanist critics fall into these positions. Roberto González Echevarría's otherwise remarkable reading of Severo Sarduy is probably the best-known example of the insufficiently critical application of the stylistic checklists of postmodernism theory to Latin American writers. See his *La ruta de Severo Sarduy* (Hanover, N.H.: Ediciones del Norte, 1987). On the other hand, Neil Larsen has consistently rejected postmodernism theory as a foreign and imperialist discourse incapable of accounting for Latin American reality. See his "Posmodernismo e Imperialismo: Teoría y Política en América Latina," *Nuevo Texto Crítico* 6 (año 3, segundo semestre de 1990): 77–94 and *Modernism and Hegemony: A Materialist Critique of Aesthetic Agency* (Minneapolis: University of Minnesota Press, 1990), especially the introduction and chapters 4 and 5. For contributions specifically addressing these positions and the "problem" of "importing" postmodernism theory into Latin America, see Yúdice, "¿Puede hablarse?" and John Beverley and José Oviedo, "Postmodernism and Latin America," *boundary 2*, 20 no. 3 (1993): 1–17, special issue on "The Postmodernism Debate in Latin America."

34 See, for example, Seymour Martin Lipset and Aldo Solari, *Elites in Latin America* (New York: Oxford University Press, 1967). See also Peter F. Klarén and Thomas J. Bossert, eds., *Promise of Development: Theories of Change in Latin America,* esp. the editors' concise discussion of modernization theory in the introduction, "Lost Promises: Explaining Latin American Underdevelopment," 9–14.

35 See Klarén and Bossert, *Promise of Development,* 9 and Cristóbal Kay, *Latin American Theories of Development and Underdevelopment* (London: Routledge, 1989), 6.

36 "Metropolis and satellite" come from Andre Gunder Frank's *Capitalism and Underdevelopment in Latin America: Historical Studies of Chile and Brazil* (New York: Monthly Review Press, 1967), 8–12. See also his *Latin America: Underdevelopment or Revolution* (New York: Monthly Review Press, 1969). Not only does the title betray this dualistic thinking, so also do chapter titles such as "Sociology of Development and Underdevelopment of Sociology," "Functionalism and Dialectics," "Economic Politics or Political Economy," "Liberal Anthropology vs. Liberation Anthropology," and "Aid or Exploitation." "Core and periphery" are developed in Immanuel Wallerstein's "world systems" theory. See his *Capitalist World Economy* (1979; reprint, Cambridge: Cambridge University Press, 1987), esp. pt. 1 on "The Inequalities of Core and Periphery."

37 For a general collection with region- and problem-specific essays, see *Industria, Estado, y Sociedad. La reestructuración industrial en América Latina y Europa* (Caracas: EURAL/Centro de Investigaciones Europeo-Latinoamericanos y Fundación Friedrich Ebert and Argentina, 1989). But see also essays in *Sociological Forum* 4, no. 4 (1990); Sistema Económico Latinoamericano, ed., *El FMI, El banco mundial, y la crisis latinoamericana* (México: Siglo vientiuno, 1986); Atilio A. Boron, *Estado, Capitalismo, y Democracia en América Latina* (Buenos Aires: Ediciones Imago Mundi, 1991); Michael Stohl and Harry R. Targ, eds., *The Global Political Economy* *in the 1980s* (Cambridge, Mass.: Schenkman Publishing, 1982); Michael Peter Smith and Joe R. Feagin, eds., *The Capitalist City* (Oxford: Basil Blackwell, 1987); Alejandro Portes, Manuel Castells, and Lauren A. Benton, eds., *The Informal Economy: Studies in Advanced and Less Developed Countries* (Baltimore: Johns Hopkins University Press, 1989); and Mike Davis, *City of Quartz: Excavating the Future in Los Angeles* (London: Verso, 1990).

38 See Ernesto Laclau, *New Reflections on the Revolution of Our Time* (London: Verso, 1990), 41–59; Martin Hopenhayn, "El debate postmoderno y la dimensión cultural del desarrollo," unpublished typescript, (ILPES), 16; and Norbert Lechner, "Un desencanto llamado posmoderno," typescript (Santiago de Chile: FLACSO, 1988), 32.

39 See, for a concise deconstruction of this opposition, Laclau, *New Reflections,* xiii–xv, and Hopenhayn, "El debate," 16–17. May I also note that already in 1956, C. L. R. James had diagnosed the illusory, if politically effective, character of this opposition? See his *State Capitalism and World Revolution,* written in collaboration with Raya Dunayevskaya and Grace Lee (1956; reprint, Chicago: Charles H. Kerr Publishing, 1986).

40 See Franz J. Hinkelammert's "fourth thesis" for "overcoming modernity" in his "Frente a la cultura de la post-modernidad. Proyecto político y utopía," *David y Goliath* 17, no. 52 (septiembre 1987): 29. Also see Hopenhayn, "El debate," 14–19.

41 Escobar, "Imagining," 22–28. See also his "Discourse and Power in Development: Michel Foucault and the Relevance of his Work to the Third World," *Alternatives* 10, no. 3 (1984): 377–400, and "Power and Visibility: The Invention and Management of Development in the Third World," *Cultural Anthropology* 3, no. 4 (1988): 428–43.

42 In the U.S. context, see Stanley Aronowitz, *The Crisis in Historical Materialism: Class, Politics, and Culture in Marxist Theory,* 2d ed. (Minneapolis: University of Minnesota Press, 1990).

43 See Hinkelammert, "Frente," Arditi, "Una Gramática," Hopenhayn, "El debate," and Lechner, "Un desencanto." Of course, for the critique of Marxism as a modern politics, the contemporary standard is Ernesto Laclau and Chantal Mouffe's *Hegemony and Socialist Strategy: Towards a Radical Democratic Politics* (London: Verso, 1985). But also see Laclau's *New Reflections,* 5–41.

44 Lechner, "Un desencanto," 5–7.

45 Ibid., 11–12 and Arditi, "Una gramática," 171–75.

46 Hopenhayn, "El debate," 6–7 and 21.

47 Hinkelammert, "Frente," 21–24 and Lechner, "Un desencanto," 7–8 and 25–27. Andreas Huyssen has similarly pointed to the emancipatory potential of postmodernism's challenge to modernization's blind valorization of progress and the new at any cost. See his *After the Great Divide: Modernism, Mass Culture, Postmodernism* (Bloomington: Indiana University Press, 1986), 185–86. James Holston's exhaustive account of Brasília makes similar points. See *The Modernist City: An*

Anthropological Critique of Brasília (Chicago: University of Chicago Press, 1989), 314–18.

48 Jean François Lyotard, *The Postmodern Condition: A Report on Knowledge*, trans. Geoff Bennington and Brian Massumi, with foreword by Fredric Jameson (1984; reprint, Minneapolis: University of Minnesota Press, 1989), xxiv.

49 In particular, see Hopenhayn, "El debate," 9–14.

50 "Anarchocapitalism," the theory of which was formulated by David Friedman, the son of Chicago-School economist Milton Friedman, advocates massive de-regulation and privatization, akin to what is being offered as a "cure" in East-ern Europe and the former Soviet Union. See Hinkelammert, "Frente," 25, and Hopenhayn, "El debate," 11.

51 For a brief account and bibliography see Escobar, "Imagining," 32–34. For a useful English-language collection, see David Slater, ed., *New Social Movements and the State in Latin America* (Amsterdam: Cedla, 1985) and Arturo Escobar and Sonia E. Alvarez, eds., *The Making of Social Movements in Latin America: Identity, Strategy, and Democracy* (Boulder, Colo.: Westview Press, 1992).

52 Compare this to Laclau's discussion of "social imaginaries," articulation, and democracy in *New Reflections*, 60–85.

53 Arditi, "Una gramática," 184.

54 Lechner, "Un desencanto," 32–34 and Hopenhayn, "El debate," 22–23.

55 See the collection of articles in a post-1990 election special issue of *Latin American Perspectives* 66 (Summer 1990). Also see special issues on "Post-Marxism, the Left, and Democracy" and "Popular Organizing and the State" in *Latin American Perspectives* 65 (Spring 1990) and 73 (Spring 1992).

56 Arditi, "Una gramática," 184, and Hopenhayn, "El debate," 23.

57 José Joaquín Brunner, "Notas sobre la modernidad y lo posmoderno en la cultura latinoamericana," *David y Goliath* 17, no. 52 (septiembre 1987), 33.

58 Ibid., 34.

59 See "El debate posmoderno en iberoamérica," *Cuadernos hispanoamericanos* 463 (enero 1989): 79–92.

60 Nestor García Canclini, *Culturas híbridas: Estrategias para entrar y salir de la modernidad* (México: Grijalbo, 1990) and *Transforming Modernity: Popular Culture in Mexico*, Trans. Lidia Lazano (Austin: University of Texas Press, 1993).

61 See also Oscar Landi, *Devórame otra vez: Que hizo la televisión con la gente, que hace la gente con la televisión* (Buenos Aires: Planeta/Espejo de la Argentina, 1992).

62 Jameson, *Postmodernism*, 6.

63 On this paradigm shift toward cultural studies, see, besides García Canclini's *Culturas híbridas* and Landi's *Devórame otra vez*, Néstor García Canclini, ed., *Políticas Culturales en América Latina* (México: Grijalbo, 1987); Alcira Argumedo, *Los laberintos de la crisis. América Latina: Poder transnacional y comunicaciones* (Buenos Aires: ILET/Punto Sur, 1984); John Beverley, *Against Literature* (Minneapolis: University of Minnesota Press, 1993); and George Yúdice, Jean Franco, and Juan

Flores, eds., *On Edge: The Crisis of Contemporary Latin American Culture* (Minneapolis: University of Minnesota Press, 1992), esp. essays by Yúdice, García Canclini, and Newmann.

2 Beyond Western Modernity?

1   Jorge Luis Borges, "Kafka y sus precursores" (1951) from *Otras inquisiciones* (1952), in *Obras Completas* (1974; reprint, Buenos Aires: Emecé, 1987), 711; and "Pierre Menard, Autor del Quijote" (1939) from *Ficciones* (1944) in *Obras Completas*, 449.
2   See, besides the numerous more recent works making this theoretical point, Hayden White's *Metahistory* (Baltimore: Johns Hopkins University Press, 1973).
3   For a general picture, see Jürgen Habermas, *The Philosophical Discourse of Modernity*, trans. Frederick G. Lawrence (1987; reprint, Cambridge, Mass.: MIT Press, 1990) and Marshall Berman, *All that Is Solid Melts into Air: The Experience of Modernity* (New York: Penguin, 1988).
4   Stuart Hall, et al., "The Siege of Cuba," *New Left Review* 7 (January–February 1961): 2.
5   François Maspero, "Preface," in Janette Habel's *Cuba: The Revolution in Peril*, trans. Jon Barnes (1989; reprint, London: Verso, 1991), xiii–xiv.
6   C. L. R. James, "Appendix: From Toussaint L'Ouverture to Fidel Castro," in *The Black Jacobins* (1963; reprint, New York: Vintage, 1989), 391.
7   Louis A. Pérez, Jr., *Cuba and the United States: Ties of Singular Intimacy* (Athens: University of Georgia Press, 1990), 242. See also, for example, among the number of conservative treatises written during the sixties and early seventies on campus protest in the United States, Seymour Martin Lipset and Gerald M. Schaflander, *Passion and Politics: Student Activism in America* (Boston: Little, Brown, 1971). Lipset, a Harvard sociologist specializing in Latin American affairs, was a foremost U.S. modernization theorist.
8   Donald C. Hodges, *Argentina, 1943–1987: The National Revolution and Resistance*, rev. and enlarged ed. (Albuquerque: University of New Mexico Press, 1988), 49.
9   Oscar Teran, *Nuestro años sesentas* (Buenos Aires: Puntosur, 1991), 135, my translation. See also Silvia Sigal, *Intelectuales y poder en la década del sesenta* (Buenos Aires: Puntosur, 1991) and a discussion by these two authors published (uncoincidentally, I would argue) in a special issue of *Punto de vista* on utopias. Silvia Sigal and Oscar Teran, "Los intelectuales frente a la política," *Punto de Vista* 42 (abril 1992): 42–48.
10   Julio Cortázar, "Acerca de la situación del intelectual latinoamericano," in *Ultimo Round*, 2 vols. (1969; reprint, México: Siglo veintiuno, 1987), 2:272, my translation.

11 "By the way," Cortázar concluded parenthetically, "what would Fidel Castro think about this? I don't think I'm mistaken in thinking that he would agree, as Che would have agreed." Julio Cortázar, "Literatura en la revolución y revolución en la literatura," in *Literatura en la revolución y revolución en la literatura*, Oscar Collazos, Julio Cortázar, Mario Vargas Llosa (1970; reprint, México: Siglo veintiuno, 1977), 44, my translation.

12 Miguel Barnet, "La Novela Testimonio. Socio-literatura," in *Testimonio y literatura*, ed. René Jara and Hernán Vidal (Minneapolis: Institute for the Study of Ideologies and Literature, 1986), 285. Barnet wrote one of the first *testimonios*, *Biografía de un Cimarrón*, in 1966. See also Doris Sommer and George Yúdice, "Latin American Literature from the 'Boom' On," in *Postmodern Fiction: A Bio-Bibliographical Guide*, ed. Larry McCaffery (Westport, Conn.: Greenwood Press, 1986), 205–6.

13 Roberto Fernández Retamar, *Caliban: Apuntes sobre la cultura de nuestra américa* (1972; reprint, México: Editorial Diógenes, 1974), 92.

14 For related documents, see a special issue of *Libre* 1 (September–November 1971): 95–145. This includes Cortázar's own statement refusing to judge, "paternistically" in his view, events that must be understood within the context of a Cuba's continuing state of emergency in the face of U.S. intervention. Similarly, Gabriel García Márquez refused to sign the telegram of protest sent to Castro.

15 Doris Sommer, *Foundational Fictions: The National Romances of Latin America* (Berkeley and Los Angeles: University of California Press, 1991).

16 Carlos Fuentes, *La nueva novela hispanoamericana* (1969; reprint, México: Joaquín, 1980), 30.

17 Mario Vargas Llosa, "Novela primitiva y novela de creación en América Latina," *Revista de la Universidad de México* 23, no. 10 (junio 1969): 31.

18 Jean Franco, "Modernización, Resistencia y Revolución: La producción literaria de los años sesenta," in *La cultura moderna en América Latina*, trans. Sergio Pitol (México: Grijalbo, 1985), 335–56.

19 Doris Sommer, "Irresistible Romance: The Foundational Fictions of Latin America," in *Nation and Narration*, ed. Homi K. Bhabha (London: Routledge, 1990), 71.

20 See Che's famous speech "El socialismo y el hombre en Cuba," delivered in March of 1965 and published in Ernesto "Che" Guevara, *Obra revolucionaria* (1967; reprint, México: Ediciones Era, 1989), 627–39.

21 Sommer and Yúdice, "Latin American Literature," 191.

22 Page numbers from *Rayuela* hereafter will be cited parenthetically in the text. The citation will include chapter number, page number from the Spanish, and page number from the English. In Spanish, I will be using the Biblioteca Ayacucho edition (Caracas, 1980), and in English, the fourth printing of Gregory Rabassa's translation (New York: Random House, 1972).

23 Steven Boldy, "The Final Chapters of Cortázar's *Rayuela:* Madness, Suicide, Conformism?" *Bulletin of Hispanic Studies* 57 (1980): 233–38.
24 I am not the first to observe this. See Saúl Sosnowski, *Julio Cortázar: Una Busqueda Mítica* (Buenos Aires: Ediciones Noé, 1973), 120 and Steven Boldy, *The Novels of Julió Cortázar* (Cambridge: Cambridge University Press, 1980), 31.
25 Randal Johnson, "Tupy or not Tupy," in *Modern Latin American Fiction,* ed. John King (1987; reprint, New York: Noonday Press, 1989), 41–59.
26 More recently, Paul Julian Smith has developed a "bodily" theory of gender and sexuality in Spanish American literature that resonates with this tradition in an interesting fashion: *The Body Hispanic* (Oxford: Clarendon, 1989). Michel de Certeau has posited the Latin American earth-body as the locus of memory and resistance; see "The Long Silence," in *Heterologies: Discourse on the Other,* trans. Brian Massumi (Minneapolis: University of Minnesota Press, 1986), 225–33. For a critique of a poststructuralist fetishization of the abject Latin American body, see Yúdice, "*Testimonio* and Postmodernism."
27 More recently, Sandinista Omar Cabezas's *testimonio, La Montaña es algo más que una inmensa esteba verde* (1982; *Fire from the Mountain,* 1985) rehearses this gendering because the mountains of Nicaragua are figured, variously, as yielding virgin, protective mother, and vengeful or capricious lover.
28 At least since 1845, when Domingo F. Sarmiento, president of Argentina from 1868–74, published his manifesto *Facundo: Civilización y barbarie* celebrating the civilizing virtues of European culture over and against the barbarism of the gauchos whom Sarmiento tellingly refers to as "white savages"; obviously a monstrous contradiction in terms for the author. Domingo F. Sarmiento, *Facundo: Civilización y barbarie* (1845; reprint, Buenos Aires: EUDEBA, 1961), 48.
29 See James Joyce, *Ulysses* (1922; reprint, New York: Vintage, 1986), 644 and Richard Ellman in his preface to this same "corrected" edition, xiii–xiv. The countless critical interpretations asserting that *Ulysses* "can be seen as a demonstration and summation of the major features of the entire [modernist] movement"—including alienation—were usefully summarized by Maurice Beebe in "*Ulysses* and the Age of Modernism," *James Joyce Quarterly* 10 (Fall 1972): 176.
30 Though he does not propose this specific thesis with respect to *Rayuela*'s "Yes," Gerald Martin, in his impressive history, argues convincingly for the centrality of *Ulysses* to twentieth-century Latin American fiction, including, or especially, *Rayuela*. Gerald Martin, *Journeys Through the Labyrinth: Latin American Fiction in the Twentieth Century* (London: Verso, 1989), esp. chaps. 5 and 7. Beebe argues that Joyce's "refusal to get involved" makes him a "Modern master" (Beebe, "*Ulysses* and the Age of Modernism," 181). Whether or not this is the case, the "refusal to get involved" will certainly contrast with what I will ultimately argue is the positive Latin American modernist content of *Rayuela:* precisely a participatory and involving leap.
31 For a useful reflection on the problem of beginnings, see Edward W. Said,

Beginnings: Intention and Method (1975; reprint, New York: Columbia University Press, 1985).

32 For examples see, Jason Wilson, "Julio Cortázar and the Drama of Reading," in King, *Modern Latin American Fiction*, 173–90; Steven Boldy, "Julio Cortázar: *Rayuela*," in *Landmarks in Modern Latin American Fiction*, ed. Philip Swanson (London: Routledge, 1990), 118–40; and Carlos Fuentes's section on *Rayuela* in *La nueva novela hispanoamericana*, 67–77.

33 Kristin Ross, *The Emergence of Social Space: Rimbaud and the Paris Commune* (Minneapolis: University of Minnesota Press, 1988), esp. 44–45 and 47–74.

34 Ross, *Emergence of Social Space*, 32, emphasis added.

35 For Cortázar, Artaud's surrealism was "not literary, anti- and extraliterary"; his lesson that "living matters more than writing, except when writing—as in so few cases—is living." He quotes Artaud: "When I recite a poem, it is not to be applauded but rather to feel the bodies of men and women, I said *the bodies* . . ." Julio Cortázar, "Muerte de Antonin Artaud," *Sur* 163 (May 1948): 80–82. Also, on the question of Cortázar's relation to surrealism, see Evelyn Picon Garfield, *¿Es Julio Cortázar un Surrealista?* (Madrid: Gredos, 1975).

36 Marx's specifically nineteenth-century conception was itself "updated" by Harry Braverman in *Labor and Monopoly Capital: The Degradation of Work in the Twentieth Century* (New York: Monthly Review Press, 1974). See also Alex Callinicos, *Marxism and Philosophy* (New York: Oxford University Press, 1985), 32–43.

37 Karl Marx, *Economic and Philosophic Manuscripts of 1844*, vol. 3 of *Karl Marx–Frederick Engels Collected Works* 3:272.

38 Ibid., 274–75. See also Marx, *Grundrisse* 28:233.

39 Marx, *Economic and Philosophic Manuscripts*, 276–77.

40 See, for example, Herbert Marcuse, *One-Dimensional Man* (Boston: Beacon Press, 1964).

41 Marx, *Economic and Philosophic Manuscripts*, 278; also see Marx, *Grundrisse* 28:381–83.

42 Marx, *Economic and Philosophic Manuscripts*, 296.

43 Ngugi wa Thiong'o, *Decolonising the Mind: The Politics of Language in African Literature* (1981; reprint, Portsmouth, N.H.: Heinemann, 1989), 18.

44 Ibid., 17. Significantly, this was Ngugi's farewell work to an only English-reading public. Henceforth he wrote only in Giyuko and Kiswahili.

45 Fidel Castro, "Olive-Green," *New Left Review* 7 (January–February 1961), 2.

46 José Martí, "Nuestra América" (1891), in *Conciencia Intelectual de América: Antología del Ensayo Hispanoamericano*, ed. Carlos Ripoll (New York: Eliseo Torres and Sons, 1974), 230, my translation.

47 Djelal Kadir, *Questing Fictions: Latin America's Family Romance* (Minneapolis: University of Minnesota Press, 1986). See also the foreword to the book, written by Terry Cochran.

48 See Marshall Berman, *All that Is Solid Melts into Air* and Smith, *Uneven Development.*

49 For excellent readings of Bello related to these questions, see Julio Ramos, *Desencuentros de la Modernidad en América Latina: Literatura y Política en el Siglo XIX* (México: Fondo de cultura económica, 1989) and Sommer, *Foundational Fictions.*

50 Andrés Bello, "Autonomía cultural de América [aka "Modo de escribir la Historia"]" (1848), in Ripoll, *Conciencia Intelectual de América*, 48–54.

51 Ibid. And, for the various Argentine responses to this problem, see Tulio Halperin Donghi, ed., *Proyecto y Construcción de una Nación (Argentina, 1845–1880)* (Caracas: Biblioteca Ayacucho, 1980).

52 On this period of Latin American history and on its relations to Europe and, later, to North America, see David Bushnell and Neil Macaulay, *The Emergence of Latin America in the Nineteenth Century* (New York: Oxford University Press, 1988); Tulio Halperin Donghi, *Historia Contemporanea de América Latina* (Madrid: Alianza, 1979); and Charles Bergquist, *Labor in Latin America: Comparative Essays on Chile, Argentina, Venezuela, and Colombia* (Stanford, Calif.: Stanford University Press, 1986).

53 Jürgen Habermas gives an account of this difficulty for European philosophy in *Philosophical Discourse of Modernity*, 5–22.

54 Collected in *Antología de Andrés Bello*, ed. Pedro Grases (Caracas: Editorial Kapelusz Venezolana, 1964).

55 Kwame Anthony Appiah, "Is the Post- in Postmodernism the Post- in Postcolonial?" *Critical Inquiry* 17, no. 2 (Winter 1991): 348.

56 David Viñas, *Literatura Argentina y realidad política* (Buenos Aires: Centro Editor de América Latina, 1982), esp. the first section of pt. 1 entitled "La mirada a europa: Del viaje colonial al viaje estético."

57 Gerald Martin has observed the importance of *Los Pasos Perdidos*—and Carpentier in general—as a precursor to *Rayuela*. Martin, *Journeys Through the Labyrinth*, 202.

58 Picon Garfield, *¿Es Julio Cortázar un Surrealista?* 209–26.

59 Ross, *Emergence of Social Space*, 54–55.

60 Gilles Deleuze, *The Logic of Sense*, trans. Mark Lester with Charles Stivale and ed. Constantin V. Boundas (New York: Columbia University Press, 1990), 299.

61 See, for a historical treatment of this role, Gayle Rubin, "The Traffic in Women: Notes on the 'Political Economy' of Sex," in *Toward an Anthropology of Women*, ed. Rayna R. Reiter (New York: Monthly Review Press, 1975), 157–210.

62 Georges Bataille, *The Accursed Share, Volume I: Consumption*, trans. Robert Hurley (New York: Zone Books, 1988), 131.

63 Bataille took as the central object of his life's work "excessive" phenomena such as death, torture, ritual sacrifice, erotism. See, besides *Accursed Share*, "The Notion of Expenditure," in *Visions of Excess: Selected Writings, 1927–1939*, ed. and trans.

Allen Stoekl (Minneapolis: University of Minnesota Press, 1986), 116–29; *Erotism: Death and Sensuality,* trans. Mary Dalwood (1962; reprint, San Francisco: City Lights, 1986), and *The Tears of Eros,* trans. Peter Connor (San Francisco: City Lights, 1989). Interestingly, some photos of a Chinese torture called *Leng-Tch'e* (cutting into pieces) from 1905 reprinted in *Tears of Eros* (204–6) seem to reappear in *Rayuela* (in chapter 14). Severo Sarduy also observes this in an interpretive essay with which I otherwise do not agree. See his essay "From *Yin* to *Yang* (About Sade, Bataille, Marmori, Cortázar, and Elizondo)" in the section entitled "Eroticisms" of *Written on a Body,* trans. Carol Meier (New York: Lumen Books, 1989), 5–17. As for insanity, see Michel Foucault, *Madness and Civilization: A History of Insanity in the Age of Reason,* trans. Richard Howard (1965; reprint, New York: Vintage, 1973). Finally, see Jürgen Habermas's criticisms of Foucault and Bataille on the grounds that these scientific attempts to disengage an irrecuperable otherness from modern Western rationality wind up reinscribing that otherness within the Western tradition. *Philosophical Discourse of Modernity,* 235–36 and 247.

64 Along these lines, see criticisms by Hernán Vidal, "Julio Cortázar y la Nueva Izquierda," *Ideologies and Literature* 2, no. 7 (May–June 1978): 45–67, and in his *Literatura hispanoamericana e ideologia liberal: Surgimiento y crisis (Una problematica sobre la dependencia en torno a la narrativa del boom)* (Buenos Aires: Ediciones Hispamérica, 1976); Jaime Concha, "Criticando *Rayuela,*" *Hispamerica* 4, no. 1 (agosto 1975): 132–51 (a special issue on "Literatura latinoamericana e ideología de la dependencia," guest edited by Vidal); and, finally, Jean Franco's "Modernización," in her *La cultura moderna en América Latina.*

65 Martin, *Journeys Through the Labyrinth,* 202.

66 Peter Bürger, "Literary Institution and Modernization," *Poetics* 12 (1983): 419–33 and for Latin America, Ramos, *Desencuentros,* and Franco, *La cultura moderna en América Latina.*

67 Huyssen, *After the Great Divide,* 183, 185–86.

68 Quoted, critically, in Rincón, "Modernidad periférica," 79, my translation. For other postmodernizing approaches, besides Linda Hutcheon's, which I treated above, see Ihab Hassan, *The Postmodern Turn: Essays in Postmodern Theory and Culture* (Columbus: Ohio State University Press, 1987); Douwe Fokkema, *Literary History, Modernism, and Postmodernism* (Amsterdam: Johns Benjamins, 1984); Gerald Graff, "The Myth of the Postmodern Breakthrough," in *Literature Against Itself: Literary Ideas in Modern Society* (1979, reprint, Chicago: University of Chicago Press, 1986); and Brian McHale, *Postmodernist Fiction* (New York: Methuen, 1987).

69 See Anthony Geist, José Monleón, and Jenaro Talens, eds., *Modernism and its Margins,* forthcoming (Minneapolis: University of Minnesota Press, 1995), and Gilles Deleuze and Felix Guattari, *Kafka: Toward a Minor Literature,* trans. Dana Polan (Minneapolis: University of Minnesota Press, 1986).

70 However, see two essays that understandably emphasize the gains for women within the Cuban revolution: Marjorie King, "Cuba's Attack on Women's Second

Shift, 1974–76," in *Women in Latin America: An Anthology*, ed. Eleanor Leacock et al. (Riverside, Calif.: Latin American Perspectives, 1979), 118–31; and Max Azicri, "Women's Development through Revolutionary Mobilization," in *The Cuba Reader: The Making of a Revolutionary Society*, ed. Philip Brenner, William M. LeoGrande, Donna Rich, and Daniel Siegel (New York: Grove Press, 1989), 457–71. See also, for a more general perspective that nonetheless articulates some of these difficulties, Nancy Saporta Sternbach, Marysa Navarro-Aranguren, Patricia Chuchryk, and Sonia E. Alvarez, "Feminisms in Latin America: From Bógota to San Bernardo," in *Making of Social Movements in Latin America*, 207–39.

71 Lucille Kerr, "Leaps Across the Board," *Diacritics* 4, no. 4 (Winter 1974): 29–34.

72 That these are in fact the values of the avant-garde is established in Peter Bürger's groundbreaking study, *Theory of the Avant-Garde*, trans. Michael Shaw (1984; reprint, Minneapolis: University of Minnesota Press, 1987).

73 Fredric Jameson, "The Ideology of the Text," in *The Ideologies of Theory*, 2 vols. (Minneapolis: University of Minnesota Press, 1988), 1:57.

74 Ramos, *Desencuentros*, 21–25.

75 Fernando Ortíz, *Contrapunteo cubano del tobaco y el azúcar* (1940; reprint, Caracas: Biblioteca Ayacucho, 1978), 86.

76 Michel de Certeau, *The Practice of Everyday Life* (1984; reprint, Berkeley and Los Angeles: University of California Press, 1988).

77 Angel Rama, *Transculturación narrativa en américa latina* (México: Siglo Veintiuno, 1982).

78 For that matter, a certain current of Latin American postmodernism theory, drawn more from European poststructuralist versions of postmodernism than from Marxist ones, has invoked this practice as evidence of Latin America's essential postmodernity *avant la lettre*. In the Caribbean, see Antonio Benítez Rojo, *La isla que se repite: El Caribe y la perspectiva posmoderna* (Hanover, N.H.: Ediciones del Norte, 1989). For a critique of this view in general, see George Yúdice, "Postmodernity and Transnational Capitalism in Latin America," in Yúdice, Franco, and Flores, *On Edge*, esp. 1–9 and of Benítez Rojo specifically see my " 'There's No Place Like Home', or, The Utopian, Uncanny Caribbean State of Mind of Antonio Benítez-Rojo," forthcoming *Siglo XX/20th Century* 12 (1994).

79 Jorge Luis Borges, "El escritor argentino y la tradición" (from *Discusión*, 1932), in *Obras Completas*, 267–74.

80 Kerr, "Leaps Across the Board," 33.

3 Toward a Latin American Modernity

1 *Sin rumbo*, besides literally meaning "without a path," is also the title of the 1885 novel by the Argentine Eugenio Cambaceres (1843–88), a quasi-naturalist tale of Argentina's identity crisis as it enters more and more deeply into European-dominated peripheral modernization; that is, as it transforms nature into agriculture.

2 *Everyday Life in the Modern World,* trans. Sacha Rabinovitch (1971; reprint, New Brunswick: Transaction, 1984), 196–97. We will have occasion below to examine more closely the relationship between Horacio's vision of dealienation and that of the New Left.

3 Manfredo Tafuri characterizes the project of Le Corbusier in *Architecture and Utopia: Design and Capitalist Development,* trans. Barbara Luigia La Penta (1976; reprint, Cambridge, Mass.: MIT Press, 1988), 125. See also Holston, *Modernist City.*

4 Charles Taylor, *Hegel* (1975; reprint, Cambridge: Cambridge University Press, 1988), 376. See also Fredric Jameson, "Morality versus Ethical Substance," in *Ideologies of Theory* 1:182 as concretized by George Yúdice's analysis of the Guatemalan *testimonio, I, Rigoberta Menchú.* See Yúdice, "Marginality and the Ethics of Survival." When Taylor rightly observes that Hegel confounds attempts to label him as liberal or reactionary (374–75), he seems to me unwittingly to reveal that insofar as Hegel's ethical substance is the basis for a revolutionary ethos, it is both progressive and conservative: rupturing tradition in the name of the future, and closing off the future in the name of the present.

5 Sigmund Freud, "Repression," vol. 14 of *Standard Edition of the Complete Psychological Notes of Sigmund Freud,* Trans. and Ed. James Strachey (London: Hogarth, 1965), 147.

6 Ibid., 78. Sigmund Freud, "Analysis of a Phobia in a Five-Year-Old Boy," vol. 10 of *Standard Edition* (London: Hogarth, 1962), 122.

7 Ibid., 80. Sigmund Freud, *Beyond the Pleasure Principle,* Trans. and Ed. James Strachey (New York: Norton, 1961), 30. See also, for a similar but more radical view, Jacques Lacan, *The Four Fundamental Concepts of Psycho-Analysis,* trans. Alan Sheridan (1977; reprint, New York: Norton, 1981), esp. 48–64.

8 See *A Thousand Plateaus,* trans. Brian Massumi (Minneapolis: University of Minnesota Press, 1987). Deleuze and Guattari apply the concept of deterritorialization to Kafka's deforming and subversive use of German. They also associate it with the wandering—nonsearching—of the nomad. In all these cases, as with Cortázar himself, the term—*deterritorialization*—recalls its Spanish cousin *destierro,* or "exile." Perhaps the political marginalization marked by exile is the rather more grim material condition of possibility for the emancipatory dimension of deterritorialization given in Deleuze and Guattari, Lefebvre, and Cortázar.

9 See Steven Boldy, "The final chapters of Cortázar's *Rayuela:* madness, suicide, conformism?"

10 On this matter, my own position owes a debt to the work of Fredric Jameson in *Political Unconscious,* as well as in his essays "Marxism and Historicism" and "Periodizing the 60s" in *Ideologies of Theory* 2:148–77 and 178–208.

11 See Vidal, "Julio Cortázar y la Nueva Izquierda" and his *Literatura hispano-americana e ideologia liberal;* also Concha, "Criticando *Rayuela.*" Though not taking *Rayuela* on specifically, Larsen provides a brilliant example of this view in *Modernism and Hegemony.*

12 See, for examples, Julio Cortázar, "Homenaje a una torre de fuego," a report written for the Uruguayan journal *Marcha, Ultimo Round* 1:194–97 and "Noticias del Mes de Mayo," a collage poem, *Ultimo Round* 1:88–120.

13 See Aronowitz, *Crisis in Historical Materialism,* esp. 59–60, 87–90, and 154–61 and Stephen A. Resnick and Richard D. Wolff, *Knowledge and Class: A Marxian Critique of Political Economy* (Chicago: University of Chicago Press, 1987), esp. 38–108.

14 George Katsiaficas, *The Global Imagination of the New Left: A Global Analysis of 1968* (Boston: South End Press, 1987), 37.

15 Ibid., 36.

16 Ernesto "Che" Guevara, *La guerra de guerrillas* in *Obra revolucionaria,* 70.

17 Regis Debray, *Revolution in the Revolution?* trans. Bobbye Ortiz (New York: Monthly Review Press, 1967), 15; Donald C. Hodges, *Argentina, 1943–1987,* 151–52; and Thomas C. Wright, *Latin America in the Era of the Cuban Revolution* (New York: Praeger, 1991), 18.

18 See, for examples, Frantz Fanon's discourses on violence and spontaneity in *Wretched of the Earth,* trans. Constance Farrington (New York: Grove, 1968) and Guy Debord's 1967 situationist manifesto, *Society of the Spectacle* (Detroit: Black and Red, 1983).

19 Louis A. Perez, Jr., *Cuba: Between Reform and Revolution* (New York: Oxford University Press, 1988), esp. 215–22. According to Saul Landau, a lieutenant in the militia said to him, "In our country everybody had the vote too, before, but we weren't able to do anything with it." Saul Landau, "Cuba: The Present Reality," *New Left Review* 9 (May–June 1961), 14.

20 See, for example, Fidel Castro, "Medio millón de campesinos en la Habana" (26 July 1959), in *La revolución cubana,* ed. Adolfo Sánchez Rebolledo (1972; reprint, México: Ediciones Era, 1983), 193.

21 Guevara, "El socialismo el hombre en Cuba," 629.

22 Pérez, *Cuba: Between Reform,* 321. According to Celso Furtado, "Conservative estimates have allowed that the sum effect of the various measures adopted between 1959 and 1961 was to transfer at least 15 percent of the Cuban national income from property-owning groups to the working peasants." *Economic Development of Latin America: Historical Background and Contemporary Problems,* 2d ed. (1976; reprint, Cambridge: Cambridge University Press, 1986), 288.

23 Fidel Castro, "La reforma agraria va" (12 July 1959), in *La revolución cubana;* 160–89.

24 Katsiaficas, *Global Imagination of the New Left,* 98–99.

25 Jean Franco, "South of your border," in Sayres et al., *60s Without Apology*, 324.

26 James, *Notes on Dialectics*, 100. The passage in Hegel comes from *The Science of Logic*, trans. A. V. Miller (1969; reprint, Atlantic Highlands, N.J.: Humanities Press, 1989), 370 and in Lenin's *Conspectus of Hegel's Book "The Science of Logic,"* in *Collected Works* (Moscow: Progress Publishers, 1981), 38:123; see also 38:282.

27 Herbert Marcuse, *Reason and Revolution: Hegel and the Rise of Social Theory* (1941; reprint, Boston: Beacon Press, 1960), 141.

28 James, *Notes on Dialectics*, 100–101.

29 Krishan Kumar, *Utopianism* (Buckingham, England: Open University Press, 1991).

30 Sir Thomas More, *Utopia* (1516; reprint, New York: Norton, 1975), 7–9.

31 Although even British Marxist (and modernist) Perry Anderson recognizes that one of three essential coordinates of the "modernist conjuncture . . . was the imaginative proximity of social revolution." Perry Anderson, "Modernity and Revolution," *New Left Review* 144 (March–April 1984): 105.

32 Lefebvre, *Everyday Life in the Modern World*, 197. And Beatriz Sarlo locates the origins of this impulse in the cultural and social forces coalescing in the wake of the first wave of modernization in Argentina; see chapters 4 and 5 on "Vanguardia y utopía" and "La revolución como fundamento" in *Una modernidad periférica*.

33 Ernesto "Che" Guevara, "Notas para el estudio de la ideología de la Revolución Cubana," in *Obra revolucionaria*, 509.

34 Beatriz Sarlo, "El campo intelectual: un espacio doblemente fracturado," in *Represión y reconstrucción de una cultura: el caso Argentino*, ed. Saúl Sosnowski (Buenos Aires: EUDEBA, 1988), 96. Sarlo adds to this that "for Argentines, the figure of Cortázar duplicated this vast Cuban space of mediation in the literary field. Cortázar was, in fact, the one that could put into communication the most diverse intellectual traditions."

35 A more comprehensive, critical but sympathetic, account of the recent crises in the revolution can be found in Janette Habel's *Cuba: The Revolution in Peril*.

36 Wright, *Latin America in the Era of the Cuban Revolution*, 19, 25.

37 Landau, "The Present Reality," 16, emphasis added.

38 Fidel Castro, "Palabras a los intelectuales" (30 June 1961), in *La revolución cubana*, 363.

39 Norbert Lechner, *La conflictiva y nunca acabada construcción del orden deseado* (Madrid: Siglo XXI and Centro de Investigaciones Sociológicas, 1986), esp. 166–70. See also Atilio A. Boron, *Estado, Capitalismo y Democracia en América Latina*.

40 José Nun, "La izquierda ante la cultura de la posmodernidad," in *La Rebelión del Coro: Estudios sobre la racionalidad política y el sentido común* (Buenos Aires: Editores Nueva Visión, 1989), 138. See also Laclau, *New Reflections*, xi.

41 Gayatri Spivak, "Who Claims Alterity?" in *Remaking History*, ed. Barbara Kruger and Phil Marini (Seattle: Bay Press and Dia Art Foundation, 1989), 282.

4 Latin American Modernity in Crisis

1   Manuel Puig, *El beso de la mujer araña* (Barcelona: Seix Barral, 1976), in English as *Kiss of the Spider Woman*, trans. Thomas Colchie (1978; reprint, New York: Vintage, 1980). Quotations from the novel will be taken from the 1980 edition of the translation unless otherwise noted and will be followed by parenthetical page references to the Spanish original and English translation, respectively.

2   For a positive evaluation of the "protective or consoling function of art, even in its commodity form," see Frances Wyers (Weber), "Manuel Puig at the Movies," *Hispanic Review* 49, no. 2 (Spring 1981): 165, 180. For less sanguine views of Puig's "contradictory strategy," see Gustavo Pellón, "Manuel Puig's Contradictory Strategy: Kitsch Paradigms *versus* Paradigmatic Structure in *Kiss of the Spider Woman* and *Pubis Angelical*," *Symposium* 36 (1983): 199; Marta Morello-Frosch, "La sexualidad opresiva en las obras de Manuel Puig," *Nueva narrativa hispanoamericana* 5, nos. 1–2 (1976): 152; and James Ray Green, Jr., "*Kiss of the Spider Woman:* Sexual Repression and Textual Repression," in *La Chispa '81: Selected Proceedings,* ed. Gilbert Paolini (New Orleans: Tulane University Press and the Louisiana Conference on Hispanic Languages and Literature, 1981), 138.

3   Manuel Puig, "Del Kitsch a Lacan," Interview by Reina Roffé, in *Espejo de Escritores,* ed. Reina Roffé (Hanover, N.H.: Ediciones del Norte, 1985), 131.

4   Ibid., 133.

5   Manuel Puig, "Manuel Puig," Interview by Marie-Lise Gazarian Gautier in her *Interviews with Latin American Writers* (Elmwood Park, Ill.: Dalkey Archive Press, 1989), 224.

6   Here Puig seems to echo Gilles Deleuze and Félix Guattari who wrote *Anti-Oedipus,* they said, to understand how people could desire their own oppression and, of course, to offer a way out of that desire. The way out may be what is no longer so clearly marked in Puig. See *Anti-Oedipus,* trans. Robert Hurley, Mark Seem, and Helen R. Lane (Minneapolis: University of Minnesota Press, 1986).

7   Among Puig critics, Alicia Borinsky has addressed this question most adequately. See her "Castration: Artifices: Notes on the Writing of Manuel Puig," trans. Norman Holland and Stephen F. Houston, *Georgia Review* 29 (1975): 95–114; and *Ver/Ser Visto: Notas para un analítica poética* (Barcelona: Bosch, 1978).

8   Hutcheon, *Narcissistic Narrative* and Lucien Dällenbach, *The Mirror in the Text,* trans. Jeremy Whitely with Emma Hughes (Chicago: University of Chicago Press, 1989).

9   Robert Alter, *Partial Magic: The Novel as a Self-Conscious Genre* (1975; reprint, Berkeley and Los Angeles: University of California Press, 1978), x.

10   For a thoughtful discussion of this view, see Martin, *Journeys Through the Labyrinth,* 247–51.

11   See Paul de Man, *Allegories of Reading: Figural Language in Rousseau, Nietsche,*

Rilke, and Proust (New Haven, Conn.: Yale University Press, 1979), esp. 57–78 and 221–45; and Jameson, *Political Unconscious*.

12 Patricia Waugh, *Metafiction: The Theory and Practice of Self-Conscious Fiction* (London: Methuen, 1984), 2. In my view, Dällenbach mistakes this essential function of metafiction for one of its "types" in his discussion of the "fiction of origins" *mise en âbyme* (Dällenbach, *Mirror in the Text*, 101–6).

13 Hutcheon, *Narcissistic Narrative*, xii.

14 Ibid., 5.

15 Ibid., 3.

16 George Yúdice provides an interesting formulation along these lines arguing that the novel effects the "conversion of imprisonment into pleasure." George Yúdice, "*Kiss of the Spider Woman* y *Pubis Angelical:* Entre el placer y el saber," in *Literature and Popular Culture in the Hispanic World: A Symposium,* ed. Rose S. Minc (Gaithersburg, Md.: Ediciones Hispamérica and Montclair State College, 1981), 43–58. I would argue however that the opposite is also the case. In this novel, the utopia of pleasure is always found to contain the seeds of imprisonment. It is precisely the dialectical nature of this dynamic that enables, or requires, the novel to represent this crisis of utopia.

17 See Barbara Harlow, *Resistance Literature* (New York: Methuen, 1987), esp. the chapter on "Prison memoirs of political detainees," 117–53.

18 Lucille Kerr also notes this in her important work on Puig: Lucille Kerr, *Suspended Fictions: Reading Novels by Manuel Puig* (Urbana: University of Illinois Press, 1987), 185.

19 Manuel Puig, "Losing Readers in Argentina," *Index on Censorship* 14, no. 5 (October 1985): 56.

20 Stephanie Merrim persuasively argues that the films function as psychoanalytical tools for the characters to work out their repressions. See Stephanie Merrim, "Through the Film Darkly: Grade 'B' Movies and Dreamwork in *Tres Tristes Tigres* and *El beso de la mujer arana,*" *Modern Language Studies* 15, no. 4 (Fall 1985): 300–312. Without disputing this possibility, I would emphasize that this is all enabled, or perhaps necessitated, by the circumstance of physical imprisonment.

21 Jorge Panesi, Laura Rice-Sayre, and Paul Julian Smith have all offered suggestive readings of the sexual politics of the novel. Rice-Sayre writes that Puig "underlines the complexity of gender formation" and links it to the "larger social ill" of "a society based on aggression and humiliation." Laura Rice-Sayre, "Domination and Desire: A Feminist Materialist Reading of Manuel Puig's *Kiss of the Spider Woman,*" in *Textual Analysis: Some Readers Reading,* ed. Mary Ann Caws (New York: Modern Language Association, 1986), 253, 255. Also see Paul Julian Smith, "*La mujer araña* and the Return of the Body," in Smith, *Body Hispanic,* 193–201; and Jorge Panesi, "Manuel Puig: Las relaciones peligrosas," *Revista Iberoamericana* 125, no. 49 (October–December 1983): 903–17.

22 This is as against the view that the characters have undergone an "inversion" of roles. See Michael Boccia, "Versions (Con-, In-, and Per-) in Manuel Puig's and Hector Babenco's *Kiss of the Spider Woman* Novel and Film," *Modern Fiction Studies* 32, no. 3 (Autumn 1986): 422.

23 Merrim, "Through the Film Darkly," 305.

24 Efraín Barradas, "Notas sobre notas: *Kiss of the Spider Woman*," *Revista de estudios hispánicos* 6 (1979): 180.

25 "The power of science consists, in the first place, in its conflation of knowledge and truth." Stanley Aronowitz, *Science as Power: Discourse and Ideology in Modern Society* (Minneapolis: University of Minnesota Press, 1988), vii.

26 Theodor Adorno, *Negative Dialectics*, trans. E. B. Ashton (1973; reprint, New York: Continuum, 1987), 5.

5 Beyond Valentín's Dream

1 This event, known as *El retorno*, "the return," in Peronist lore, is the focal point for Tomás Eloy Martínez's *La novela de Perón*, taken up in chapter 7 of this volume.

2 Richard Gillespie, in 1982, referred to the *montoneros* as "Latin America's foremost urban guerrilla force to date." *Soldiers of Perón: Argentina's Montoneros* (Oxford: Clarendon Press, 1982), v.

3 Joseph Page, *Perón: A Biography* (New York: Random House, 1983), 462–66, and David Rock, *Argentina, 1516–1987: From Spanish Colonization to Alfonsín* (Berkeley and Los Angeles: University of California Press, 1987), 360.

4 Hodges, *Argentina, 1943–1987*, 121 and Gillespie, *Soldiers of Perón*, 152–53.

5 Rock, *Argentina, 1516–1987*, 363.

6 Puig's 1973 detective novel, *The Buenos Aires Affair,* was censored by the Peronist regime. Puig wrote that "in 1973, there was room only for praise, all criticism was blasphemous." Puig, "Losing Readers in Argentina," 85. Pamela Bacarisse has addressed the question of Peronism with respect to *La traición de Rita Hayworth* (1967), *The Buenos Aires Affair* (1973), and *Pubis Angelical* (1979) in her essay "The Projection of Peronism in the Novels of Manuel Puig," in *The Historical Novel in Latin America: A Symposium,* ed. Daniel Balderston (Gaithersburg, Md.: Ediciones Hispamérica, 1986), 185–200.

7 Bergquist, *Labor in Latin America,* 85–95, James Scobie, *Argentina,* 2d ed. (New York: Oxford University Press, 1971), 119–20, and Furtado, *Economic Development of Latin America,* 51.

8 Ronaldo Munck, with Ricardo Falcon and Bernardo Galitelli, *Argentina from Anarchism to Peronism: Workers, Unions, and Politics, 1855–1985* (London: Zed, 1987), 24–33.

9 Bergquist, *Labor in Latin America,* 132, and Munck, with Falcon and Galitelli, *Argentina from Anarchism to Peronism,* 85–89.

10 Hodges, *Argentina, 1943–1987*, 4.

11 Lenin, in 1916—the year of the middle-class Radical party electoral victory at the polls in Argentina—cited Argentina as an example of what he called the "semi-colony": " 'South America, and especially Argentina,' " Lenin began, quoting a work on British imperialism, " 'is so dependent financially on London that it ought to be described as almost a British commercial colony.' It is not difficult to imagine what strong connections British finance capital (and its faithful 'friend,' diplomacy) thereby acquires with the Argentine bourgeosie, with the circles that control the whole of the country's economic and political life." Lenin, *Imperialism*, 101–2.

12 Furtado, *Economic Development of Latin America*, 56.

13 Bergquist, *Labor in Latin America*, 141.

14 Hodges, *Argentina, 1943–1987*, 6.

15 Munck, with Falcon and Galitelli, *Argentina from Anarchism to Peronism*, 123.

16 Bergquist, *Labor in Latin America*, 169 and Munck with Falcon and Galitelli, *Argentina from Anarchism to Peronism*, 127–29.

17 Hodges, *Argentina, 1943–1987*, 26–31.

18 See Page, *Perón*, 264, Rock, *Argentina: 1516–1987*, 306–7, and Hodges, *Argentina, 1943–1987*, 32.

19 Eva Perón, *La razón de mi vida* (Buenos Aires: Ediciones Pereusa, 1951), 65.

20 Ibid., 84.

21 Ibid., 314.

22 Quoted in Hodges, *Argentina, 1943–1987*, 30.

23 Guevara, "El socialismo," 637–38.

24 Hodges, *Argentina, 1943–1987*, 32–39.

25 Juan Perón, in *Diario secreto de Perón*, anotado por Enrique Pavón Pereyra (Buenos Aires: Sudamericana/Planeta, 1986), 134.

26 *Perón-Cooke Correspondencia*, 2 vols. (Buenos Aires: Granica, 1973), 2:35.

27 Hodges, *Argentina, 1943–1987*, 49.

28 Ibid., 154, and 307.

29 See Daniel James, *Resistance and Integration: Peronism and the Argentine Working Class, 1946–1976* (Cambridge: Cambridge University Press, 1988).

30 Gillespie, *Soldiers of Perón*, 37.

31 Juan Perón, *La hora de los pueblos* (Buenos Aires: Editorial Norte, 1968).

32 Hodges, *Argentina, 1943–1987*, 54–55.

33 Quoted in ibid., 55.

34 For accounts, see Munck, with Falcon and Galitelli, *Argentina from Anarchism to Peronism*, 171–74; Rock, *Argentina, 1516–1987*, 349–52; Hodges, *Argentina, 1943–1987*, 60–61; Gillespie, *Soldiers of Perón*, 65; Ernesto Laclau, "Argentina—Imperialist Strategy and the May Crisis," *New Left Review* 62 (July–August 1970): 3–21; and James, *Resistance and Integration*, 221–23.

35 Gillespie, *Soldiers of Perón*, 90–91.

36 Wright, *Latin America in the Era of the Cuban Revolution*, 104–5. Also see James

Kohl and John Litt, *Urban Guerrilla Warfare in Latin America* (Cambridge, Mass.: MIT Press, 1974), 185.

37 Hodges, *Argentina, 1943–1987*, 65–66.

38 Gillespie, *Soldiers of Perón*, 100.

39 Alicia Partnoy, *The Little School: Tales of Disappearance and Survival in Argentina* (San Francisco: Cleis Press, 1986), 11.

40 For other examples see Gillespie, *Soldiers of Perón*, 103–9 and Perón, *Diario secreto de Perón*. These contradictions are also discussed by Hodges in *Argentina, 1943–1987*.

41 Quoted in Gillespie, *Soldiers of Perón*, 157.

42 Mandel, *Late Capitalism*, 131.

43 Lipietz, *Mirages and Miracles*, 29.

44 Mandel, *Late Capitalism*, 121.

45 Ibid.

46 Lipietz, *Mirages and Miracles*, 41.

47 William C. Smith, *Authoritarianism and the Crisis of the Argentine Political Economy* (1989; reprint, Stanford: Stanford University Press, 1991), 239.

48 Ernest Mandel, *The Second Slump: A Marxist Analysis of Recession in the Seventies*, trans. Jon Rothschild (London: Verso, 1978), 42–46.

49 Ibid., 45.

50 Harvey, *Condition of Postmodernity*.

51 Pellón, "Manuel Puig's Contradictory Strategy," 199.

52 Beverley and Oviedo, "Postmodernism in Latin America," 6.

6 Resuscitating History

1 James D. Cockroft, *Neighbors in Turmoil: Latin America* (New York: Harper and Row, 1989), 516, 514.

2 Hodges, *Argentina, 1943–1987*, 199. See also Hodges's more recent work, *Argentina's Dirty War: An Intellectual Biography* (Austin: University of Texas Press, 1991).

3 Ricardo Piglia, *Respiración artificial* (1980; reprint, Buenos Aires: Sudamericana, 1988), in English as *Artificial Respiration*, trans. Daniel Balderston (Durham: Duke University Press, 1994). Quotations will be taken from this translation unless otherwise noted and will be followed by parenthetical page references to the Spanish original and English translation, respectively.

4 Taken from a document called "Basic Goals and Objectives of the Process of National Reorganization," which appeared just five days after the 24 March coup. This quote and many others that made up the military's discourse on culture come from the Andrés Avellaneda's very useful compilation *Censura, autoritarismo y cultura: Argentina 1960–1983*, 2 vols. (Buenos Aires: Biblioteca Política Argentina/

Centro Editor de América Latina, 1986). The quote above appears in 1:134. See also, for an analysis of one of the military's more conspicuous attempts in this regard, Neil Larsen, "Sport as Civil Society: The Argentinean Junta Plays Championship Soccer," in *The Discourse of Power: Culture, Hegemony and the Authoritarian State in Latin America*, ed. Neil Larsen (Minneapolis: Institute for the study of Ideologies and Literature, 1983), 113–28.

5 Tulio Halperín Donghi, "Estilos nacionales de institucionalización de la cultura e impacto de la represión: Argentina y Chile," in Sosnowski, *Represión y reconstrucción*, 27–48.

6 See Andrés Avellaneda, "Introducción," in Avellaneda, *Censura, autoritarismo y cultura* 1:36–53, for a summary of the different practices of censorship and the different forms of culture they affected.

7 "Documento Final de la Junta Militar," *La Nación* (Buenos Aires), 29 April 1983, p. 13. See also Jorge Rafael Videla, *Discursos y Mensajes del Presidente de la Nación* (Buenos Aires: Secretaria de Información Pública, 1977).

8 Quoted from the daily *La Prensa* (Buenos Aires), 18 December 1977, in Avellaneda, *Censura, autoritarismo y cultura* 2:162–63.

9 Quoted from *La Prensa* (Buenos Aires), 11 August 1978, in Avellaneda, *Censura, autoritarismo y cultura* 2:172.

10 Quoted from various sources in Avellaneda, *Censura, autoritarismo y cultura* 2:185–91.

11 A detailed account of the various historical and philosophical sources of the military's discourse is given by Hodges, *Argentina's "Dirty War."*

12 Rock, *Argentina, 1516–1987*, 366.

13 For an excellent account of these two historical "truths," see José Pablo Feinmann, "Política y verdad," in Sosnowski, *Represión y reconstrucción de una cultura*, 79–94.

14 On the *Proceso's* attempt to identify itself as a new *"generación del 80"*—the generation that consolidated the Argentine republic and its initially prosperous role in the world economy at the end of the nineteenth century—see Gabriel Montergous, *La generación del 80 y el proceso militar* (Buenos Aires: Biblioteca Política Argentina/Centro Editor de América Latina, 1985).

15 Feinmann, "Política y verdad," 93.

16 Michel Foucault, *Discipline and Punish: The Birth of the Prison*, trans. Alan Sheridan (1977; reprint, New York: Vintage, 1979), 201.

17 This phenomenon, not just in Argentina but throughout the Southern Cone, has been very usefully analyzed in terms of a "culture of fear." See Corradi, Fagen, and Garretón, *Fear at the Edge*.

18 The Madres de la Plaza de Mayo—a fairly heterogeneous group of Argentine mothers who circled the government square in Buenos Aires every Thursday demanding the appearance, alive, of their disappeared loved ones—can, in this respect, be seen as forging an extraliterary (though not extrasymbolic) resistance practice parallel to Piglia's in its attention to absence in the historical record. See chapter 8 in this volume.

19 Ariel Dorfman, "La muerte como acto imaginativo en *Cien años de soledad*," *Imaginación y violencia en América* (1970; reprint, Barcelona: Anagrama, 1972), 151–98.

20 Kathleen Newman provides an extremely deft deciphering of the various local political allusions embedded in *Respiración artificial*. See her "Historical Knowledge in the Post-Boom Novel," in Balderston, *Historical Novel in Latin America*, 209–19.

21 My sense of the institutional function of literature during the *Proceso* owes a debt to the various essays collected in Daniel Balderston et al., *Ficción y política: La narrativa argentina durante el proceso militar* (Buenos Aires: Alianza Editorial; Minneapolis: Institute for the Study of Ideologies and Literature, 1987), also to Luis Gregorovich, "Literatura, una descripción del campo: narrativa, periodismo, ideología"; Juan Carlos Martini, "Especificidad, alusiones y saber de una escritura"; Noé Jitrik, "Miradas desde el borde: el exilio y la literatura argentina"; and Jorge Lafforgue, "La narrativa argentina"—all in Sosnowski, *Represión y reconstrucción de una cultura*, and finally, to Beatriz Sarlo, "Strategies of the Literary Imagination," in Corradi, Fagen, and Garretón, *Fear at the Edge*, 236–49. My relationship to these accounts, I believe, is essentially to inscribe the literature they describe within the larger historical and conceptual framework of postmodernity.

22 Michel Foucault, "Nietzsche, Genealogy, History," trans. Donald F. Bouchard and Sherry Simon, in *Language, Counter-Memory, Practice: Selected Essays and Interviews*, ed. Donald F. Bouchard (1977; reprint, Ithaca, N.Y.: Cornell University Press, 1988), 139.

23 Ramos, *Desencuentros*.

24 Marta Morello-Frosch, "Borges and Contemporary Argentine Writers: Continuity and Change," in *Borges and His Successors: The Borgesian Impact on Literature and the Arts*, ed. Edna Aizenberg (Columbia: University of Missouri Press, 1990), 34.

25 Walter Benjamin, "Theses on the Philosophy of History," in *Illuminations: Essays and Reflections*, ed. Hannah Arendt, and trans. Harry Zohn (New York: Harcourt Brace and World, 1968), 256.

26 Julia Kristeva, "Word, Dialogue, and Novel," in *Desire in Language: A Semiotic Approach to Literature and Art*, ed. Leon S. Roudiez and trans. Thomas Gora, Alice Jardine, and Leon S. Roudiez (New York: Columbia University Press, 1980), 64–91 and "An Interview with Julia Kristeva," interview by Margaret Waller, trans. Richard Macksey, in *Intertextuality and Contemporary American Fiction*, ed. Patrick O'Donnell and Robert Con Davis (Baltimore: Johns Hopkins University Press, 1989), 280–93; Roland Barthes, "From Work to Text," in *Image, Music, Text*, selected and trans. Stephen Heath (New York: Hill and Wang, 1977), 155–64; V. N.

Volosinov, *Marxism and the Philosophy of Language*, trans. Ladislav Matejka and I. R. Titunik (1973; reprint, Cambridge: Harvard University Press, 1986); and Antoine Compagnon, *La seconde main, ou le travail de la citation* (Paris: Seuil, 1979).

27 Again, for a related discussion of the *cita*, and of Piglia's view of it, see Ramos, *Desencuentros*, 19–34.

28 From *The Oxford Dictionary of English Etymology*, ed. C. T. Onions with the assistance of G. W. S. Friedrichsen and R. W. Burchfield (Oxford: Clarendon, 1991), 178 and 761.

29 Larsen, "Sport as Civil Society, 113.

30 Alain Rouquié, *The Military and the State in Latin America*, trans. Paul E. Sigmund (Berkeley and Los Angeles: University of California Press, 1989), esp. chap. 3, "Modernization by the Army."

31 Robert Potash, *The Army and Politics in Argentina: 1928–1962*, 2 vols. (Stanford, Calif.: Stanford University Press, 1969 and 1980). Also, Brian Loveman and Thomas M. Davies, Jr., *The Politics of Antipolitics: The Military in Latin America*, 2d ed., rev. and exp. (Lincoln: University of Nebraska Press, 1989).

32 What follows draws from Emilio Mignone, *Witness to the Truth: The Complicity of Church and Dictatorship in Argentina*, trans. Phillip Berryman (Maryknoll, N.Y.: Orbis Books, 1988).

33 Quoted in Mignone, *Witness*, 89.

34 Larsen, "Sport as Civil Society," 113.

35 Annie L. Cot, "Neoconservative Economics, Utopia, and Crisis," *Zone* 1/2 (1986): 293.

36 Smith, *Authoritarianism*, 234.

37 Ibid., 235.

38 Ibid., 236; Julian Martel [pseud.], "Domination by Debt: Finance Capital in Argentina," *NACLA Report on the Americas* 12, no. 4 (1978): 20–39; and Roberto Frenkel and José María Fanelli, "Argentina y el FMI en la última década," *El FMI*, 105–61, esp. 124–38.

39 Smith, *Authoritarianism*, 260.

40 Ibid., 260 and Sue Branford and Bernardo Kucinski, *The Debt Squads: The U.S., The Banks, and Latin America* (London: Zed, 1988), 73–76 and 88–93.

41 Harvey, *Condition of Postmodernity*, 196. See also Branford and Kucinski, *Debt Squads*, 35, 45.

42 Yúdice, "¿Puede hablarse?" 106.

7   The Importance of Writing History

1   Karl Marx, *The Class Struggles in France, 1848–1850*, vol. 10 of *Karl Marx–Frederick Engels Collected Works* (London: Lawrence and Wishart, 1978), 10:81.

2 See Marx's letter to Engels on 9 December 1851 in *Briefe: Januar 1851 bis Dezember 1851*, in *Marx/Engels Gesamtausgabe* (Berlin: Dietz Verlag, 1984), vol. 3, pt. 4, no. 1:264–65. See also, for an excellent biographical account of this period, Jerrold Siegel, *Marx's Fate: The Shape of a Life* (University Park: Pennsylvania State University Press, 1978), 193–216.

3 Marx, *The Eighteenth Brumaire of Louis Bonaparte*, vol. 11 of *Karl Marx–Frederick Engels Collected Works* (London: Lawrence and Wishart, 1979), 11:103.

4 Ibid.

5 Ibid.

6 Ibid., 104.

7 Neil Larsen has convincingly rescued a materialist Marx from modernist readings of the *Eighteenth Brumaire* which have justified the displacement of political agency to the realm of an autonomous aesthetic. Larsen usefully points out, in effect, that Marx can observe and grant the victory of illusion in that particular battle without conceding the war. I would modify this observation only slightly by recalling that the lessons Marx's dialectic elsewhere offers are that what one observes—the farce of Louis Bonaparte—is what one must work with, though not what one must remain satisfied with. See Larsen, *Modernism and Hegemony,* chap. 1. Also, for accounts from different angles, see Michel Chaouli, "Masking and Unmasking: The Ideological Fantasies of the *Eighteenth Brumaire*," *Qui Parle* 3, no. 1 (Spring 1989): 53–71 and Paul Bové, "The Metaphysics of Textuality: Marx's *Eighteenth Brumaire* and Nietzsche's *Use and Abuse of History*," *Dalhousie Review* 64, no. 2 (Summer 1984): 401–22.

8 Tomás Eloy Martínez, *La novela de Perón* (Buenos Aires: Legasa, 1985), in English as *The Perón Novel,* trans. Asa Zatz (New York: Pantheon, 1988). Quotations from the novel will be taken from this edition of the translation unless otherwise noted and will be followed by parenthetical page references to the English and Spanish original.

9 Marx, *Class Struggles in France,* 143.

10 Friedrich Nietzsche, "On the Uses and Disadvantages of History for Life," in *Untimely Meditations,* trans. R. J. Hollingdale (Cambridge: Cambridge University Press, 1986), 59–123.

11 On the Nietzsche-Marx relation, see Bové, "Metaphysics of Textuality."

12 Feinmann, "Política y verdad," 93.

8 Speculations Toward Articulating Latin American Postmodernities

1 Though see, for a view of testimonial narrative in the Southern Cone, my "Latin America and the Problem of Resistance Culture," *Polygraph* 4 (1990): 92–110 and Mabel Moraña, *Memorias de la generación fantasma* (Montevideo: Monte Sexto, 1988).

2 A recent statement that is nevertheless paradigmatic of this early view by the individual generally considered the founder of the form can be found in Barnet, "La novela testimonio."

3 With the understanding that his view has changed somewhat, see George Yúdice, "El conflicto de posmodernidades," *Nuevo Texto Crítico* 7 (1er semestre de 1991): 19–33.

4 See Tim Golden, "Exiled Indian from Guatemala awarded the Nobel Peace Prize," *New York Times*, 12 October 1992, v142, p. 1, col 2.

5 Jameson, *Postmodernism*, 159. For an explicit expression of the view that *testimonio* constitutes an opposition to "hegemonic" or "imperialist" postmodernism, see (again with the caveat that his views have been modified) Yúdice, "*Testimonio* and Postmodernism" and Larsen, "Postmodernismo e imperialismo."

6 See John Beverley and Marc Zimmerman, *Literature and Politics in the Central American Revolutions* (Austin: University of Texas Press, 1990), xii–xiii and 172–207, and John Beverley, Against Literature.

7 See Doris Sommer, "Rigoberta's Secrets," *Latin American Perspectives* 70 (Summer 1991): 32–50.

8 Dinesh D'Souza, *Illiberal Education* (New York: Free Press, 1991), 71–73.

9 Laclau, *New Reflections*, 38.

10 Beverley, *Against Literature*, 157, n.1.

11 Marjorie Woodford Bray and Jennifer Dugan Abassi, "Introduction," *Latin American Perspectives* 66 (Summer 1990): 4.

12 What follows draws heavily from Jean-Pierre Bousquet, *Les "folles" de la place de Mai* (Paris: Stock, 1982), Maria del Carmen Feijoó, "The Challenge of Constructing Civilian Peace: Women and Democracy in Argentina," in *The Women's Movement in Latin America*, ed. Jane S. Jaquette (Boston: Unwin Hyman, 1989), 72–94, and Maria del Carmen Feijoó and Mónica Gogna, "Las Mujeres en la Transición a la Democracia," in Jelín, *Los Nuevos Movimientos Sociales*, 41–82.

13 See Inés González Bombal, "Madres de Plaza de Mayo: ¿Un signo en la historia?," *David y Goliath* 17, no. 52 (Setiembre 1987): 79–82. Some measure of support for the connection between resistance, history, new social movements, and postmodernism comes from the fact that this is a special issue on "Identidad Latinoamericana, premodernidad, modernidad, y postmodernidad." See also Luis Puenzo's 1985 film *La historia oficial*, which represents, in part, the middle-class' unsavory complicity with the *Proceso* through the story of a woman whose husband secretly secures for her the adoption of a child of disappeared parents. It is then the activity of the *Madres* that, in the film, reveals the middle-class' role in the terror and forces its confrontation with that role.

14 Feijoó, "Challenge of Constructing Civilian Peace."

15 George Yúdice, "We Are *Not* the World," *Social Text* 31, no. 2 (1992): 212.

16 Marta Traba, *En Cualquier Lugar* (Bogotá: Siglo veintiuno, 1984). Don't pass up Elena Poniatowska's moving and intelligent introduction to this edition. And see also Traba's *Conversación al sur* (México: Siglo veintiuno, 1981).

17 See Parizad T. Dejbord, "Cristina Peri Rossi: Escritora del exilio," (Ph.D. diss., University of Michigan, 1994).

18 See José Joaquín Brunner, "Políticas culturales y democracia: hacia una teoría de las oportunidades," in Canclini, *Políticas culturales en América Latina,* 175–203.

19 See Judith Adler Hellman, "The Study of New Social Movements in Latin America and the Question of Autonomy," in Escobar and Alvarez, *Making of Social Movements in Latin America,* 52–61.

20 See Jean Franco, "Going Public: Reinhabiting the Private," in Yúdice, Franco, and Flores, *On Edge,* esp. 67–69.

21 Judith Butler, *Gender Trouble: Feminism and the Subversion of Identity* (New York: Routledge, 1990), 14–15. See also Fraser, "Rethinking the Public Sphere" and essays in *Feminists Theorize the Political,* ed. Judith Butler and Joan W. Scott (New York: Routledge, 1992), esp. Ana María Alonso, "Gender, Power, and Historical Memory: Discourses of *Serrano* Resistance," 404–25.

22 Laclau, *New Reflections,* xiv. See also Laclau and Mouffe, *Hegemony and Socialist Strategy.*

23 Jean Franco, "Death Camp Confessions and the Resistance to Violence in Latin America," *Socialism and Democracy* 2 (Spring/Summer 1986): 15–16.

24 Laclau and Mouffe, *Hegemony and Socialist Strategy,* 192. See also Laclau's, "New Social Movements and the Plurality of the Social," in *New Social Movements in Latin America,* 27–42.

Bibliography

Adler Hellman, Judith. "The Study of New Social Movements in Latin America and the Question of Autonomy." In *The Making of Social Movements in Latin America: Identity, Strategy, and Democracy,* edited by Arturo Escobar and Sonia E. Alvarez, 52–61. Boulder, Colo.: Westview Press, 1992.

Adorno, Theodor. *Negative Dialectics.* Translated by E. B. Ashton. 1973. Reprint, New York: Continuum, 1987.

Aglietta, Michel. *A Theory of Capitalist Regulation: The U.S. Experience.* Translated by David Fernbach. 1979. Reprint, London: Verso, 1987.

Agosti, Brig. Gen. Orlando R. "Los documentos de marzo de 1976 . . ." In *Censura, autoritarismo y cultura: Argentina 1960–1983,* edited by Andrés Avellaneda, 2:172. Buenos Aires: Biblioteca Política Argentina/Centro Editor de América Latina, 1986.

Ahmad, Aijaz. "Jameson's Rhetoric of Otherness and the 'National Allegory.'" *Social Text* 17 (Fall 1987): 3–25.

Alonso, Ana María. "Gender, Power, and Historical Memory: Discourses of *Serrano* Resistance." In *Feminists Theorize the Political,* ed. Judith Butler and Joan Scott (N.Y.: Routledge, 1992) 404–25.

Alter, Robert. *Partial Magic: The Novel as a Self-Conscious Genre.* 1975. Reprint, Berkeley and Los Angeles: University of California Press, 1978.

Amin, Samir. *Unequal Development: An Essay on the Social Formations of Peripheral Capitalism.* Translated by Brian Pearce. New York: Monthly Review, 1976.

Anderson, Perry. "Modernity and Revolution." *New Left Review* 144 (March–April 1984): 96–113.

Appadurai, Arjun. "Disjuncture and Difference in the Global Cultural Economy." *Public Culture* 2, no. 2 (Spring 1990): 1–24.

Appiah, Kwame Anthony. "Is the Post- in Postmodernism the Post- in Postcolonial?" *Critical Inquiry* 17, no. 2 (Winter 1991): 336–55.

Arditi, Benjamín. "Una gramática postmoderna para pensar lo social." In *Cultura, política, y democratización,* edited by Norbert Lechner, 169–87. Santiago de Chile: FLACSO/CLASCO/ICI, 1987.

Argumedo, Alcira. *Los laberintos de la crisis. América Latina: Poder transnacional y comunicaciones.* Buenos Aires: ILET/Punto Sur, 1984.

Aronowitz, Stanley. *The Crisis in Historical Materialism: Class, Politics, and Culture in Marxist Theory.* 2d ed. Minneapolis: University of Minnesota Press, 1990.

———. *Science as Power: Discourse and Ideology in Modern Society.* Minneapolis: University of Minnesota Press, 1988.

Avellaneda, Andrés. "Introducción." In *Censura, autoritarinismo y cultura: Argentina 1960–1983,* edited by Andrés Avellaneda, 10–53. Buenos Aires: Biblioteca Política Argentina/Centro Editor de América Latina, 1986.

———, ed. *Censura, autoritarinismo y cultura: Argentina 1960–1983.* 2 vols. Buenos Aires: Biblioteca Política Argentina/Centro Editor de América Latina, 1986.

Azicri, Max. "Women's Development through Revolutionary Mobilization." In *The Cuba Reader: The Making of a Revolutionary Society,* edited by Philip Brenner, William M. LeoGrande, Donna Rich, and Daniel Siegel, 457–71. New York: Grove, 1989.

Bacarisse, Pamela. "The Projection of Peronism in the Novels of Manuel Puig." In *The Historical Novel in Latin America: A Symposium,* edited by Daniel Balderston, 185–200. Gaithersburg, Md.: Ediciones Hispamérica, 1986.

Balderston, Daniel, ed. *The Historical Novel in Latin America: A Symposium.* Gaithersburg, Md.: Ediciones Hispamérica, 1986.

Balderston, Daniel, David William Foster, Tulio Halperin Donghi, Francine Masiello, Marta Morello-Frosch, Beatriz Sarlo. *Ficción y política: La narrativa argentina durante el proceso militar.* Buenos Aires: Alianza Editorial; Minneapolis: Institute for the Study of Ideologies and Literature, 1987.

Barnet, Miguel. "La Novela Testimonio. Socio-Literatura." In *Testimonio y literatura,* edited by René Jara and Hernán Vidal, 280–302. Minneapolis: Institute for the Study of Ideologies and Literature, 1986.

Barradas, Efraín. "Notas sobre notas: *Kiss of the Spider Woman.*" *Revista de estudios hispánicos* 6 (1979): 177–82.

Barthes, Roland. "From Work to Text." In *Image, Music, Text,* selected and translated by Stephen Heath, 155–64. New York: Hill and Wang, 1977.

Bataille, Georges. *The Accursed Share, Volume I: Consumption.* Translated by Robert Hurley. New York: Zone Books, 1988.

———. *Erotism: Death and Sensuality.* Translated by Mary Dalwood. 1962. Reprint, San Francisco: City Lights, 1986.

———. "The Notion of Expenditure." In *Visions of Excess: Selected Writings, 1927–1939,* edited and translated by Allen Stoekl, 116–29. Minneapolis: University of Minnesota Press, 1986.

———. *The Tears of Eros.* Translated by Peter Connor. San Francisco: City Lights, 1989.

Baudrillard, Jean. *In the Shadow of the Silent Majorities or, The End of the Social and Other Essays.* Translated by Paul Foss, John Johnston, and Paul Patton. New York: Semiotext(e), 1983.

Beebe, Maurice. "*Ulysses* and the Age of Modernism." *James Joyce Quarterly* 10 (Fall 1972): 172–88.

Bello, Andrés. *Antología de Andrés Bello.* Edited by Pedro Grases. Caracas: Editorial Kapelusz Venezolana, 1964.

———. "Autonomía cultural de América." In *Conciencia Intelectual de América: An-*

tología del Ensayo Hispanoamericano, edited by Carlos Ripoll, 48–54. New York: Eliseo Torres and Sons, 1974.

Benítez Rojo, Antonio. *La isla que se repite: El caribe y la perspectiva posmoderna.* Hanover, N.H.: Ediciones del Norte, 1989.

Benjamin, Walter. "Theses on the Philosophy of History." In *Illuminations: Essays and Reflections,* edited by Hannah Arendt and translated by Harry Zohn, 255–66. New York: Harcourt Brace and World, 1968.

Bergquist, Charles. *Labor in Latin America: Comparative Essays on Chile, Argentina, Venezuela, and Colombia.* Stanford, Calif.: Stanford University Press, 1986.

Berman, Marshall. *All That Is Solid Melts into Air: The Experience of Modernity.* New York: Penguin, 1988.

Bertens, Hans. "The Postmodern *Weltanschauung* and Its Relations with Modernism: An Introductory Survey." In *Approaching Postmodernism,* edited by Douwe Fokkema and Hans Bertens, 9–52. Amsterdam: Johns Benjamins, 1986.

Beverley, John. *Against Literature* (Minneapolis: University of Minnesota Press, 1993).

Beverley, John and José Oviedo. "Postmodernism and Latin America." *boundary2* 20 no. 3 (1993): 1–17, special issue on "The Postmodernism Debate in Latin America."

Beverley, John, and Marc Zimmerman. *Literature and Politics in the Central American Revolutions.* Austin: University of Texas Press, 1990.

Boccia, Michael. "Versions (Con-, In-, and Per-) in Manuel Puig's and Hector Babenco's *Kiss of the Spider Woman* Novel and Film." *Modern Fiction Studies* 32, no. 3 (Autumn 1986): 417–26.

Boldy, Steven. "The Final Chapters of Cortázar's *Rayuela:* madness, suicide, conformism?" *Bulletin of Hispanic Studies* 57 (1980): 233–38.

——. "Julio Cortázar: *Rayuela.*" In *Landmarks in Latin American Fiction,* edited by Philip Swanson, 118–40. London: Routledge, 1990.

——. *The Novels of Julio Cortázar.* Cambridge: Cambridge University Press, 1980.

Borges, Jorge Luis. "El escritor argentino y la tradición" (from *Discusión,* 1932). In *Obras Completas,* 267–74. Buenos Aires: Emecé, 1987.

——. "Kafka y sus precursores" (from *Otras Inquisiciones,* 1952). In *Obras Completas,* 710–12. Buenos Aires: Emecé, 1987.

——. *Obras Completas.* 1974. Reprint, Buenos Aires: Emecé, 1987.

——. "Pierre Menard, Autor del Quijote" (from *Ficciones,* 1944). In *Obras Completas,* 444–50. Buenos Aires: Emecé, 1987.

Borinsky, Alicia. "Castration: Artifices: Notes on the Writing of Manuel Puig." Translated by Norman Holland and Stephen F. Houston. *Georgia Review* 29 (1975): 95–114.

——. *Ver/Ser Visto: Notas para una analítica poética.* Barcelona: Bosch, 1978.

Borón, Atilio A. *Estado, Capitalismo, y Democracia en América Latina.* 2d ed. Buenos Aires: Ediciones Imago Mundi, 1992.

Bousquet, Jean-Perre. *Les "folles" de la place de Mai.* Paris: Stock, 1982.

Bové, Paul. "The Metaphysics of Textuality: Marx's *Eighteenth Brumaire* and Nietzsche's *Use and Abuse of History.*" *Dalhousie Review* 64, no. 2 (Summer 1984): 401–22.

Branford, Sue, and Bernardo Kucinski. *The Debt Squads: The U.S., the Banks, and Latin America.* London: Zed, 1988.

Braverman, Harry. *Labor and Monopoly Capital: The Degradation of Work in the Twentieth Century.* New York: Monthly Review Press, 1974.

Brewer, Anthony. *Marxist Theories of Imperialism: A Critical Survey.* 1980. Reprint, New York: Routledge and Kegan Paul, 1987.

Brunner, José Joaquín. "Notas sobre la modernidad y lo posmoderno en la cultura latinoamericana." *David y Goliath* 17, no. 52 (septiembre 1987): 30–39.

———. "Políticas culturales y democracia: hacia una teoría de las oportunidades." In *Políticas culturales en América Latina,* ed. Nestor García Canclini México Grijalbo, 175–203 1987.

Bürger, Peter. "Literary Institution and Modernization." *Poetics* 12 (1983): 419–33.

———. *Theory of the Avant-Garde.* Translated by Michael Shaw. 1984. Reprint, Minneapolis: University of Minnesota Press, 1987.

Bushnell, David, and Neil Macauley. *The Emergence of Latin America in the Nineteenth Century.* New York: Oxford University Press, 1988.

Butler, Judith. *Gender Trouble: Feminism and the Subversion of Identity.* New York: Routledge, 1990.

Butler, Judith, and Joan Scott, eds. *Feminists Theorize the Political.* New York: Routledge, 1992.

Cabezas, Omar. *La montaña es algo más que una inmensa estepa verde.* México: Siglo veintiuno, 1982.

Callinicos, Alex. *Marxism and Philosophy.* New York: Oxford University Press, 1985.

Castro, Fidel. "Medio millón de campesinos en la Habana" (26 July 1959). In *La revolución cubana: 1953–1962,* edited by Adolfo Sánchez Rebolledo, 190–213. 1972. Reprint, México: Ediciones Era, 1983.

———. "Olive-Green." *New Left Review* 7 (January–February 1961): 2.

———. "Palabras a los intelectuales" (30 June 1961). In *La revolución cubana: 1953–1962,* edited by Adolfo Sánchez Rebolledo, 356–79. México: Ediciones Era, 1983.

———. "La reforma agraria va" (12 July 1959). *La revolución cubana: 1953–1962,* edited by Adolfo Sánchez Rebolledo, 160–89. México: Ediciones Era, 1983.

Chaoli, Michel. "Masking and Unmasking: The Ideological Fantasies of the *Eighteenth Brumaire.*" *Qui Parle* 3, no. 1 (Spring 1989): 53–71.

Cochran, Terry. "Foreword." In *Questing Fictions: Latin America's Family Romance,* by Djelal Kadir, ix–xix. Minneapolis: University of Minnesota Press, 1986.

Cockroft, James D. *Neighbors in Turmoil: Latin America.* New York: Harper and Row, 1989.

Colás, Santiago. "Latin America and the Problem of Resistance Culture." *Polygraph* 4 (1990): 92–110.

———. "'There's No Place Like Home,' or, The Utopian, Uncanny Caribbean State of Mind of Antonio Benítez-Rojo." forthcoming *Siglo XX/20th Century* 12 (1994).

Compagnon, Antoine. *La seconde main, ou le travail de la citation.* Paris: Seuil, 1979.

Concha, Jaime. "Criticando *Rayuela.*" *Hispamérica* 4, no. 1 (Agosto 1975): 132–51.

Cooke, John William. *Perón-Cooke Correspondencia.* 2 vols. Buenos Aires: Granica, 1973.

Corradi, Juan E., Patricia Weiss Fagen, and Manuel Antonio Garretón, eds. *Fear at the Edge: State Terror and Resistance in Latin America.* Berkeley and Los Angeles: University of California Press, 1992.

Cortázar, Julio. "Acerca de la situación del intelectual latinoamericano." In *Ultimo Round,* 2:265–80. 1969. Reprint, México: Siglo veintiuno, 1987.

———. "Homenaje a una torre de fuego." *Ultimo Round,* 1:194–97. México: Siglo veintiuno, 1987.

———. *Hopscotch.* Translated by Gregory Rabassa. 1966. Reprint, New York: Random House, 1972.

———. "Literatura en la revolución y revolución en la literatura." Collazos, Oscar, Julio Cortázar and Mario Vargas Llosa. *Literatura en la revolución y revolución en la literatura.* 1970. Reprint, México: Siglo veintiuno, 1977. 38–77.

———. "Muerte de Antonin Artaud." *Sur* 163 (mayo 1948): 80–82.

———. "Noticias del mes de mayo." *Ultimo Round* 1:88–120.

———. *Rayuela.* 1963. Reprint, Caracas: Biblioteca Ayacucho, 1980.

Cot, Annie L. "Neoconservative Economics, Utopia, and Crisis." *Zone* 1/2 (1990): 293–311.

Dällenbach, Lucien. *The Mirror in the Text.* Translated by Jeremy Whitely with Emma Hughes. Chicago: University of Chicago Press, 1989.

Davis, Mike. *City of Quartz: Excavating the Future in Los Angeles.* London: Verso, 1990.

Debord, Guy. *Society of the Spectacle.* Detroit: Black and Red, 1983.

Debray, Regis. *Revolution in the Revolution?* Translated by Bobbye Ortiz. New York: Monthly Review Press, 1967.

de Certeau, Michel. "The Long Silence." In *Heterologies: Discourse on the Other,* translated by Brian Massumi, 225–33. Minneapolis: University of Minnesota Press, 1986.

———. *The Practice of Everyday Life.* 1984. Reprint, Berkeley and Los Angeles: University of California Press, 1988.

Dejbord, Parizad T. "Cristina Peri Rossi: Escritora del exilio." Ph.D. diss., University of Michigan, 1994.

Deleuze, Gilles. *The Logic of Sense.* Translated by Mark Lester with Charles Stivale and edited by Constantin V. Boundas. New York: Columbia University Press, 1990.

Deleuze, Gilles, and Félix Guattari. *Anti-Oedipus.* Trans. Robert Hurley, Mark Seem and Helen R. Lane. Minneapolis: University of Minnesota Press, 1986.

———. *Kafka: Towards a Minor Literature.* Translated by Dana Polan. Minneapolis: University of Minnesota Press, 1986.

———. *A Thousand Plateaus.* Translated by Brian Massumi. Minneapolis: University of Minnesota Press, 1987.

De Man, Paul. *Allegories of Reading: Figural Language in Rousseau, Nietzsche, Rilke, and Proust.* New Haven, Conn.: Yale University Press, 1979.

"Documento Final de la Junta Militar." *La Nación* (Buenos Aires), 29 April 1983.

Dorfman, Ariel. "La muerte como acto imaginativo en *Cien años de soledad.*" In *Imaginación y violencia en América Latina.* 1970. Reprint, Barcelona: Anagrama, 1972. 151–98.

D'Souza, Dinesh. *Illiberal Education.* New York: Free Press, 1991.

Ellman, Richard. "Preface." In *Ulysses: The Corrected Text,* by James Joyce. New York: Vintage, 1986.

Escobar, Arturo. "Discourse and Power in Development: Michel Foucault and the Relevance of his Work to the Third World." *Alternatives* 10, no. 3 (1984): 377–400.

———. "Imagining a Post-Development Era? Critical Thought, Development and Social Movements." *Social Text* 31/32 (1992): 20–56.

———. "Power and Visibility: The Invention and Management of Development in the Third World." *Cultural Anthropology* 3, no. 4 (1988): 428–43.

Escobar, Arturo, and Sonia E. Alvarez, eds. *The Making of Social Movements in Latin America: Identity, Strategy, and Democracy.* Boulder, Colo.: Westview Press, 1992.

Eysteinsson, Astradur. *The Concept of Modernism.* Ithaca, N.Y.: Cornell University Press, 1990.

Fanon, Frantz. *Wretched of the Earth.* Translated by Constance Farrington. New York: Grove, 1968.

Feijoó, María del Carmen. "The Challenge of Constructing Civilian Peace: Women and Democracy in Argentina." In *The Women's Movement in Latin America,* edited by Jane S. Jaquette, 72–94. Boston: Unwin and Hyman, 1989.

Feijoó, María del Carmen, and Mónica Gogna. "Las mujeres en transición a la democracia." In *Los Nuevos Movimientos Sociales,* edited by Elizabeth Jelín, 41–82. Buenos Aires: Centro Editor de América Latina, 1988.

Feinmann, José Pablo. "Política y verdad." In *Represión y reconstrucción de una cultura: El caso argentino,* edited by Saúl Sosnowski, 79–94. Buenos Aires: EUDEBA, 1988.

Fernández Retamar, Roberto. *Caliban: Apuntes sobre la cultura de nuestra américa.* 1972. Reprint, México: Editorial Diógenes, 1974.

Fokkema, Douwe. *Literary History, Modernism, and Postmodernism.* Amsterdam: Johns Benjamins, 1984.

Foucault, Michel. *Discipline and Punish: The Birth of the Prison.* Translated by Alan Sheridan. 1977. Reprint, New York: Vintage, 1979.

———. *Madness and Civilization: A History of Insanity in the Age of Reason.* Translated by Richard Howard. 1965. Reprint, New York: Vintage, 1973.

———. "Nietzsche, Genealogy, History." Translated by Donald F. Bouchard and Sherry Simon. *Language, Counter-Memory, Practice: Selected Essays and Interviews,* edited by Donald F. Bouchard, 139–64. 1977. Reprint, Ithaca, N.Y.: Cornell University Press, 1988.

Franco, Jean. "Modernización, Resistencia y Revolución: La producción literaria de los años sesenta." In *La cultura moderna en américa latina,* translated by Sergio Pitol, 335–56. México: Grijalbo, 1985.

———. "Death Camp Confessions and the Resistance to Violence in Latin America." *Socialism and Democracy* 2 (Spring/Summer 1986): 5–17.

———. "Going Public: Reinhabiting the Private." In *On Edge: The Crisis of Contemporary Latin American Culture,* edited by George Yúdice, Jean Franco, and Juan Flores, 65–83. Minneapolis: University of Minnesota Press, 1992.

———. "South of your border." In *The 60s Without Apology,* edited by Sohnya Sayres, Anders Stephanson, Stanley Aronowitz, Fredric Jameson. 324–26. Minneapolis: University of Minnesota Press, 1984.

Frank, Andre Gunder. *Capitalism and Underdevelopment in Latin America: Historical Studies of Chile and Brazil.* New York: Monthly Review Press, 1967.

———. *Latin America: Underdevelopment or Revolution.* New York: Monthly Review Press, 1969.

Fraser, Nancy. "Rethinking the Public Sphere: Towards a Critique of Actually Existing Democracy." *Social Text* 25/26 (1990): 56–81.

Frenkel, Roberto, and José María Fanelli. "Argentina y el FMI en la última década." In *El FMI, el banco mundial y la crisis latinoamericana,* by Sistema Económico Latinoamericano. México: Siglo veintiuno, 1986. 105–61.

Freud, Sigmund. "Analysis of a Phobia in a Five-Year-Old Boy." *Standard Edition of the Complete Pyschological Works of Sigmund Freud.* Trans. and Ed. James Strachey. London: Hogarth, 1953–1973. Vol. 10.

———. *Beyond the Pleasure Principle.* Trans. and Ed. James Strachey. New York: Norton, 1962.

———. "Repression." *Standard Edition.* Vol. 14.

Fuentes, Carlos. *La nueva novela hispanoamericana.* 1969. Reprint, México: Joaquín Mortíz, 1980.

Furtado, Celso. *Economic Development of Latin America: Historical Background and Contemporary Problems.* 2d ed. Cambridge: Cambridge University Press, 1986.

García Candini, Nestor. "Cultural Reconversion." In *On Edge: The Crisis of Contemporary Latin American Culture,* edited by George Yúdice, Jean Franco, and Juan Flores, 29–43. Minneapolis: University of Minnesota Press, 1992.

——. *Culturas híbridas: Estrategias para entrar y salir de la modernidad.* México: Grijalbo, 1990.

——. "El debate posmoderno en iberoamérica." *Cuadernos hispanoamericanos* 463 (Enero 1989): 79–82.

——, ed. *Políticas culturales en américa latina.* México: Grijalbo, 1987.

Geist, Anthony, José Monleón, and Jenaro Talens, eds. *Modernism and Its Margins.* Forthcoming, Minneapolis: University of Minnesota Press, 1995.

Gillespie, Richard. *Soldiers of Perón: Argentina's Montoneros.* Oxford: Clarendon Press, 1982.

Golden, Tim. "Exiled Indian from Guatemala awarded the Nobel Peace Prize." *New York Times,* 12 October 1992, Section 1, page 2.

González Bombal, Inés. "Madres de Plaza de Mayo: ¿Un signo en la historia?" *David y Goliath* 17, no. 52 (Septiembre 1987): 79–82.

González Echevarría, Roberto. *La ruta de Severo Sarduy.* Hanover, N.H.: Ediciones del Norte, 1987.

Graff, Gerald. "The Myth of the Postmodern Breakthrough." In *Literature Against Itself: Literary Ideas in Modern Society.* 1979. Reprint, Chicago: University of Chicago Press, 1986. 31–62.

Graffigna, Brig. gen. Omar D. "Los argentinos de hoy tenemos . . ." (27 March 1980). In *Censura, autoritarismo y cultura: Argentina 1960–1983,* edited by Andrés Avellaneda, 2:191. Buenos Aires: Biblioteca Política Argentina/Centro Editor de América Latina, 1986.

——. "En los últimos años . . ." (17 November 1979). In *Censura, autoritarismo y cultura: Argentina 1960–1983,* edited by Andrés Avellaneda 2:188. Buenos Aires: Biblioteca Argentina/Centro Editor de América Latina, 1986.

——. "Más que una dimensió geográfica . . ." (24 August 1979). In *Censura, autoritarismo y cultura: Argentina 1960–1983,* edited by Andrés Avellaneda, 2:185. Buenos Aires: Biblioteca Política Argentina/Centro Editor de América Latina, 1986.

Green, James Ray, Jr. "*Kiss of the Spider Woman:* Sexual Repression and Textual Repression." In *La Chispa '81: Selected Proceedings,* edited by Gilbert Paolini, 133–39. New Orleans: Tulane University Press and the Louisiana Conference on Hispanic Language and Literatures, 1981.

Gregorovich, Luis. "Literatura, una descripción del campo: narrativa, periodismo, ideología." In *Represión y reconstrucción de una cultura: el caso Argentino,* 109–24.

Guevara, Ernesto. *La guerra de guerrillas.* In *Obra revolucionaria,* Prologo y selección de Roberto Fernández Retamar. 23–109. 1967. Reprint, México: Ediciones Era, 1989.

——. "Notas para el estudio de la ideología de la Revolución Cubana." In *Obra revolucionaria*, Prologo y selección de Roberto Fernández Retamar. México: Ediciones Era, 1989. 507–14.

——. "El socialismo y el hombre en Cuba" (March 1965). In *Obra revolucionaria*, Prologo y selección de Roberto Fernández Retamar. México: Ediciones Era, 1989. 627–39.

Habel, Janette. *Cuba: The Revolution in Peril.* Translated by Jon Barnes. London: Verso, 1991.

Habermas, Jürgen. "Modernity—An Incomplete Project." Translated by Seyla Ben-Habib. In *The Anti-Aesthetic: Essays in Postmodern Culture*, edited by Hal Foster, 3–15. Port Townsend, Wash.: Bay Press, 1983.

——. *The Philosophical Discourse of Modernity.* Translated by Frederick G. Lawrence. 1987. Reprint, Cambridge, Mass.: MIT Press, 1990.

Hall, Stuart et al. "The Siege of Cuba." *New Left Review* 7 (January–February 1961): 2–3.

Halperin Donghi, Tulio. "Estilos nacionales de institucionalización de la cultura e impacto de la represión: Argentina y Chile." In *Represión y reconstrucción de una cultura: el caso argentino*, edited by Saúl Sosnowski, 27–48. Buenos Aires: EUDEBA, 1988.

——. *Historia Contemporanea de América Latina.* Madrid: Alianza, 1979.

——, ed. *Proyecto y Construcción de una Nación (Argentina, 1845–1880).* Caracas: Biblioteca Ayacucho, 1980.

Harlow, Barbara. *Resistance Literature.* New York: Methuen, 1987.

Harvey, David. *The Condition of Postmodernity.* Oxford: Basil Blackwell, 1989.

——. *The Limits to Capital.* Chicago: University of Chicago Press, 1982.

Hassan, Ihab. *The Postmodern Turn: Essays in Postmodern Theory and Culture.* Columbus: Ohio State University Press, 1987.

Hegel, G. W. F. *Science of Logic.* Translated by A. V. Miller. 1969. Reprint, Atlantic Highlands, N.J.: Humanities Press International, 1989.

Henriquez Ureña, Pedro. *Literary Currents in Hispanic America.* 1945. Reprint, New York: Russell and Russell, 1963.

Hinkelammert, Franz J. "Frente a la cultura de la post-modernidad. Proyecto político y utopía." *David y Goliath* 17, no. 52 (septiembre 1987): 21–29.

Hodges, Donald C. *Argentina, 1943–1987: The National Revolution and Resistance.* Rev. and enlarged ed. Albuquerque: University of New Mexico Press, 1988.

——. *Argentina's "Dirty War": An Intellectual Biography.* Austin: University of Texas Press, 1991.

Holston, James. *The Modernist City: An Anthropological Critique of Brasília.* Chicago: University of Chicago Press, 1989.

Hopenhayn, Martin. "El debate postmoderno y la dimensión cultural del desarrollo." Unpublished typescript. ILPES.

Hutcheon, Linda. *Canadian Postmodernism.* New York: Oxford University Press, 1988.

———. *Narcissistic Narrative: The Metafictional Paradox.* 1980. Reprint, New York: Methuen, 1984.

———. *A Poetics of Postmodernism: History, Theory, Fiction.* New York: Routledge, 1988.

———. *The Politics of Postmodernism.* New York: Routledge, 1989.

———. *Splitting Images: Contemporary Canadian Ironies.* New York: Oxford University Press, 1991.

———. *A Theory of Parody: The Teachings of Twentieth-Century Art Forms.* New York: Methuen, 1985.

Huyssen, Andreas. *After the Great Divide: Modernism, Mass Culture, Postmodernism.* Bloomington: Indiana University Press, 1986.

Industria, Estado, y Sociedad. La reestructuración industrial en América Latina y Europa. Caracas: EURAL/Centro de Investigaciones Europeo-Latinoamericanos y Fundación Friedrich Ebert, 1989.

James, C. L. R. "Appendix: From Toussaint L'Ouverture to Fidel Castro." In *The Black Jacobins,* 391–418. 1963. Reprint, New York: Vintage, 1989.

———. *Notes on Dialectics: Hegel-Marx-Lenin.* 1948. Reprint, Westport, Conn.: Lawrence Hill, 1980.

———. *State Capitalism and World Revolution,* with Raya Dunayevskaya and Grace Lee. 1956. Reprint, Chicago: Charles H. Kerr Publishing, 1986.

James, Daniel. *Resistance and Integration: Peronism and the Argentine Working Class, 1946–1976.* Cambridge: Cambridge University Press, 1988.

Jameson, Fredric. *The Political Unconscious: Narrative as a Socially Symbolic Act.* Ithaca, N.Y.: Cornell University Press, 1981.

———. "The Ideology of the Text." In *The Ideologies of Theory: Essays 1971–1986,* 1:17–71. Minneapolis: University of Minnesota Press, 1988.

———. "Marxism and Historicism." In *The Ideologies of Theory: Essays 1971–1986,* 2:148–47. Minneapolis: University of Minnesota Press, 1988.

———. "Morality versus Ethical Substance." In *The Ideologies of Theory: Essays 1971–1986,* 1:181–85. Minneapolis: University of Minnesota Press, 1988.

———. "Periodizing the 60s." In *The 60s Without Apology,* edited by Sohnya Sayres, Anders Stephanson, Stanley Aronowitz, Fredric Jameson, 171–208. Minneapolis: University of Minnesota Press, 1984.

———. "Postmodernism and Utopia." In *Utopia Post-Utopia: Configurations of Nature and Culture in Recent Sculpture and Photography,* ed. by David Ross, 11–32. Boston: Institute of Contemporary Art, 1988.

———. *Postmodernism, or, The Cultural Logic of Late Capitalism.* Durham, N.C.: Duke University Press, 1990.

———. "Regarding Postmodernism—A Conversation with Fredric Jameson." By Anders Stephanson. *Social Text* 17 (Fall 1987): 29–54.

———. "Third World Literature in the Era of Multinational Capitalism." *Social Text* 15 (Fall 1986): 65–88.

Jitrik, Noé. "Miradas desde el borde: el exilio y la literatura argentina." In *Represión y reconstrucción de una cultura: el caso Argentino,* edited by Saúl Sosnowski, 133–47. Buenos Aires: EUDEBA, 1988.

Johnson, Randal. "Tupy or not Tupy." In *Modern Latin American Fiction,* edited by John King, 41–59. 1987. Reprint, New York: Noonday Press, 1989.

Joyce, James. *Ulysses.* 1922. Reprint, New York: Vintage, 1986.

Kadir, Djelal. *Questing Fictions: Latin America's Family Romance.* Minneapolis: University of Minnesota Press, 1986.

Katsiaficas, George. *The Imagination of the New Left: A Global Analysis of 1968.* Boston: South End Press, 1987.

Kay, Cristóbal. *Latin American Theories of Development and Underdevelopment.* London: Routledge, 1989.

Kerr, Lucille. "Leaps Across the Board." *Diacritics* 4, no. 4 (Winter 1974): 29–34.

———. *Suspended Fictions: Reading Novels by Manuel Puig.* Urbana: University of Illinois Press, 1987.

King, Marjorie. "Cuba's Attack on Women's Second Shift, 1974–76." *Women in Latin America: An Anthology,* edited by Eleanor Leacock, Elinor C. Burkett, Carmen Diana Deere, Margaret Towner, Mary K. Vaughan, María Linda Apodaca, Nancy Ca-o Hollander, Marjorie King, Margaret Randall, Deena Metzger, Norma Stoltz Chinchilla, María Amalia Irías de Rivera and Irma Violela Alfaco de Carpio, 118–31. Riverside: Latin American Perspectives, 1979.

Klarén, Peter F., and Thomas J. Bossert. "Introduction." In *Promise of Development: Theories of Change in Latin America,* edited by Peter F. Klarén and Thomas J. Bossert, 9–14. Boulder, Colo.: Westview Press, 1986.

Klarén, Peter F., and Thomas J. Bossert, eds. *Promise of Development: Theories of Change in Latin America.* Boulder, Colo.: Westview Press, 1986.

Kohl, James, and John Litt. *Urban Guerrilla Warfare in Latin America.* Cambridge, Mass.: MIT Press, 1974.

Kristeva, Julia. "An Interview with Julia Kristeva." By Margaret Waller. Translated by Richard Macksey. In *Intertextuality and Contemporary American Fiction,* edited by Patrick O'Donnell and Robert Con Davis, 280–93. Baltimore: Johns Hopkins University Press, 1989.

———. "Word, Dialogue, and Novel." *Desire in Language: A Semiotic Approach to Literature and Art,* edited by Leon S. Roudiez and translated by Thomas Gora, Alice Jardine, and Leon S. Roudiez, 64–91. New York: Columbia University Press, 1980.

Kumar, Krishnan. *Utopianism.* Buckingham, England: Open University Press, 1991.

Lacan, Jacques. *The Four Fundamental Concepts of Psycho-Analysis.* Translated by Alan Sheridan. 1977. Reprint, New York: Norton, 1981.

Laclau, Ernesto. "Argentina—Imperialist Strategy and the May Crisis." *New Left Review* 62 (July–August 1970): 3–21.

——. *New Reflections on the Revolution of Our Time*. London: Verso, 1990.

Laclau, Ernesto, and Chantal Mouffe. *Hegemony and Socialist Strategy: Towards a Radical Democratic Politics*. London: Verso, 1985.

Lafforgue, Jorge, "La narrativa argentina." In *Represión y reconstrucción de una cultura: el caso Argentino,* edited by Saúl Sosnowski, 149–66. Buenos Aires: EUDEBA, 1988.

Landau, Saul. "Cuba: The Present Reality." *New Left Review* 9 (May–June 1961): 12–22.

Landi, Oscar. *Devórame otra vez: Que hizo la televisión con la gente, que hace la gente con la televisión.* Buenos Aires: Planeta/Espejo de la Argentina, 1992.

Laplanche, J., and J.-B. Pontalis. *The Language of Psycho-Analysis.* Translated by Donald Nicholson-Smith. New York: Norton, 1973.

Larsen, Neil. *Modernism and Hegemony: A Materialist Critique of Aesthetic Agency.* Minneapolis: University of Minnesota Press, 1990.

——. "Posmodernismo e Imperialismo." *Nuevo Texto Crítico* 6 (Año 3, segundo semestre de 1990): 77–94.

——. "Sport as Civil Society: The Argentinean Junta Plays Championship Soccer." In *The Discourse of Power: Culture, Hegemony, and the Authoritarian State in Latin America,* edited by Neil Larsen, 113–28. Minneapolis: Institute for the Study of Ideologies and Literature, 1983.

——, ed. *The Discourse of Power: Culture, Hegemony, and the Authoritarian State in Latin America.* Minneapolis: Institute for the Study of Ideologies and Literature, 1983.

Lash, Scott, and John Urry. *The End of Organized Capitalism.* Madison: University of Wisconsin Press, 1987.

Latin American Perspectives 65 (Spring 1990). Special Issue: "Post-Marxism, the Left, and Democracy."

Latin American Perspectives 66 (Summer 1990). Special Issue: "The Sandinista Legacy: The Construction of Democracy."

Latin American Perspectives 73 (Spring 1992). Special Issue: "Popular Organizing and the State."

Lechner, Norbert. *La conflictiva y nunca acabada construcción del orden deseado.* Madrid: Siglo Veintiuno and Centro de Investigaciones Sociologicas, 1986.

——. "Un desencanto llamado posmoderno." Typescript. Santiago de Chile: FLACSO, 1988.

——. "Some People Die of Fear." In *Fear at the Edge: State Terror and Resistance in Latin America,* edited by Juan E. Corradi, Patricia Weiss Fagen, and Manuel Antonio Garretón, 26–35. Berkeley and Los Angeles: University of California Press, 1992.

Lefebvre, Henri. *Everyday Life in the Modern World.* Translated by Sacha Rabino-vitch. 1971. Reprint, New Brunswick, N.J.: Transaction, 1984.

Lenin, V. I. *Conspectus of Hegel's Book "The Science of Logic."* In *Collected Works*, 38:86–237. Ed. Stewart Smith. Moscow: Progress Publishers, 1981.

———. *Imperialism, The Highest Stage of Capitalism.* 1916. Reprint, Peking: Foreign Languages Press, 1973.

Leonard, Irving A. *Books of the Brave: Being an account of books and men in the Spanish conquest and settlement of the 16th century new world.* Cambridge: Harvard University Press, 1949.

Libre 1 (septiembre–noviembre 1971): 95–145.

Lipietz, Alain. *Mirages and Miracles: The Crises of Global Fordism.* Translated by David Macey. London: Verso, 1987.

Lipset, Seymour Martin, and Aldo Solari. *Elites in Latin America.* New York: Oxford University Press, 1967.

Lipset, Seymour Martin, and Gerald M. Schaflander. *Passion and Politics: Student Activism in America.* Boston: Little, Brown, 1971.

Loveman, Brian, and Thomas M. Davies, Jr., eds. *The Politics of Anti-Politics: The Military in Latin America.* 2d ed., rev. and expanded. Lincoln: University of Nebraska Press, 1989.

Lyotard, Jean-François. *The Postmodern Condition: A Report on Knowledge.* Translated by Geoff Bennington and Brian Massumi. Foreword by Fredric Jameson. 1984. Reprint, Minneapolis: University of Minnesota Press, 1989.

Mandel, Ernest. *Late Capitalism.* Translated by Joris DeBres. 1975. Reprint, London: Verso, 1987.

———. *The Second Slump: A Marxist Analysis of Recession in the Seventies.* Translated by Jon Rothschild. London: Verso, 1978.

Marcuse, Herbert. *One-Dimensional Man.* Boston: Beacon, 1964.

———. *Reason and Revolution: Hegel and the Rise of Social Theory.* 1941. Boston: Beacon Press, 1960.

Martel, Julian [pseud.]. "Domination by Debt: Finance Capital in Argentina." *NACLA Report on the Americas* 12, no. 4 (1978): 20–39.

Martí, José. "Nuestra América." In *Conciencia Intelectual de América: Antología del Ensayo Hispanoamericano,* edited by Carlos Ripoll, 228–36. New York: Eliseo Torres and Sons, 1974.

Martin, Gerald. *Journeys Through the Labyrinth: Latin American Fiction in the Twentieth Century.* London: Verso, 1989.

Martínez, Tomás Eloy. "Ficción e historia en *La novela de Perón.*" *Hispamérica* 49 (1988): 41–49.

———. *La novela de Perón.* Buenos Aires: Legasa 1985.

———. *The Perón Novel.* Translated by Asa Zatz. New York: Pantheon, 1988.

Martini, Juan Carlos. "Especificidad, alusiones y saber de una escritura." In *Represión y reconstrucción de una cultura: el caso Argentino,* edited by Saúl Sosnowski, 125–32. Buenos Aires: EUDEBA, 1988.

Marx, Karl. *The Class Struggles in France, 1848–1850.* Trans. Barbara Ruhemann. Vol. 10 of *Karl Marx–Frederick Engels Collected Works,* 10:43–145. Ed. by Tatyana Yeremeyeva. 50 vols. London: Lawrence and Wishart, 1979.

———. *Economic and Philosophic Manuscripts of 1844.* Trans. Martin Milligan and Dirk J. Strüik. Vol. 3 of *Karl Marx–Frederick Engels Collected Works,* 3:229–346. Ed. Lev Golman. 50 vols. Moscow: Progress Publishers, 1975.

———. *The Eighteenth Brumaire of Louis Bonaparte.* Vol. 11 of *Karl Marx–Frederick Engels Collected Works,* 11:99–197. Ed. Lev Golman. 50 vols. London: Lawrence and Wishart, 1979.

———. *Grundrisse.* Trans. Ernst Wangerman. Vols. 28–29 of *Karl Marx–Frederick Engels Collected Works.* Ed. Lev Golman and Vladimir Brushlinsky. 50 vols. New York: International Publishers, 1986.

———. "Karl Marx and Friedrich Engels in Manchester: London, 9. Dezember 1851." *Karl Marx Friedrich Engels Gesamtausgabe (MEGA),* vol. 3, pt. 4, no. 1, pp. 364–65. Ed. Wera Morosowa. Gen. ed. Günter Heyden and Anatoli Jegorow. Berlin: Dietz Verlag, 1984.

Marx, Karl, and Frederick Engels. *Manifesto of the Communist Party.* Vol. 6 of *Karl Marx–Frederick Engels Collected Works.* Ed. Lev Golman. 50 vols. New York: International Publishers, 1976.

Maspero, François. "Preface." In *Cuba: The Revolution in Peril,* by Janette Habel, vii–xxx. Translated by Jon Barnes. London: Verso, 1991.

McHale, Brian. *Postmodernist Fiction.* New York: Methuen, 1987.

Merrim, Stephanie. "Through the Film Darkly: Grade 'B' Movies and Dreamwork in *Tres Tristes Tigres* and *El beso de la mujer araña.*" *Modern Language Studies* 15, no. 4 (Fall 1985): 300–312.

Mignone, Emilio. *Witness to the Truth: The Complicity of Church and Dictatorship in Argentina.* Translated by Phillip Berryman. Maryknoll, N.Y.: Orbis Books, 1988.

Montergous, Gabriel. *La generación del 80 y el proceso militar.* Buenos Aires: Biblioteca Política Argentina/Centro Editor de América Latina, 1985.

Moraña, Mabel. *Memorias de la generación fantasma.* Montevideo: Monte Sexto, 1988.

More, Sir Thomas. *Utopia.* 1516. Reprint, New York: Norton, 1975.

Morello-Frosch, Marta. "Borges and Contemporary Argentine Writers: Continuity and Change." In *Borges and His Successors: The Borgesian Impact on Literature and the Arts,* edited by Edna Aizenberg, 26–43. Columbia: University of Missouri Press, 1990.

———. "La sexualidad opresiva en las obras de Manuel Puig." *Nueva narrativa hispanoamericana* 5, nos. 1–2 (1976): 151–57.

Munck, Ronaldo, with Ricardo Falcón and Bernardo Galitelli. *Argentina from Anarchism to Peronism: Workers, Unions, and Politics, 1855–1985.* London: Zed, 1987.

Nation 255, no. 3 (July 20–27 1992).

Newmann, Kathleen. "Historical Knowledge in the Post-Boom Novel." In *The His-*

torical Novel in Latin America: A Symposium, Ed. Daniel Balderston. Gaithersburg, Md.: Ediciones hispamérica, 1986. 209–19.

Ngugi wa Thiong'o. *Decolonising the Mind: The Politics of Language in African Literature.* 1981. Reprint, Portsmouth, N.H.: Heinemann, 1989.

Nietzsche, Friedrich. "On the Uses and Disadvantages of History for Life." Translated by R. J. Hollingdale. In *Untimely Meditations,* Intro. by J. P. Stern, 59–123. Cambridge: Cambridge University Press, 1986.

Nun, José. "La izquierda ante la cultura de la posmodernidad." In *La rebelión del coro: Estudios sobre la racionalidad política y el sentido común,* 133–48. Buenos Aires: Editores Nueva Visión, 1989.

Offe, Claus. *Disorganized Capitalism: Contemporary Transformations of Work and Politics.* Cambridge, Mass.: MIT Press, 1985.

O'Gorman, Edmundo. *La idea del descubrimiento de América: historia de esa interpretación y crítica de sus fundamentos.* México: Centro de estudios filosóficos, 1951.

———. *La invención de América: El universalismo de la cultura de occidente.* México: Fondo de cultura económica, 1958.

Ortíz, Fernando. *Contrapunteo cubano del tobaco y el azúcar.* 1940. Reprint, Caracas: Biblioteca Ayacucho, 1978.

Page, Joseph. *Perón: A Biography.* New York: Random House, 1983.

Panesi, Jorge. "Manuel Puig: Relaciones Peligrosas." *Revista Iberoamericana* 125 (octubre–diciembre 1983): 903–17.

Partnoy, Alicia. *The Little School: Tales of Disappearance and Survival in Argentina.* San Francisco: Cleis Press, 1986.

Pellón, Gustavo. "Manuel Puig's Contradictory Strategy: Kitsch Paradigms *versus* Paradigmatic Structure in *Kiss of the Spider Woman* and *Pubis Angelical.*" *Symposium* 36 (1983): 186–201.

Pérez, Louis A., Jr. *Cuba and the United States: Ties of Singular Intimacy.* Athens: University of Georgia Press, 1990.

———. *Cuba: Between Reform and Revolution.* New York: Oxford University Press, 1988.

Perón, Eva. *La razón de mi vida.* Buenos Aires: Ediciones Pereusa, 1951.

Perón, Juan. *Diario Secreto de Perón.* Anotado por Enrique Pavón Pereyra. Buenos Aires: Sudamericana/Planeta, 1986.

———. *La hora de los pueblos.* Buenos Aires: Editorial Norte, 1968.

Picon Garfield, Evelyn. *¿Es Julio Cortázar un surrealista?* Madrid: Gredos, 1975.

Piglia, Ricardo. *Respiración artificial.* 1980. Reprint, Buenos Aires: Sudamericana, 1988.

———. *Artificial Respiration.* Translated by Daniel Balderston. Durham, N.C.: Duke University Press, 1994.

Poniatowska, Elena. "Marta Traba o el salto al vació." In *En cualquier lugar,* by Marta Traba, 7–28. México: Siglo veintiuno, 1984.

Portes, Alejandro, Manuel Castells, and Lauren A. Benton, eds. *The Informal Econ-*

omy: Studies in Advanced and Less Developed Countries. Baltimore: Johns Hopkins University Press, 1989.

Potash, Robert C. *The Army and Politics in Argentina: 1928–1962.* 2 vols. Stanford, Calif.: Stanford University Press, 1969 and 1980.

Prasad, Madhava. "On the Question of a Theory of (Third World) Literature." *Social Text* 31/32 (1992): 57–83.

"Propósitos y objetivos básicos del Proceso de Reorganización Nacional." In *Censura, autoritarinismo y cultura: Argentina 1960–1983,* edited by Andrés Avellaneda, 1:134. Buenos Aires: Biblioteca Política Argentina/Centro Editor de América Latina, 1986.

Puig, Manuel. *El beso de la mujer araña.* Barcelona: Seix Barral, 1976.

———. "Del Kitsch a Lacan." Interview by Reina Roffe. *Espejo de Escritores,* edited by Reina Roffé, 131–45. Hanover, N.H.: Ediciones del Norte, 1985.

———. *Kiss of the Spider Woman.* Translated by Thomas Colchie. 1978. Reprint, New York: Vintage, 1980.

———. "Losing Readers in Argentina." *Index on Censorship* 14, no. 5 (October 1985): 55–57.

———. "Manuel Puig." Interview by Marie-Lise Gazarian Gautier. In *Interviews with Latin American Writers,* edited by Marie-Lise Gazarian Gautier, 217–33. Elmwood Park, Ill.: Dalkey Archive Press, 1989.

Rama, Angel. *Transculturación narrativa en américa latina.* México: Siglo Veintiuno, 1982.

Ramos, Julio. *Desencuentros de la Modernidad en América Latina: Literatura y Política en el Siglo XIX.* México: Fondo de cultura ecónomica, 1989.

Resnick, Stephen A., and Richard D. Wolff. *Knowledge and Class: A Marxian Critique of Political Economy.* Chicago: University of Chicago Press, 1987.

Rice-Sayre, Laura. "Domination and Desire: A Feminist Materialist Reading of Manuel Puig's *Kiss of the Spider Woman.*" In *Textual Analysis: Some Readers Reading,* edited by Mary Ann Caws, 245–56. New York: Modern Language Association, 1986.

Rincón, Carlos. "Modernidad periférica y el desafío de lo postmoderno: perspectivas del arte narrativo latinoamericano." *Revista de crítica literaria latinoamericana* 29 (Primer semestre de 1989): 61–104.

Rock, David. *Argentina, 1516–1987: From Spanish Colonization to Alfonsín.* Berkeley and Los Angeles: University of California Press, 1987.

Ross, Kristin. *The Emergence of Social Space: Rimbaud and the Paris Commune.* Minneapolis: University of Minnesota Press, 1988.

Rouquié, Alain. *The Military and the State in Latin America.* Translated by Paul E. Sigmund. Berkeley and Los Angeles: University of California Press, 1989.

Rubin, Gayle. "The Traffic in Women: Notes on the 'Political Economy' of Sex." In *Toward an Anthropology of Women,* edited by Rayna R. Reiter, 157–210. New York: Monthly Review Press, 1975.

Ruffinelli, Jorge. "Los 80: ¿Ingreso a la posmodernidad?" *Nuevo Texto Crítico* 6 (Año 3, segundo semestre de 1990): 31–42.

Said, Edward W. *Beginnings: Intention and Method.* 1975. Reprint, New York: Columbia University Press, 1985.

Saporta Sternbach, Nancy, Marysa Navarro-Aranguren, Patricia Chuchryk, and Sonia E. Alvarez. "Feminisms in Latin America: From Bógota to San Bernardo." In *The Making of Social Movements in Latin America,* edited by Arturo Escobar and Sonia E. Alvarez, 207–39. Boulder, Colo.: Westview, 1992.

Sarduy, Severo. "From *Yin* to *Yang* (About Sade, Bataille, Marmori, Cortázar, and Elizondo)." In *Written on a Body,* translated by Carol Meier, 5–17. New York: Lumen Books, 1989.

Sarlo, Beatriz. "El campo intelectual: un espacio doblemente fracturado." In *Represión y reconstrucción de una cultura: el caso Argentino,* edited by Saúl Sosnowski, 95–107. Buenos Aires: EUDEBA, 1988.

———. *Una modernidad periférica: Buenos Aires 1920–1960.* Buenos Aires: Ediciones Nueva Visión, 1988.

———. "Strategies of the Literary Imagination." In *Fear at the Edge: State Terror and Resistance in Latin America,* edited by Juan E. Corradi, Patricia Weiss Fagen, and Manuel Antonio Garretón, 236–49. Berkeley and Los Angeles: University of California Press, 1992.

Sarmiento, Domingo F. *Facundo: Civilización o barbarie.* 1845. Reprint, Buenos Aires: EUDEBA, 1961.

Sistema económico latinoamericano. *El FMI, el banco mundial, y la crisis latinoamericana.* México: Siglo Veintiuno, 1986.

Schwarz, Henry. "Provocations Toward a Theory of Third World Literature." *Mississippi Review* 49/50 (1989): 177–201.

Scobie, James. *Argentina.* 2d ed. New York: Oxford University Press, 1971.

Siegel, Jerrold. *Marx's Fate: The Shape of a Life.* University Park: Pennsylvania State University Press, 1978.

Sigal, Silvia. *Intelectuales y poder en la década del sesenta.* Buenos Aires: Puntosur, 1991.

Sigal, Silvia, and Oscar Teran. "Los intelectuales frente a la política." *Punto de Vista* 42 (abril 1992): 42–48.

Slater, David, ed. *New Social Movements and the State in Latin America.* Amsterdam: CEDLA, 1985.

Smith, Michael Peter, and Joe R. Feagin, eds. *The Capitalist City.* Oxford: Basil Blackwell, 1987.

Smith, Neil. *Uneven Development: Nature, Capital, and the Production of Space.* Oxford: Basil Blackwell, 1984.

Smith, Paul Julian. *The Body Hispanic.* Oxford: Clarendon, 1989.

Smith, William C. *Authoritarianism and the Crisis of the Argentine Political Economy.* 1989. Reprint, Stanford, Calif.: Stanford University Press, 1991.

Sociological Forum 4, no. 4 (1990).

Soja, Edward. *Postmodern Geographies: The Reassertion of Space in Critical Social Theory.* London: Verso, 1989.

Sommer, Doris. *Foundational Fictions: The National Romances of Latin America.* Berkeley and Los Angeles: University of California Press, 1991.

——. "Irresistible romance: the foundational fictions of Latin America." In *Nation and Narration,* edited by Homi K. Bhabha, 71–98. London: Routledge, 1990.

——. "Rigoberta's Secrets." *Latin American Perspectives* 70 (Summer 1991): 32–50.

Sommer, Doris, and George Yúdice. "Latin American Literature from the 'Boom' On." In *Postmodern Fiction: A Bio-Bibliographical Guide,* edited by Larry McCaffery, 189–214. Westport, Conn.: Greenwood Press, 1986.

Sosnowski, Saúl. *Julio Cortázar: Una busquedá mítica.* Buenos Aires: Ediciones Noé, 1973.

——, ed. *Represión y reconstrucción de una cultura: el caso argentino.* Buenos Aires: EUDEBA, 1988.

Speaks, Michael. "Chaos, Simulation and Corporate Culture." *Mississippi Review* 49/50 (1989): 159–76.

——. "Modernizing Postmodern Literature: Historiographic Metafiction and the 'Downtown Writing.'" *Dagens Nyuter* (Stockholm), 27 April 1991, Lorsdag (Saturday), "Kultur and Nöjen," p. 23.

Spivak, Gayatri. "Who Claims Alterity?" In *Remaking History,* edited by Barbara Kruger and Phil Marini, 269–92. Seattle: Bay Press and Dia Art Foundation, 1989.

Stohl, Michael, and Harry R. Targ, eds. *The Global Political Economy in the 1980s.* Cambridge, Mass.: Schenkman Publishing, 1982.

Sumner, General Gordon. "Estoy visitando Buenos Aires . . ." In *Censura, autoritarismo y cultura: Argentina 1960–1983,* edited by Andrés Avellaneda, 2:187–88. Buenos Aires: Biblioteca Política Argentina/Centro Editor de América Latina, 1986.

Tafuri, Manfredo. *Architecture and Utopia: Design and Capitalist Development.* Translated by Barbara Luigia La Penta. 1976. Reprint, Cambridge, Mass.: MIT Press, 1988.

Taylor, Charles. *Hegel.* 1975. Reprint, Cambridge: Cambridge University Press, 1988.

Teran, Oscar. *Nuestros Años Sesentas.* Buenos Aires: Puntosur, 1991.

Traba, Marta. *Conversación al sur.* México: Siglo veintiuno, 1981.

——. *En cualquier lugar.* Bogotá: Siglo veintiuno, 1984.

Vargas Llosa, Mario. "Novela primitiva y novela de la creación en América Latina." *Revista de la Universidad de México* 23, no. 10 (junio 1969): 29–36.

Vidal, Hernán. "Julio Cortázar y la Nueva Izquierda." *Ideologies and Literature* 2, no. 7 (May–June 1978): 45–67.

——. *Literatura hispanoamericana e ideologia liberal: Surgimiento y crisis (Una pro-*

blemática sobre la dependencia en torno a la narrativa del boom). Buenos Aires: Ediciones Hispamérica, 1976.

Videla, Jorge Rafael. "La argentina es un país occidental y cristiano . . ." (18 December 1977). *Censura, autoritarismo y cultura: Argentina 1960–1983,* edited by Andrés Avellaneda, 2:162–63. Buenos Aires: Biblioteca Política Argentina/ Centro Editor de América Latina, 1986.

———. *Discursos y mensajes del Presidente de la Nación.* Buenos Aires: Secretaria de Información Pública, 1977.

Viñas, David. *Literatura Argentina y realidad política.* Buenos Aires: Centro Editor de América Latina, 1982.

Volosinov, V. N. *Marxism and the Philosophy of Language.* Translated by Ladislav Matejka and I. R. Titunik. 1973. Reprint, Cambridge: Harvard University Press, 1986.

Wallerstein, Immanuel. *The Capitalist World Economy.* 1979. Reprint, Cambridge: Cambridge University Press, 1987.

Waugh, Patricia. *Metafiction: The Theory and Practice of Self-Conscious Fiction.* London: Methuen, 1984.

White, Hayden. *Metahistory.* Baltimore: Johns Hopkins University Press, 1973.

Wilson, Jason. "Julio Cortázar and the Drama of Reading." In *Modern Latin American Fiction,* edited by John King, 173–90. 1987. Reprint, New York: Noonday, 1989.

Woodford Bray, Marjorie, and Jennifer Dugan Abassi. "Introduction." *Latin American Perspectives* 66 (Summer 1990): 3–9.

Wright, Thomas C. *Latin America in the Era of Cuban Revolution.* New York: Praeger, 1991.

Wyers (Weber), Frances. "Manuel Puig at the Movies." *Hispanic Review* 49, no. 2 (Spring 1981): 163–81.

Yúdice, George. "El conflicto de posmodernidades." *Nuevo Texto Crítico* 7 (1er semestre de 1991): 19–33.

———. *"Kiss of the Spider Woman* y *Pubis Angelical:* Entre el placer y el saber." In *Literature and Popular Culture in the Hispanic World,* edited by Rose S. Minc, 43–58. Gaithersburg, Md.: Ediciones Hispamérica and Montclair State College, 1981.

———. "Marginality and the Ethics of Survival." In *Universal Abandon? The Politics of Postmodernism,* edited by Andrew Ross, 214–36. Minneapolis: University of Minnesota Press, 1988.

———. "Postmodernity and Transnational Capitalism in Latin America." In *On Edge: The Crisis of Contemporary Latin American Culture,* edited by George Yúdice, Jean Franco, and Juan Flores, 1–28. Minneapolis: University of Minnesota Press, 1992.

———. "¿Puede hablarse de posmodernidad en américa latina?" *Revista de crítica literaria latinoamericana* 29 (1er semestre de 1989): 105–128.

——. "*Testimonio* and Postmodernism." *Latin American Perspectives* 70 (Summer 1991): 15–31.

——. "We Are *Not* the World." *Social Text* 31/32 (1992): 202–16.

Yúdice, George, Jean Franco, and Juan Flores, eds. *On Edge: The Crisis of Contemporary Latin American Culture*. Minneapolis: University of Minnesota Press, 1992.

Index

Adorno, Theodor, 91
Agosti, Brig. Gen. Orlando, 125
Alienation: and colonization, 35; and
  modernity, 33–35; in *Rayuela*, 29–30,
  36–40, 38–41, 52, 56–59, 63–64; re-
  introduced in Latin American mo-
  dernity, 72–75; struggle against in
  Cuban revolution, 68
Allende, Salvador, 165
Alter, Robert, 80
Althusser, Louis, 10, 175 n.10
Appiah, K. Anthony, 37
Aramburu, Gen. Pedro, 108
Arditi, Benjamín, 11, 15–16, 170
Argentina: economic history of, 102–4;
  intellectuals in, 25, 72; left resistance
  in, 24, 86–87, 100–17

Barnet, Miguel, 25
Bataille, George, 41
Baudrillard, Jean, 174 n.8
Bello, Andrés, 30, 36–37
Bergquist, Charles, 103–4
Boom (narrative), 24–26
Borges, Jorge Luis, 23, 48, 132
Brunner, José Joaquín, 16
Butler, Judith, 171

Cámpora, Hector, 110
Capitalism: and alienation, 33–35; development of, 8–13, 16, 116; "flexible," 114, 145–48; "late," 5–10, 111–
  14
Carpentier, Alejo, 6, 30, 40
Castro, Fidel, 35, 68, 95

Citation (*cita*): in Latin American liter-
  ary history, 46–48; in *Respiración ar-
  tificial,* 132–44
Clinton, Bill, 165
Cockroft, James, 121
Cooke, Dr. John William, 107–8
Cortázar, Julio: and Antonin Artaud,
  183 n.35; and Georges Bataille, 184
  n.63; and Cuban Revolution, 25;
  Rayuela, 27–75
Culture, 30, 38. *See also* Language

Dällenbach, Lucien, 80
Debray, Régis, 68
de Certeau, Michel, 47
Deleuze, Gilles, 40, 60, 187 n.8, 190 n.6
de Man, Paul, 80
Democracy, 14, 68, 116–17, 166
Dependency Theory, 9, 12–14, 46
Dorfman, Ariel, 128
D'Souza, Dinesh, 163

Eroticism, 40–41
Escobar, Arturo, 11, 13–14
Ethics, 52–53, 62–64
Ezeiza Airport Massacre, 100–1, 110–
  11, 150

Feinmann, José Pablo, 156
Fernández Retamar, Roberto, 26, 30,
  48
Foucault, Michel, 127, 130
Franco, Jean, 26, 70, 172
Freud, Sigmund, 54–55, 59
Fuentes, Carlos, 26

Gallegos, Rómulo, 40
García Canclini, Nestor, 16–17
Graffigna, Brig. Gen. Omar, 125
Guevara, Ernesto "Che," 68–69, 72,
    102, 105–6

Habermas, Jürgen, 185 n.63
Harvey, David, 10, 113–14, 145–47
Hegel, Georg Wilhelm Friedrich, 53,
    70–71, 187 n.4
Historical Representation: and Argen-
    tine postmodernity, 148, 151–52; and
    Latin American modernity, 116–17;
    and Process of National Reorganiza-
    tion (Proceso), 122, 128; and public–
    private distinction, 126–27; in Re-
    spiración artificial, 129–34
Historicity, 6–7
Hodges, Donald, 107
Hopenhayn, Martin, 16
Hutcheon, Linda, 1–5, 80–81
Huyssen, Andreas, 43

Immanence, 52, 61
Impurity, 11–17, 96–97, 166
Isaacs, Jorge, 41

James, C. L. R., xiii, 70–71
Jameson, Fredric: narrative theory of,
    80; theory of postmodernism of, 5–
    11, 18
Joyce, James, 30–31

Kadir, Djelal, 35
Katsiaficas, George, 67
Kerr, Lucille, 46, 48–49

Laclau, Ernesto, 164
Language, 35, 38–41, 53–55, 59–60
Larsen, Neil, 144, 146, 198 n.7
Latin America: and colonial alienation,
    35–38; concept of, 11, 18, 70, 162;
    development of capitalism in, 9; and
    materiality, 30; and nature, 30, 37;
    "New Social Movements" in, 15; in

theories of postmodernism, xii, xiv,
    1–5
Leap, 62–72, 110. See also Modernity,
    Latin American; Utopia
Lechner, Norbert, 9, 16
Lefebvre, Henri, 60, 72
Lenin, V. I., 8, 70–71, 193 n.11
Lipietz, Alain, 112
López Rega, José, 100–1
Lyotard, Jean-François, 14

Madres de la Plaza de Mayo, 166–67,
    170–72
Mandel, Ernest, 5, 9, 111–13
Marcuse, Herbert, 71
Mármol, José, 41
Martí, José, 30, 35
Martin, Gerald, 42
Martínez, Tomás Eloy, La Novela de
    Perón, 152–57
Martínez de Hoz, José, 146
Marx, Karl: on alienation, 33–35; on
    capitalist development, 8–11; on
    communism, 53; on historical repre-
    sentation, 149–51; and Nietzsche,
    155
Mass Culture, xi, 16, 77–79
Materiality, 52–55
Medina, Fernando Abal, 108
Menchú, Rigoberta, 163
Metafiction, 79–82
Modernity, Latin American: and Boom
    narrative, 24; and Cuban Revolution,
    24; introduced, 23–27; and disen-
    chantment, 150; and historical repre-
    sentation, 116–17; and the Leap, 63–
    75; and repression, 27; and utopia,
    72; and Western modernity, 26–27
Modernity, Western: and alienation,
    33–35; and Latin American theories
    of postmodernity, 12; and Rayuela,
    41, 43–44, 46–49; and reason, 39
Modernization Theory, 12
Montoneros, 100–14
More, Thomas, 95
Morello-Frosch, Marta, 132

Nature, 6, 30, 40–41
New Left, 42, 66, 69–71
Ngugi wa Thiong'o, 35
Nietzsche, Friedrich, 130, 155
Nixon, Richard, 145
Nonsense, 40–41

Olmos, Amado, 107
Orthel, Hanns-Josef, 43
Ortíz, Fernando, 47
Osinde, Lt. Col. Jorge, 100, 110

Palma, Ricardo, 40–41
Peri Rossi, Cristina, 170
Perón, Eva, 105–6
Perón, Gen. Juan D.: and Argentine National Left, 107–12; and Argentine postmodernity, 152; and Cooke, Dr. John William, 107; and Ezeiza massacre, 100–1; and historical representation, 152–56; and Louis Bonaparte, 151, 154–55; political career of, 104–6; return of and Argentine economy, 112–13; and *semana trágica*, 103
Peronism, 105–12, 125–26
Piglia, Ricardo, *Respiración artificial*, 121–48
Postmodernism, theories of: xi; as "cultural dominant," 5; and democracy, xii; and imperialism, xi, xiv; and "late capitalism," 111–12; and Latin America, xii–xiv, 65, 148; in Latin America, 11–19, 35, 72, 116–17, 186 n.78; and mass culture, xi; as "style," 5
Postmodernity: in Latin America, 17–19, 23–24, 117, 151–52
Process of National Reorganization (*Proceso*): forms of repression of, 127–28; and historical representation, 123–29; and Peronism, 125; political economy of, 145–48; statistics on, 121–22
Puig, Manuel: *El beso de la mujer araña*, 76–117; and crisis of Argentine National Left, 78; relation of work to

women's writing, 78–79; role of mass culture in work of, 77–79; work of viewed as escapist, 77–79

Rama, Angel, 47
Ramos, Julio, 46–47
Reason, 53–55, 59–60
Repetition compulsion, 59
Repression: in *El beso de la mujer araña*, 81–92, 97; and Boom narrative, 27; and complexity, 78; and Cuban Revolution, 27, 72–75; and Process of National Reorganization (*Proceso*), 127–28; psychoanalytic theory of, 54–55; and reason, 91
Revolution, Cuban: and alienation, 72–75; and Argentine National Left, 106–12, 115–16; and *foco* theory, 68, 72, 101–2, 108; and Latin American Modernity, 24, 26, 101–2; and New Left, 42, 66–68; and *Rayuela*, 42, 69–74; and repression, 72–75; and Western Modernity, 24
Revolution, Nicaraguan, 164–66
Rimbaud, Arthur, 31–33
Rock, David, 125
Rodó, José Enrique, 30
Ross, Kristin, 31–33

Sarmiento, Domingo F., 47, 132
Sarlo, Beatriz, 72
Searching, 29–31, 51–52
Smith, William C., 146–47
Sommer, Doris, 26, 69, 105
Speaks, Michael, 10–11
Sumner, Gen. Gordon, 125

Testimonial narrative (*testimonio*), 25, 162–66
Third World, 5–10
Traba, Marta *En cualquier lugar*, 167–70
Transculturation (*transculturación*), 47

Utopia: and Argentine National Left, 115–16; in *El beso de la mujer araña*, 76, 81, 83–90, 94–99; and Boom nar-

rative, 26; and colonization, 72; and
Cuban Revolution, 26, 115–16; in
Jameson's theory of postmodernism,
7–8; and Latin American modernity,
72; in Latin American theories of
postmodernism, 14; and the Leap,
71; in *Rayuela* 29; and representation,
121; and Western modernity, 14, 72

Vandor, Augusto, 107
Vargas Llosa, Mario, 26
Videl, Gen. Jorge, 123

Waugh, Patricia, 80

Yúdice, George, 148, 167

Santiago Colás

is Assistant Professor of Latin American and
Comparative Literature at the University of Michigan.
He has published articles in *Social Text, Nuevo texto
crítico, Architecture New York,* and *The American Book Review.*

Library of Congress Cataloging-in-Publication Data

Colás, Santiago, 1965–
Postmodernity in Latin America: The Argentine Paradigm
Santiago Colás.
p.   cm. — (Post-contemporary interventions)
Includes bibliographical references.
ISBN 0-8223-1508-4 (alk. paper). —
ISBN 0-8223-1520-3 (pbk. : alk. paper)
1. Argentine fiction—20th century—History and criticism.
2. Postmodernism (Literature).   3. Cortázar, Julio. Rayuela.
4. Puig, Manuel. Beso de la mujer araña.   5. Piglia, Ricardo.
Respiración artificial.   6. Literature and society—Argentina.
7. Literature and society—Latin America.   I. Title.   II. Series.
PQ7703.C65   1994
863—dc20   94-11348   CIP